# WomanWisdom

# WomanWisdom

## A Feminist Lectionary
and Psalter

## Women of the Hebrew Scriptures

PART ONE

## Miriam Therese Winter

Illustrated by Meinrad Craighead

CROSSROAD • NEW YORK

1991

The Crossroad Publishing Company
370 Lexington Avenue, New York, NY 10017

Printed in the United States of America

Cover illustration and text illustrations: Meinrad Craighead

Manufactured in the United States of America
Typesetting output: TEXSource, Houston

---

**Library of Congress Cataloging-in-Publication Data**

Winter, Miriam Therese.
    WomanWisdom : a feminist lectionary and psalter : women of the
Hebrew scriptures: part one / Miriam Therese Winter ; illustrated by
Meinrad Craighead.
    p. cm.
    ISBN 0-8245-1100-X (pbk.)
    1. Women in the Bible. 2. Women—Prayer-books and devotions—
English. 3. Bible. O.T.—Devotional literature. I. Title.
II. Title: Woman wisdom.
BS575.W55 1991
264'.13'082—dc20                                              91-15126
                                                                   CIP

# Contents

### III ◇ MEMORABLE WOMEN

# Psalms

# PREFACE

COUNTLESS GENERATIONS OF WOMEN AND MEN have turned to the Hebrew Scriptures (Christianity's Old Testament) for perspective and inspiration. Countless generations have allowed these ancient texts to shape attitudes and values, behaviors and beliefs. Without hesitation. Without question. Until now.

Today women, and even men, are rejecting much of what seems to be the Bible's perspective on women and challenging certain assertions and assumptions of biblical texts and their interpretations. But isn't the Bible God's word, the sourcebook of divine revelation? How dare we question the word of God?

The biblical word is a word that has passed through the filters and frameworks of cultures. The Bible reflects the social, political, and theological conditions of various voices living at various times. Biblical history is the history written by J (the Yahwist) and E (the Elohist) and P (the Priest/s) and D (the Deuteronomist) and assembled by R (the Redactor), biblical writers whose documents say something about themselves as they tell of the myths and the mysteries of God in the midst of human experience. The Bible is not solely God's perspective. It is also the perspective of priests, prophets, and ordinary people, especially those who prepared its texts and whose perspectives are essentially male.

If the biblical perspective is predominantly male, or so it seems at present, how can the scriptures remain normative for those generations that are yet to come? Women are asking hard questions, determined to address the doubts arising within those who still believe. Do the biblical texts reflect the full extent of biblical tradition or is there more to our story than the records suggest? Is there more to the texts than present awareness suggests? For example, what about women, biblical women? Who are they? Where are they? What have they to tell us? Some women are convinced that we have yet to feel the full force of God's liberating word as transmitted through the Bible. Some of us are probing its pages for words of womanwisdom on behalf of women everywhere. Feminist scholars have provided us with a framework for recovering our matriarchal traditions. If we would only take time now to know the narratives that tell of women's experience, to know the women, their numbers, and where possible, their names, we might come to a more inclusive understanding of the biblical word.

Many women inhabit the Hebrew Scriptures — powerful women, persuasive women. As I went in search of their stories, seeking some tangible access to the charisma of their lost lives, I was blessed with a sense of their presence. Over the space of a single summer, these women who are my sisters became my intimate friends. It was their testimony I was assembling, their truth I sought to recover, their spirit I longed to express. I asked each woman to tell me something about who she really was, to help me break through the barrier of silence surrounding her memory. We sat with each other, prayed together, laughed, wept, rejoiced together as I reconstructed their lives. I set out to prepare a lectionary, but it was clear to me as their stories emerged that this was in fact their testament and they were writing it themselves. They told their own stories, raised their own questions, set the themes for their psalms. They have so much more to tell us if we would only take the time.

The women of *WomanWisdom* are extraordinary yet ordinary women. All are biblical women. Some of their stories are familiar to us, others have yet to be told. Covering a broad spectrum of female experience and female agendas, their narratives offer a new appreciation of what biblical women had to contend with and how much they had to lose. Many suffered the loss of their children, their husbands, their own lives. They were abused, used, insulted, and far too often ignored. They endured rape, incest, slavery, and had to function within a patriarchal system that silences and diminishes and routinely disempowers.

There were also women, many women, who took charge of their lives and their world. Sarah, Rebekah, Rachel, and Leah, when confronted with their sterility, decided themselves that their husbands should impregnate their slaves. The matriarchs all the way back to Eve, with the exception of invisible Milcah, speak and act with an authority that comes as a surprise. Eve takes the initiative toward becoming fully human. Sarah shapes the future for both Isaac and Ishmael. Hagar makes it against all odds and gives birth to a parallel tradition that has the blessing of God. Rebekah's daring duplicity ensures that the covenant will continue through Jacob, her favored son. Leah's convincing charade is her guarantee of marriage. Rachel risks her father's wrath when she steals his household gods. Miriam is a charismatic leader who is cherished by her people as they move toward the promised land. Memorable women can be found throughout biblical tradition, women of uncommon valor who are unsung heroines. Widows call forth miracles in their struggle to survive. Women foresee the future, communicate with the dead, stand up for foundational values, slay the enemy, and influence their leaders as mothers, lovers, wives.

This lectionary says a lot about women. It says something also about men. The heroes of our tradition probably looked considerably different to the women who shared their lives. Abraham seems assertive in the narratives best known to us, yet in the earliest sources of Sarah and Abraham he is overshadowed by his wife. Joseph, salvation of his people during a devastating famine, is clearly the child of Rachel who kept those household gods. In light of this connection, his own religious inclinations are no longer all that clear. What about Moses as a husband? What of his command to slaughter all those women and men out there in the wilderness? Samson, a legendary hero, was responsible for the arbitrary death of many, including his wife. The history of David, God's beloved, is incomplete without the perspective of Michal and his other wives and those ten concubines. Solomon, praised for his wisdom and prolific accomplishments, had a harem of a thousand women who were his wives and concubines. The man who built the temple in Jerusalem also worshiped other gods. Hosea's poetic prophecies have touched the hearts of many, yet the specter of Gomer now haunts us every time we hear his words.

This lectionary offers another perspective, not only of the women and a few of their men, but also of the tradition seen afresh through women's lives. We are well aware of the patriarchs, for we have grown up in their shadow and have been conditioned by their response, not only to God but to their environments rife with political intrigue. We know more now of the matriarchs, those staunch women whose ancient traditions are all but lost to us because of patriarchal overlays. Savina Teubal and other scholars are suggesting that the Genesis narratives may go back to an oral tradition about women, and Harold Bloom in *The Book of J* says that J the author of the Yahwist source probably was a woman. What do these narratives tell us?

Women in the Bible from earliest times had their own spiritual heritage and continued to worship the deity of their choice in the manner of their own choosing. Those on the margins had staying power, women who came from other cultures and worshiped in other ways. Women's validation as bearers of children, the importance of having sons, the privileged place of the firstborn son — these unchallenged pillars of patriarchy were not always so firmly in place. For example, child-bearing was always essential, yet women crucial to the covenant were barren for lengths of time. This juxtaposition of barrenness and fruitfulness should not be overlooked, for it suggests some vital relationship between emptiness and fertility, between promise and fulfillment. Sarah, Rebekah, Rachel, Hannah, even Samson's mother, were childless women loved by husbands who chose to remain with them, a statement of some significance in a tradition that allows a man legally to dismiss his childless wife. In a number of instances matriarchal influence reaches to the sons. Although tradition has taught us that God's preference has been for the firstborn male, younger sons inherit. God rejects Cain's offering, although he is Eve's first child. The covenant made with Abraham and Sarah continued through their offspring, through Isaac, Jacob, Joseph, Moses, through David and Solomon, yet none of these was a firstborn son. The accent on sons, on firstborn sons, grows stronger in the sources that build upon J, yet the narratives hint that continuity is contingent on the women, on their wit as well as their wombs.

After viewing the tradition through women's experience, questions are bound to arise. Are the interpretations of commentators and their editorial adjustments responsible for the Bible's patriarchal focus, and not the stories themselves? Was Miriam's leprous condition really a punishment from God? Or was it made to look that way in order to diffuse some of the charismatic power of her role? Could some of Isaiah's prophetic poetry have been written by his wife? Was the episode of the Levite who destroyed his concubine also a metaphor for a larger issue involving the behavior and attitudes of priests? Which of the words of scripture are God's and which are the words of mere men? What is the real issue underlying all the rhetoric on foreign women, especially foreign wives? Hebrew men are continually chastised for marrying foreign women. At the heart of this xenophobia is certainly the fear that Israel's religion, race, and culture will be severely compromised. In the face of this threat Ezekiel and other prophets and writers compare unfaithful Israel to a woman who is a foreigner, which meant inferior and a slut. Yet there are no words of caution or concern about foreign husbands. And Hebrew men continue to marry women of other cultures, as they had done down through the centuries, just as Joseph and Moses had done, and David and Solomon.

So many of us structure our private and public lives according to biblical values that are not always accurately portrayed. Not everything in the Bible is necessarily the intention of God. Revelation encompasses more than scripture. It begins with everyday life. Women whose frame of reference is rooted in experience are a key to a fuller understanding of the ways and the will of God. We have much to learn from the women of the Bible. Their stories are a lot like ours.

*WomanWisdom* is a lectionary with a gallery of images, a prayerbook, and a psalter celebrating women's lives. It presents the stories of biblical women in a context of ritual and prayer. Ritual is how we remember best, for ritual takes us out of our heads and into our experience. Ritual gives us permission and the means to interact with scripture. We take time to listen, reflect, and respond, to connect to the core of the message, to compare with our own experience, to grapple and to grow. Through ritual we learn something about the women, yes, but we also learn something about ourselves. Given the opportunity to confront our own pain and prejudice, to challenge our own assumptions, to tell and retell our own stories, we are encouraged and empowered through collective wisdom shared. The genius of ritual that is open to the Spirit is its ability to link past and present. Such potentially transformative ritual is really, after all, about us, about our lives, our world, our desire to grow more deeply into God.

*WomanWisdom* is the first of two volumes. Together with the companion volume, *WomanWitness*, it comprises a lectionary with all the texts of all the women mentioned in that portion of the Bible that is prior to what Christian churches call the New Testament. Broader than the Hebrew Scriptures, it includes narratives from that body of literature labeled deuterocanonical and known as the Apocrypha. These narratives are part of the Old Testament canon of the Roman Catholic and Orthodox traditions. It is important to include these narratives for they tell of women whose stories are becoming more and more common to all: Judith, Susanna, Anna the wife of Tobit, Sarah the wife of Tobias, and women whose stories are recorded in the writings of the Maccabees. The Index of Women includes only those women featured in this volume, either as individual entries or as part of the collectives entitled Widows, Wives, and Concubines. A complete index of all the women in the Hebrew Scriptures will appear in *WomanWitness*.

The scriptural lections are set in a style that facilitates an aural rendition. When a wife or a mother was not mentioned in the text but her presence was implied, for instance, in the Genesis genealogies and in the narrative of Noah's ark, I included her in the lection. Once, perhaps twice, you will find in the lections a female pronoun for God. It was difficult at times to reconcile the confusion regarding conflicting texts, due perhaps to different sources or traditions, or to errors in transmission or to an editorial stance. A listing in Chronicles occasionally differed from other references.

The following definitions or explanations may be a helpful guide:

- levirate: the practice of marrying the widow of one's brother as required by ancient Hebrew law

- Midrash: "investigation" or "explanation" - the designation for certain forms of postbiblical religious literature in Hebrew or Aramaic

- *Nyame:* the Ghanaian (West African) name for God

- redactor: compiler or editor; the main biblical Redactor integrated various sources into a single comprehensive version of the Bible

- Shaddai: a biblical name for God that appears primarily in Genesis, from the Hebrew root meaning "mountain" or "breast"; in ancient times may well have meant "God, the Breasted One."

- Shekinah: "to live" or "sojourn"; Aramaic designation for God that alludes to God's presence among the people

- Ur: a city in ancient Mesopotamia, which is modern Iraq

The following resources are recommended for those who might like some additional reading beyond the sources cited in the Context commentaries: *The Book of J* by Harold Bloom with a translation by David Rosenberg (1990); *The Israelite Woman* by Athalya Brenner (1985); *Who Wrote the Bible?* by Richard Elliott Friedman (1987); *An Introduction to the Old Testament: A Feminist Perspective* by Alice L. Laffey (1988); *The Lost Tradition of the Matriarchs: Hagar the Egyptian* by Savina J. Teubal (1990).

I am forever grateful to the women who entrusted to me the stories of their lives; to Meinrad Craighead whose images bring to life the power of our lost sisterhood and its deepest aspirations; to the Eaglesons, John for his editorial sensitivity and patience, Mary Ellen for her technological assist; and to my sisters and brothers who nurture and support the Spirit-spirit within me.

Thank You, Sophia, Shekinah, Shaddai,
my Shelter, my Shadow, my Shalom.

———— ◇ ————

# CHRONOLOGY

The Dawn of Civilization
    Eve / Cain's Wife / Noah's Wife

B.C.E.

| | |
|---|---|
| 1800–1700 | The Age of the Matriarchs/Settlements in Canaan<br>    Sarah / Milcah / Hagar / Lot's Wife<br>    Keturah / Rebekah / Leah / Rachel<br>    Zilpah / Bilhah / Esau's Wives |
| 1700–1600 | Israelites go down into Egypt<br>    Asenath |
| c. 1280 | The Exodus<br>    Miriam / Zipporah / Cushite Woman / Elisheba / Cozbi |
| c. 1250–1020 | Conquest of Canaan/Period of the Judges<br>    Levite's Concubine / Wives of the Benjaminites<br>    Samson's Wife / Heroine of Thebez / Orpah / Hannah |
| c. 1020–1000 | The Reign of Saul<br>    Witch of Endor |
| c. 1000–961 | United Monarchy of David<br>    David's Wives and Concubines<br>    Woman of Tekoa / Wise Woman of Abel-beth-maacah<br>    Rizpah / Woman of Bahurim / Abishag |
| c. 961–922 | Empire of Solomon<br>    Solomon's Wives and Concubines |
| c. 922–722 | Divided Kingdom<br>    Wife of Jeroboam / Widow of Zarephath / Prophet's Widow<br>    Shunammite Woman / Slave to Naaman's Wife<br>    Gomer / The Prophet |
| c. 721–650 | After the Fall of the Northern Kingdom<br>    Anna / Sarah, Wife of Tobias |
| c. 639–609 | The Reign of Josiah<br>    Huldah |
| After 500 | After the Return from Exile and Reconstruction<br>    Cleopatra / Bride of Jambri |

## ◇ WOMANWISDOM: A PSALM ◇

*All*    She wades
in a wisdom
all her own,
virgin,
lover,
caregiver,
crone,

*Choir 1*    trusts her experience,
for it has taught her
how to be grandmother,
mother, daughter,

*Choir 2*    to birth the future,
to unearth, recast
some pain remaining
from the past,

*Choir 1*    ensuring a cycle of reaping
and sowing,

*Choir 2*    nurturing,
empowering,
all the while
knowing

*Choir 1*    that who she is now
and who she has been

*Choir 2*    flows from a wellspring
deep within,

*All*    for woman's
intuitive
intimacy
is from
a God-given
wellspring
of
womanwisdom.

By M. T. Winter, Crossroad Pub. Co., © 1991 Medical Mission Sisters *WomanWisdom* / **XV**

# ◇ I ◇
# Matriarchs

# EVE

◇ **Scripture Reference**    Gen 1–3; 4:1–2, 8, 16, 25; 5:1–2

◇ **Biography**

Genesis presents Eve as the first woman created by God. It may be more accurate to say that she is the first female with an identity and a name in the recorded history of both Jews and Christians. As wife of the first man, Adam, she gave birth to three sons — Cain, Abel, and Seth — somewhere outside the Garden of Eden. Through the pain of giving birth and the loss of both Abel and Cain, Eve experienced a dimension of being human which she had not known in the Garden. The Genesis genealogy lists other sons born to Adam — and therefore to Eve — and states that there were also daughters of whom not a single memory remains. As scholars struggle to separate fact from mythology and interpretation in the narrative of Eve, she as original woman continues to be a symbol of both the domination and the liberation of her gender.

◇ **Context**

Generations have grown up with negative associations for Eve and the female gender. Adam's rib has symbolized woman's derivative and subservient nature; the serpent has been sign of female gullibility and disobedience; and the apple is still the archetypal symbol of humanity's fall from grace. Eve and through her all women have been blamed for originating sin and, consequently, for its punishment, but women are challenging such age-old assumptions and the guilt these have engendered. Feminist biblical scholars and theologians continue to peel away the patriarchy inherent in the Genesis texts and their traditional interpretation as they seek a new understanding.

Most scholars today agree that two separate creation accounts were combined to make the first three chapters of Genesis. In Genesis 1:1–2:4a which is the later, more ordered, more liturgical Priestly account of postexilic theologians, God creates 'adham, the human species, both female and male. In the earlier Yahwist narrative of chapters 2:4b–3:24, it has been suggested that God also creates androgynous humanity, 'adham, subsequently differentiating male and female with the creation of 'ezer, "helper," a term which connotes a beneficial relationship (see Phyllis Trible's "Eve and Adam: Genesis 2–3 Reread" in Carol P. Christ and Judith Plaskow, *Womanspirit Rising*, Harper & Row, 1979, pp. 74–83). With 'ishshah (woman), 'adham for the first time is 'ish (man) and declares 'ishshah his equal. "This at last is bone of my bones and flesh of my flesh." It is only after their act of disobedience that 'ish actually names 'ishshah, thereby severing the mutuality of their relationship and making woman subordinate to the man.

The Yahwist account is probably an aetiological narrative, a myth of origins which explains how things came into being and why things are the way they are. Augustine developed his theory of original sin on the basis of this story, and so much of present culture is shaped by his interpretations. The assumption that human nature is now corrupt, that humans inherit original sin at the very moment of their conception, and that sexual desire is a consequence of original sin are tenets that influence far beyond the circle of those who hold them to be true. In tracing the problems of human existence back to some primeval Fall and its subsequent punishment, the patriarchal culture which gave us the text and so much of its interpretation has succeeded in diminishing the positive aspects of the same Genesis narrative, obliterating an original gender equality which reflects a humanity created in the image of God with original freedom and responsibility. A major question remains. Was eating the apple a sin or was it in fact a blessing? Could the fullness of humanity ever have happened within the confines of the Garden? Procreation and the extension of the human race seem to be consequences of Eve's initiative. What a difference it would make to women and men if her action were seen as responsible free choice and not flagrant disobedience. The creation story also gave rise to the intriguing legend of Lilith. Preserved as Jewish midrash, it tells of Adam's first wife created when God created humanity female and male. Lilith remained with Adam only a short time because she insisted on full equality with her husband based on their identical origin, which she insisted accorded her equal rights. When this did not seem achievable, Lilith flew away.

◇ **Lectionary Reading**
### Genesis 1
### THE CREATION STORY:
### A Liturgical Reconstruction

In the beginning
God created the heavens
and the earth.
God's spirit
filled the void,
hovered above the formless depths,
called forth from darkness
terrestrial light.
God saw that light was good.
God called light Day
and darkness Night
as evening turned to morning
on that first day of creation.
◇
God lifted the sky
above the waters,
creating a space
between the waters

as evening came
and morning came
that second day of creation.

◊

God gathered the waters together
into designated places
and let dry land appear.
God called the new land Earth,
the surrounding waters Seas,
and saw that it was good.
Earth brought forth vegetation,
seeds and seedlings of every kind,
fruit-bearing, food-bearing
plants and trees,
and flowers and foliage
of every kind,
and all of it was good,
as evening gave way to morning
on that third day of creation.

◊

God fashioned lights
for the days
and the nights,
sun, moon, constellations
and galaxies of stars,
measured the months,
marked the years
and set aside the seasons
and saw that it was good,
as evening came
and morning came
that fourth day of creation.

◊

Global waters
teemed with life
and winged creatures
took to the sky
as God Creator
blessed them all,
the birds of the air,
the fish of the sea,
and watched them multiply
and saw that it was good,
as evening passed into morning
on that fifth day of creation.

◊

Wild animals
covered the earth,
animals of every conceivable kind,
creeping creatures,
carnivorous creatures,
cattle and similar
cud-chewing creatures.
The earth was filled with living creatures.
God saw that it was good.
Then God created humankind
in the image of God.
Created them
female and male.
Created them
according to God's own likeness
and made them responsible
for and to
the birds of the air,
the fish of the sea,
the animals of the earth.
God blessed them and said,
"Be fruitful.
Multiply.
Fill the earth.
Eat of its food,
its seeds and plants,
and share its fruits
with birds, beasts,
and all who have the breath of life.
God looked upon everything
God had made,
and indeed,
it was very good.
Evening came
and morning came
the sixth day of creation.

◊

After having created
the heavens and the earth
and all who inhabited
heaven and earth,
on the seventh day,
God rested.
God blessed
and consecrated
the seventh day,

for on that day
God Creator
enjoyed Her new creation.

◇ ◇ ◇

**Genesis 2–3**
**THE CREATION STORY:**
**An Ancient Myth**

Here is how
the heavens and the earth
came to be created.
When God first fashioned
earth and heaven,
before the grain
had sown its seed,
before an initial harvest,
before there was need
to till the field,
before the rains
had fallen to earth
to make the forests fruitful,
when no human life existed,
God made a form
from the dust of earth
and breathed into it
the breath of life
and made a living being.
And God planted
a primordial garden
somewhere in the east,
where the four great rivers
that water the earth
flow outward from their sources,
a garden filled
with flowering trees
and fruit-bearing trees
to fill and thrill
the senses,
and in its midst
the tree of life
and the tree of the knowledge
of good and evil.
God made the living being
the caretaker of the garden, saying,
"Eat of the fruit

of any tree
but the tree of the knowledge
of good and evil,
for should you eat
of the fruit of that tree,
on that day
you will die."
Then God said,
"So that you are not alone,
I will create for you a partner."
From the earth God created
animals of field and forest
and birds of the bush and the air
as companions to the human
who gave to every living creature
its own appropriate name,
but the human did not find among any of these
a partner or an equal.
So God put the human creature to sleep,
took a rib and made another.
When the human being awoke and saw
another human being, it said,
"Here at last
is bone of my bones
and flesh of my flesh.
Woman is the one
who is equal to man."
The man and the woman
lived in the garden
naked and unashamed.

◇

Now the serpent
who was wiser than any wild animal
the living God had created,
said one day to the woman,
"Did God really say
you shall not eat
from any one tree in the garden?"
And the woman said to the serpent,
"We may eat of the fruit
of all the trees
but that tree
in the middle of the garden.
God said that if we touch it,
we will die."
The serpent said to the woman,

"You will not die immediately;
God means that if you eat of the fruit
your eyes will be opened
to a whole new level of awareness,
you will know something of good and evil,
you will be a little more like God."
The woman saw that the fruit was good
and enticing to the eyes.
She was drawn to the tree
for she longed to be wise,
so she took some fruit and ate it
and gave some to her husband
who ate the fruit with her.
Then the eyes of both were opened.
Suddenly they knew the meaning of life,
and they wove fig leaves together
to cover their nakedness.
When they heard God moving
through the garden
in the coolness of the evening,
the man and the woman
hid themselves
from the presence of the living God.
God called to the man,
"Where are you?"
The man said,
"I heard you in the garden,
and I hid from you
because I was naked
and because I was afraid."
God said, "Who told you
that you were naked?
Have you eaten the fruit
I forbid you to eat?"
The man said, "The woman
whom you made to be with me
gave me fruit from the tree,
and I ate it."
Then God said to the woman,
"Tell me what you have done."
The woman said,
"The serpent convinced me,
so I ate the fruit of the tree."
Then God said to the serpent,
"You must now experience
what it means to be a serpent:

you will slither through dirt
all the days of your life,
despised by other creatures,
and the distance between you
and the woman and her children
will be so great
that at every opportunity
you will hiss at their heels
and they will strike your head."
Then God said to the woman,
"You must now experience
both desire and pain,
pain in bringing children to life —
in bringing them forth
and in bringing them up —
and you will long to be one
with your husband,
who will persist in dominating you."
Then God said to the man,
"Because you participated
in the choice of your wife
to be more fully human,
the land will suffer because of you;
you must work for your food
all the days of your life,
sowing seeds among thorns and thistles,
laboring to plant and harvest your fields,
and you will eat your bread
by the sweat of your brow
until you yourself are put into the earth,
the earth from which you were formed
and to which you shall return."
The man named his wife Eve
because she was mother of all the living.
Then God made skins into garments
to clothe the man and the woman.
And God said,
"Now that humans share with God
the knowledge of good and evil,
they may want to reach out to the tree of life
and eat and live forever."
Therefore, God sent them
out of the garden
to cultivate the earth
from which they were formed,
placing cherubim

and a flaming sword
at the east of the garden of Eden
to guard the tree of life.
Hereafter man and woman
would cling to one another
and become one flesh,
leaving father and mother
to be husband and wife.

◇ ◇ ◇

### Genesis 4, 5
### BEYOND THE GARDEN OF EDEN

Now Eve conceived a child by Adam
and gave birth to a son named Cain, meaning,
"I have produced with the help of God."
Soon after, she gave birth to his brother, Abel,
who grew up to be a shepherd,
while Cain cultivated the land.
Cain killed Abel.
Then Cain went away from the presence of God
and settled east of Eden.
Once again Eve gave birth to a child
and named her new son Seth, saying,
"God has given me another child
to love in place of Abel."

◇ ◇ ◇

### Genesis 5
### THE LIST OF GENERATIONS

Here are the descendants of Adam and Eve.
When God created humankind,
God created them in the image of God,
female and male God made them,
then blessed them and named them "humankind"
when they were first created.

◇

When Adam was one hundred thirty years old,
he became the father of a son named Seth,
then lived for another eight hundred years,
and he and his wife Eve had other sons
and daughters.

⬦ **Points for Shared Reflection**

- What have been some of the consequences for women as a result of the traditional understanding of Eve?

- Share some of the burden of guilt women feel simply by being female. Do you feel any of this guilt? Do you sometimes feel second-class simply because of your gender? How do you overcome those feelings?

- Do you think Eve's act was original sin or original blessing? Either way, do you think we automatically inherit either sin or blessing by our participation in her humanity?

- After eating the apple, Eve and Adam became fully human. Discuss the pros and cons of their condition before and after the apple. Where would we be if Eve had not done what she did?

⬦ **A Psalm of All the Living** (see page 13)

⬦ **Prayer**

Creator of all who live and move
and have reflected being,
we thank You for the universe
so securely wrapped around us,
for earth which is our garden of life
and for all its living creatures.
How blessed we are
to be born into so much variety
and beauty
and to know precisely what it means
to be fully, freely human.
We thank You for ourselves
and our need to give ourselves
to others.
May we never refuse the responsibility
to take life in our hands
and seek to understand its meaning,
which comes from You
and remains in You,
Creator of All the Living.
Amen.

## ◇ A PSALM OF ALL THE LIVING ◇

*Refrain*   Sing, creation,
sing your praise
to the wonderful, wonder-filled One always:
Maker of all,
Mother of all,
Lover of all the living.

*Choir 1*   Sing, star-studded galaxies
and cosmic, seismic infinities,

*Choir 2*   sunlight and moonlight, planet-at-play light,
red-apple dawn and fading-away light;

*Choir 1*   vault of the sky to the outermost reaches
of orbits and black holes and magnetic beaches;

*Choir 2*   billowing clouds in wide-open spaces
and winds that blow you to faraway places:

*Refrain*   Sing, creation,
sing your praise
to the wonderful, wonder-filled One always:
Maker of all,
Mother of all,
Lover of all the living.

*Choir 1*   Sing, you rivers, oceans and seas
that wash away all our inadequacies;

*Choir 2*   crystal-clear wellsprings of life-giving waters
that run through our sons and remain in our daughters;

*Choir 1*   mountains and meadows, deserts and canyons,
and hills, every valley's eternal companions;

*Choir 2*   mud, soil, sand, stone,
the earth of our solitude, never alone:

*Refrain*   Sing, creation,
sing your praise
to the wonderful, wonder-filled One always:
Maker of all,
Mother of all,
Lover of all the living.

*Choir 1*   Grain and grape, seedlings and flowers,
towering trees whose presence empowers;

*Choir 2*   herbs and pines, cedar grove chapel,
vegetables, fruits, especially the apple;

By M. T. Winter, Crossroad Pub. Co., © 1991 Medical Mission Sisters     *WomanWisdom* / **13**

| | |
|---|---|
| *Choir 1* | songbirds and seabirds, all birds on the wing<br>that symbolize freedom and teach us to sing; |
| *Choir 2* | dogs and elephants, koalas and all<br>earth's family of animals, large and small: |
| *Refrain* | Sing, creation,<br>sing your praise<br>to the wonderful, wonder-filled One always:<br>Maker of all,<br>Mother of all,<br>Lover of all the living. |
| *Choir 1* | Sing, humanity, women and men,<br>the faith-filled and all who would have faith again; |
| *Choir 2* | all races, all ages, all cultures, all sizes:<br>from you the Spirit-filled harmony rises, |
| *Choir 1* | touching the stars, encircling the planet,<br>and spiraling back to the One Who began it; |
| *Choir 2* | we sing in the name of all the living<br>a psalm of gratitude and thanksgiving. |
| *Refrain* | Sing, creation,<br>sing your praise<br>to the wonderful, wonder-filled One always:<br>Maker of all,<br>Mother of all,<br>Lover of all the living. |

   By M. T. Winter, Crossroad Pub. Co., © 1991 Medical Mission Sisters

# SARAH

◇ **Scripture Reference**    Gen 11:27–32; 12; 13; 16; 17:1–8,15–21
Gen 18:1–15; 20; 21:1–14; 22:1–14
Gen 23; 24:36,67; 25:10; 49:31
Is 51:2

◇ **Biography**

Sarah was born in Ur of the Chaldeans, where she married her brother
Abraham. Their father was Terah, but they had different mothers whose
names we do not know. Before God established a covenant with them,
their names were Sarai and Abram. They left Ur to settle in the land of
Canaan and lived for a while in Egypt and the Negeb before pitching
their tent near the oaks of Mamrah in Kiriath-arba, which is Hebron.
Childless until the age of ninety, Sarah bore a son named Isaac when
her husband was one hundred years old. She died at the age of one
hundred twenty-seven and was buried in a cave at Machpelah in a field
once owned by Ephron the Hittite in Hebron in the land of Canaan.

15

Sarah's story is a patchwork of highly selective, carefully edited remnants from two distinct traditions which Savina Teubal calls the "Abraham tradition" of cultural and religious patriarchy and an earlier "Sarah tradition" associated with the Genesis matriarchs (see her *Sarah the Priestess*, Swallow Press, 1984). The "Sarah tradition" was part of a non-patriarchal system in which women were dominant, descent was matrilineal (traced through the mother), residence was matrilocal (in the mother's homeland), and ultimogeniture (succession through the youngest child) not primogeniture (through the firstborn) was the norm.

The narratives of the Genesis matriarchs reflect this earlier tradition's struggle to survive, and clues to its strength and to Sarah's importance can be found in the texts. God's covenant with Abraham on Israel's behalf was a covenant made through Sarah and the child that would come from her womb. Two separate accounts (chapters 17 and 18) stress this. Persons of status ("kings") would descend from Abraham, but rulers ("kings of people") would descend from Sarah (17:16); nations would be created out of Abraham, but Sarah would be the one through whom those nations would come into being, she would be a "mother of nations" (17:16, RSV, 1952). In the face of Abraham's incredulity, God repeated a second time that Sarah would bear a son and told Abraham to name the boy "Laughter" (Isaac). Sarah herself made the decisions concerning Hagar and the child Abraham had by her. When Abraham protested, God said to him, "Do whatever Sarah tells you to do" (21:12). When Sarah died, much stress was placed on securing for her a proper burial place, emphasizing its importance, and Abraham's own story virtually ended with hers.

Clues to patriarchal tradition and redaction also abound in the narratives of Sarah. All the women of Genesis except Sarah named their own children and the children they adopted through their slaves, but Abraham named both Ishmael and Isaac with the names that God had revealed. The text always lists a person's father and often the father's father, but who was Sarah's mother? Who for that matter was Abraham's mother? Who were the mothers of Milcah, Rebekah, Rachel, and Leah? The practice of eliminating the mother's name contributed significantly to the loss of this matriarchal tradition with its matrilineal focus. Yet no matter how much the text stresses the importance of male identification through lineage and Jewish identity through circumcision, every child was — and still is — automatically a Jew who was born of a Jewish mother. There are many examples of patriarchal redaction. The child of a woman's slave was considered the woman's child (see stories of Leah, Rachel, Zilpah, and Bilhah), yet Ishmael was clearly Abraham's son. Abraham fell on his face in a fit of laughter at the news that he would father a child (17:17) while Sarah laughed quietly to herself in her tent (18:10,12), yet the text suggests that Sarah was reprimanded by God for having laughed (18:13–15). Patriarchy condoned Abraham's passing his wife Sarah off as his sister because the molestation of her body was less an issue than his own physical safety. Patriarchy fostered the blind obedience that brought Abraham to the brink of slaughtering his own child for God.

Sarah the matriarch and Abraham the patriarch are symbols of two distinct traditions that merged in the telling of their stories which were reconstructed in the writing of the texts. More evidence exists regarding the latter tradition, but Sarah's story assures us that the former is not entirely lost. A bit of midrash recorded in Lewis Ginzberg's *The Legends of the Jews* (1925) supports the assumption that Sarah was a figure of prominence in her time. "The death of Sarah was a loss not only for Abraham and his family, but for the whole country. So long as she was alive, all went well in the land. After her death confusion ensued. The weeping, lamenting, and wailing over her going hence was universal . . . " (vol. 1, p. 287–88).

◊ **Lectionary Reading**

These are the descendants of Terah.
When Terah had lived for seventy years,
he became the father of Abram, Nahor, and Haran;
and Haran was the father of Lot.
Haran died before his father did,
in Ur of the Chaldeans, his birthplace.
Abram and Nahor both took wives.
Nahor married Milcah,
the daughter of Haran
who was the father of Milcah and Iscah;
and Abram married Sarai.
Abram and Sarai were childless.
Terah took Abram, Sarai, and Lot
and went out from Ur of the Chaldeans
to go to the land of Canaan,
but they settled in Haran instead.
Terah died in Haran
when he was two hundred and five years old.

◊

Now God said to Abram,
"Leave your country, your family,
and your father's house
for the land that I will show you.
I will make of you a great nation.
I will bless you and make you famous,
so that your name will be used as a blessing.
Whoever blesses you, I will bless,

whoever curses you, I will curse.
All families of the earth
will be blessed because of you."
So when he was seventy-five years old,
Abram took Sarai and Lot
and all he possessed
and set forth for the land of Canaan.
He moved through Canaan to Shechem,
where God appeared to him
beside the oak at Moreh, saying,
"I will give this land to your children."
So Abram built an altar there,
then moved on to the hill country east of Bethel
and pitched his tent between Bethel and Ai
where he built an altar and invoked God's name
before moving on toward the Negeb.
Now there was a famine in the land of Canaan,
so Abram decided they would go down to Egypt,
but when they reached the Egyptian border,
Abram said to Sarai,
"You are such a beautiful woman,
when the Egyptians see you
they will surely say,
'Look at his wife!'
and then they will kill me
in order to have access to you.
Say that you are my sister,
so that they may spare my life."
When Abram and Sarai entered Egypt,
the Egyptians were taken with her beauty.
Pharaoh's officials praised her,
so Pharaoh took Sarai into his house
and was generous with Abram because of her,
giving him sheep, oxen, donkeys, camels,
and male and female slaves.
But God afflicted Pharaoh and his house with plagues
because of Sarai, Abram's wife.
So Pharaoh summoned Abram and said,
"Why have you done this to me?
You should have told me she was your wife.
Why did you say, 'She is my sister,'
so that I took her for my wife?
Here, take your wife, and be gone."
So Pharaoh's men escorted Abram to the border
with his wife and all his possessions.

◇

They left for the land of the Negeb
and settled between Kadesh and Shur.
While they were there in Gerar,
once again Abram said of Sarai his wife,
"She is my sister,"
and Abimelech king of Gerar
had Sarai brought to him.
But God appeared to Abimelech in a dream, saying,
"You are about to die
because you have taken a married woman."
Abimelech, who had not yet come near her, said,
"My God, will you destroy an innocent people?
Did he not say to me, 'She is my sister'?
And she herself said, 'He is my brother.'
I acted with integrity and I am without guilt."
Then God responded to him in his dream.
"Yes, I know that you acted with integrity.
Therefore, I prevented you from sinning against me
by not allowing you to touch her.
Return the man's wife, for he is a prophet,
and he will intercede for you
and you will not lose your life.
But if you do not give her back,
know that you and your people will die."
Abimelech rose early the next morning
and told his servants about his dream
and they were terrified.
Abimelech summoned Abram and said to him,
"What have you done to us?
How have I offended you
that you should bring such guilt
on me and my kingdom?
You should not have treated me this way.
What possessed you to do such a thing?"
Abram answered Abimelech.
"I thought there would be no fear of God
in this place,
and that I would be killed
because of my wife,
so I said to Sarai,
wherever we travel,
say of me, He is my brother.
Besides, she is my sister,
the daughter of my father,
but not of my mother,
and she became my wife."

Then Abimelech took sheep, oxen,
male and female slaves,
and gave them to Abram
and returned his wife, saying,
"My whole land lies before you.
Settle wherever you will."
To Sarai he said,
"I have given your brother
one thousand pieces of silver
as compensation on your behalf
before all who accompany you."
Then Abram prayed
and God healed Abimelech
and his wife and his female slaves
so that they could again bear children,
for God had closed the wombs of all
because of Sarai, Abram's wife.

◇

So Abram and Sarai and Lot and their retinue
went up into the Negeb
rich in livestock and silver and gold.
They journeyed on to Bethel,
to the site of Abram's first altar,
and again Abram called on God.
Now Lot was also wealthy
with an abundance of flocks
and herds and tents.
The two had so many possessions
they could no longer live together,
for the land could not support them
and there was dissension between the herders
of the livestock of both men.
Then Abram said to Lot,
"We are kindred.
Let there be no friction between you and me,
between my herders and your herders.
The whole land lies before us.
Separate yourself from me.
If you go left, I will turn right,
or if you turn right,
I will journey to the left."
Lot looked all around him,
and he saw that the plain along the river Jordan
was like the garden of God
or like the fertile land of Egypt,
so he chose for himself this well-watered plain

and set out on his journey eastward,
while Abram settled in the land of Canaan.
Lot moved into the cities of the Jordan plain
and pitched his tent in Sodom,
where a great many wicked people
were sinners in the eyes of God.
After Lot had departed, God said to Abram,
"Look now to the four horizons,
to the farthest reaches of the land.
All that you see I will give to you
and to your progeny forever.
I will make your descendants
like the dust of the earth,
too numerous to be counted."
So Abram moved his tent
and came and settled by the oaks of Mamre,
just outside of Hebron,
and he built an altar there.

◇

Ten years had passed in the land of Canaan
when Sarai, still childless,
took her Egyptian slave, Hagar,
and gave her to Abram as a wife
so that they might have children through her.
Hagar conceived, and when she knew she was pregnant,
she treated her mistress with contempt.
Then Sarai said to Abram,
"May this injustice be turned on you.
I handed my slave over to you,
and now that she is pregnant,
she treats me with disdain.
May God be the judge between us."
Then Abram said to Sarai,
"Your slave is at your disposal.
Do with her what you will."
Then Sarai dealt with her so severely
that Hagar ran away from her.
An angel of God found Hagar
by a spring of water
in the wilderness on the way to Shur.
"Hagar," said the angel,
"slave of Sarai,
where have you come from
and where are you going?"
"I am running away from my mistress,"
she replied, and the angel said to her,

"Return to Sarai and be obedient to her,
for I will make your descendants
too numerous to be counted.
You have conceived and you will bear a son,
and you shall name him Ishmael,
for God has heard you in your affliction.
A wild ass of a man will he be,
with his hand against everyone
and everyone's hand against him,
in defiance of his kin."
Hagar gave a name to the voice of God.
"You are El-roi," she said.
"Surely here in this place
I have seen the one who sees me."
So Hagar gave birth to a son
and Abram named him Ishmael.
Abram was eighty-six years old
when Hagar bore Ishmael.

◇

When Abram was ninety-nine years old,
God appeared to him and said,
"I am El Shaddai.
Be blameless in my presence.
I will make a covenant between me and you
and I will greatly increase your numbers."
Abram bowed low to the ground.
"This is my covenant with you," said God.
"Your name is no longer Abram.
Your name now is Abraham.
I will make you exceedingly fruitful.
You shall be ancestor to a multitude of nations,
and kings shall descend from you.
I will establish my covenant between me and you
and your offspring
from generation to generation,
an everlasting covenant
to be God to you and to your descendants.
And I will give you
and all who come after you
this land in which you are living,
all of the land of Canaan,
I will give to you forever;
and I will be your God."
Then God said to Abraham,
"Do not call your wife Sarai any longer.
Sarah is her name.

I will bless her
and give you a son by her.
She shall give birth to nations,
and kings of people shall descend from her."
Then Abraham fell to the ground and laughed
as he reasoned within himself,
"Can a child be born to a man
who is one hundred years old?
Can Sarah, who is ninety, bear a child?"
Aloud, Abraham said to God,
"O let Ishmael live in your presence!"
God said, "Sarah will bear you a son
and you shall name him Isaac.
I will establish my covenant with him
as an everlasting covenant
with his offspring after him.
And I will grant your request for Ishmael.
I will bless him and make him fruitful
and greatly increase his numbers.
He will be the father of twelve princes
and I will make of him a great nation.
But my covenant I will establish with Isaac,
whom Sarah will bring to birth
at precisely this time next year."

◊

Once again God appeared to Abraham
as he sat at the entrance to his tent
in the heat of the day
beside the oaks of Mamre.
He looked up and saw three men nearby
and he ran from the tent to greet them
and bowed low to the ground.
"My lords," he said,
"if I find favor with you,
do not pass your servant by.
Let me bring you a little water.
You can wash your feet and rest a bit
beneath the shade of the tree.
Let me bring you some bread
to refresh yourselves
before you continue on.
Surely that is why you have come this way."
They replied, "Let it be as you say."
He hurried into the tent to find Sarah.
"Quickly, prepare three bushels of flour
and knead it into loaves."

Then Abraham ran to the herd,
took a tender calf,
and gave it to his servant
to make into a meal.
Taking cream and milk
with the newly cooked calf,
he set these before his guests,
then stood nearby while they ate.
"Where is your wife Sarah?" they asked.
And he answered, "She is there in the tent."
Then one of the guests responded,
"When I visit you again this time next year,
Sarah will have had a son."
Now Sarah and her husband
were advanced in years
and her periods had ceased long ago.
She was listening
behind the entrance to the tent,
when suddenly she laughed.
"Shall my husband and I
have pleasure again,
now that we are old?"
she chuckled to herself.
God said to Abraham,
"Why did Sarah laugh?
Why did she say,
shall I bear a child,
now that I am old?
Is any wonder too much for God?
This time next year,
I will return to you,
and Sarah will have a son."
"I did not laugh,"
Sarah insisted,
for she was suddenly afraid.
"Oh yes, you laughed," said God.

◊

God kept that promise to Sarah.
She conceived and gave birth to Abraham's son
at the time that God had foretold.
Abraham named him Isaac
and circumcised the boy
when he was eight days old,
just as God had commanded.
Abraham was one hundred years old
when Isaac was born to him.

"God has given laughter to me," Sarah said,
"and all who hear of this will laugh with me.
Whoever would have said to Abraham
that Sarah would nurse a child!
Yet I have borne him a son in his old age."
Isaac grew and Abraham gave a banquet
on the day the boy was weaned.
After watching the son
whom Hagar the Egyptian had borne to Abraham
playing with her son Isaac,
Sarah finally said to Abraham,
"Dismiss this slave and her offspring,
for the son of a slave must not inherit
along with my son Isaac."
Abraham was deeply distressed, but God said to him,
"Do not be distressed because of the boy
and because of his mother, Hagar.
Do whatever Sarah tells you,
for it is through Isaac that your name will be carried on.
I will also make a nation of Hagar's son,
for he too is your child."
So early in the morning Abraham arose
and took some bread and a skin of water
and gave them to Hagar,
wrapped her arm around their son,
and sent them both away.

◊

One day God tested Abraham, saying:
"Take your son Isaac, whom you love,
and go to the land of Moriah
and sacrifice him as a burnt-offering there
on the mountain that I point out to you."
So Abraham rose early in the morning,
saddled his donkey, cut wood for the offering,
and took Isaac and two of his young men with him
and set off on his journey.
On the third day
he saw in the distance
the place that God had indicated,
and he said to the two young men,
"Stay here with the donkey;
the boy and I will go over there to worship,
and then we will return to you."
Abraham gave the wood to Isaac
and he carried the knife and the fire.
"Father," said Isaac, "we have wood and fire,

but where is the lamb for the offering?"
"God will provide, my son," he replied,
and the two walked on together.
When they came to the place revealed by God,
Abraham built an altar, arranged the wood,
bound his son Isaac, laid him on the altar,
then raised his knife to kill him.
But the voice of God called out to him,
"Abraham, do not lay your hand on the boy
or do anything to harm him.
Now I know that you fear God,
for you have not withheld your son from me."
Looking up Abraham saw a ram
caught in a thicket,
and he made a burnt-offering of the ram
in place of his son Isaac.
Abraham called the place,
"God will provide,"
and that is the source of the saying,
"On the mountain God provides."

◇

Sarah lived one hundred twenty-seven years
and died in the land of Canaan,
at Kiriath-arba, which is Hebron,
and Abraham grieved for her.
Then Abraham approached the Hittites and said,
"I am a stranger among you.
Let me purchase from you a burial plot,
that I might bury my wife."
The Hittites answered Abraham,
"You are a prince among us.
Take the choicest piece of property
as a burial ground for your dead."
Abraham rose and bowed to the Hittites,
the people of the land.
"Ask Ephron son of Zohar
to give me the cave of Machpelah
which is at the end of his field.
Let him give it to me in your presence
for its full purchase price
that I might own it for a burial plot."
Now Ephron was among those gathered there,
and he answered so that all might hear.
"My lord, hear me,
in the presence of my people,
I give you the field and the cave that is in it

as a place to bury your dead."
Then Abraham bowed before the people of the land
and said to Ephron the Hittite,
"Listen to me!
I want to give you the price of the field.
Please accept it from me."
And Ephron answered Abraham,
"A piece of land worth four hundred shekels of silver —
what is that between you and me?
Take it and bury your dead."
So Abraham weighed out the amount of silver
Ephron had named in the hearing of the Hittites,
and the field in Machpelah,
to the east of Mamre,
with the cave and the trees that were in the field,
became the possession of Abraham
in the presence of the Hittites
and of all who entered the gate of the city.
So Abraham buried Sarah his wife
in the cave in the field of Machpelah,
there in the land of Canaan.

◇ **Points for Shared Reflection**

- Reflect on Sarah the matriarch. What new information have you learned about her from hearing all of her story in the context of this ritual? What are Sarah's particular strengths? How might she serve as an inspiration and a role model for you?

- Why did Sarah laugh? Why did Abraham laugh? How do the reasons for their laughter relate to your understanding of females and males? Did God really reprimand Sarah for laughing? Was their laughter negative or positive or both? Give reasons for your response.

- Although Sarah is not mentioned in the narrative about the sacrifice of Isaac by Abraham, in what ways can you perceive her presence? How would she have felt about what was happening? About Abraham who nearly slaughtered her son? About God who supposedly asked him to do it? Do you think God really did? How would you have felt? What would you have done?

- Talk about the "Sarah tradition" and the role of the matriarch as you perceive it from the narratives. Can you trace a matriarch tradition through your own family? Through the religious institution of your experience? Spend some time on these last two questions.

◇ **Sarah's Psalm** (see page 29)

◇ **Prayer**

O One Who Laughs
at the incongruity
of life
and human nature,
name us not Mara,
which means Bitterness,
but name every one of us
Laughter,
for we laugh
at the incongruity
of our frail, fallible, gullible selves
formed in the image of You.
Laugh us to light-hearted life
in the Spirit
so that we are able to face
and endure
times of sacrifice
and doubt.
Sustain us in the tradition
which our matriarchs have established.
May we live by their vision
and move with their strength,
now and forever.
Amen.

# ◇ SARAH'S PSALM ◇

*Voice*   Sing to us of the Matriarchs:

*Choir 1*   wise women
descended from women
who nursed at the breasts
of wise women,

*Choir 2*   women who walked
in the strength of She power,
weaving a thread
of unbroken tradition
through every generation.

*All*   Blessed be the Matriarchs!
We are the matriarchs,
images of Shaddai.

*Voice*   Sing to us of Laughter:

*Choir 1*   she who laughs,
wears herself lightly,
lets go of limits,
sheds inhibition,

*Choir 2*   and miracles happen
all of a sudden
to take the world
by surprise.

*All*   Blessed be Laughter!
May we be Laughter,
imaging Shaddai.

*Voice*   Sing to us of Womb-Power:

*Choir 1*   the force that pushes
reluctance to life,

*Choir 2*   bringing to birth
what will be born —
nothing on earth
can stop it.

*All*   Blessed be Womb-Power!
Fill us with Womb-Power,
the power of Shaddai.

By M. T. Winter, Crossroad Pub. Co., © 1991 Medical Mission Sisters   *WomanWisdom* / **29**

*Voice*   Sing to us of Circles:

*Choir 1*   circles cast around sacred space,
circles of power
where women know
empowering grace,

*Choir 2*   sister circles
where heart touches heart
as Her Spirit encircles.

*All*   Blessed be Circles!
Let us form Circles,
daughters of Shaddai.

*Voice*   Sing to us of our Lost Tradition:

*Choir 1*   deep in our ancestral memories
flicker of recognition arises,

*Choir 2*   an ache
for the lost horizon of hope
and its once transforming vision.

*All*   Blessed be our Lost Tradition!
Let us find our Lost Tradition
and return again to Shaddai.

*Voice*   Let us sing of Sarah's Sisters:

*Choir 1*   all who would weave
from newspun thread
a dream of a new tomorrow,

*Choir 2*   all who would dance
free and unashamed
in Her uncompromising Spirit,
all are Sarah's Sisters.

*All*   Blessed be Sarah's Sisters!
We are Sarah's Sisters!
Praise to You, Shaddai!

 By M. T. Winter, Crossroad Pub. Co., © 1991 Medical Mission Sisters

# MILCAH

◇ **Scripture Text**   Gen 11:26–29; 22:20–24; 24:15, 24, 47

◇ **Biography**

Milcah was the daughter of Haran, who was the brother of Sarah and Abraham, and the wife of their other brother Nahor. She was the sister of Iscah and the sister of Lot, the mother of eight children, and the grandmother of Rebekah, who married Isaac, the son of Abraham and Sarah.

◇ **Context**

Milcah was Sarah's niece. Although scripture records some biographical information, not a shred of her story survives. She is not listed among the matriarchs, and except for her brief genealogical data, she is virtually unknown. Her relationship to Sarah and Abraham is complex. She was the daughter of one of their two brothers and the wife of the other one. Her granddaughter Rebekah married the son of Sarah and Abraham.

Patriarchal redaction is evident in the focus on Abraham's male lineage and the concerted effort to link all the people of the covenant to those four patriarchs — Terah, Abram, Nahor, and Haran — and thereby to Abraham. But what of the matriarchal tradition that was said to have coexisted along with the patriarchal one? (See "Context," page 16.) Its invisible thread weaves through the lives of Milcah and her sister Iscah. There must have been a strong tradition supporting the retention of Iscah's name, even though she lacks any identifying phrase. However, no force was strong enough to preserve their mother's name or the name of their brother Lot's mother. It seems that their father may have had two wives, just as his father had two wives, the mothers of Sarah and Abraham (Gen 20:12). Although no mention is made of Milcah's daughters, there may have been one or more females among her eight children who are named. Savina Teubel gives cogent reasons for suggesting that Bethuel, Rebekah's father, was in fact Rebekah's mother, pointing out that Bethuel, according to Philo, was a feminine name which the oracles gave to Sophia (Wisdom) and meant "daughter of God" (*Sarah the Priestess*, 1984, pp. 62, 171). Rebekah identifies herself as a descendant of Milcah through Bethuel and the story's narrator does the same. If Bethuel were Milcah's daughter, that would establish an unbroken matriarchal line through women named and unnamed back to the mothers of Sarah and Abraham. Although most women do not even know her name and her story may be irretrievably lost, Milcah was a matriarch in the Genesis tradition. That is how we remember her here.

◇ **Lectionary Reading**

These are the descendants of Terah.
When Terah had lived for seventy years,
he became the father of Abram, Nahor, and Haran;
and Haran was the father of Lot.
Haran died before his father did,
in Ur of the Chaldeans, his birthplace.
Abram and Nahor both took wives.
Nahor married Milcah, the daughter of Haran
who was the father of Milcah and Iscah;
and Abram married Sarai.

◇

Now these things were told to Abraham.
"Milcah also has borne children to your brother Nahor:
Uz the firstborn, Buz his brother, Kemuel the father of Aram,
Chesed, Hazo, Pildash, Jidlaph, and Bethuel."
Now Bethuel had a child named Rebekah.
These eight children Milcah bore to Nahor, Abraham's brother.
Moreover his concubine, whose name was Reumah,
bore Tebah, Gaham, Tahash, and Maacah.

◇

Before Abraham's servant had finished praying,
Rebekah daughter of Bethuel,
who was the child of Milcah,
the wife of Nahor, Abraham's brother,
came out with her water jar on her shoulder.
She said to him, "I am the daughter of Bethuel, Milcah's child,
whom she bore to Nahor."

◇ **Points for Shared Reflection**

- Would you personally list Milcah among the matriarchs? If so, why? If not, why not?

- From the fragments of information you know about her, try to imagine Milcah's story. Form a circle with several other women and tell her story to one another to create a collective image of this lost matriarch.

- Who was Iscah? Who was she for Milcah? Whatever happened to her? Have you lost touch with a sister, either a biological or a spiritual one? How might you renew your relationship? Is there some specific action you might take this week to revitalize that sisterly bond?

- What was the relationship between Milcah and Sarah? Did they know each other well? Did they keep in touch? How well do you know your sister(s)-in-law? Your niece(s)? What do you share with them?

◇ **A Psalm to "I Am"** (see page 34)

◇ **Prayer**

I lift my anonymity to You,
O One Who is the "I Am"
of my very soul and being.
Who on earth really knows me?
Only You Who placed me
in my mother's womb
before I took form
as flesh and bone
know who I really am.
Reveal to me the meaning of me
so that I can reveal it to others,
so that others may know
the "I Am" of You
in knowing who I am.
Praise be to You, Shekinah-Shaddai.
Amen.

| | |
|---|---|
| *Choir 1* | She said,<br>I Am<br>the rising sun. |
| *Choir 2* | Be dawn in us, O Holy One. |
| *All* | Praise to You, I Am. |
| *Choir 1* | She said,<br>I Am<br>the whispering wind. |
| *Choir 2* | Speak to us kindly when we have sinned. |
| *All* | Praise to You, I Am. |
| *Choir 1* | She said,<br>I Am<br>the cresting sea. |
| *Choir 2* | Let Your waves wash over me. |
| *All* | Praise to You, I Am. |
| *Choir 1* | She said,<br>I Am<br>the singing bird. |
| *Choir 2* | Sing to me a healing word. |
| *All* | Praise to You, I Am. |
| *Choir 1* | She said,<br>I Am<br>a little child. |
| *Choir 2* | I looked into Your eyes. You smiled. |
| *All* | Praise to You, I Am. |
| *Choir 1* | She said,<br>I Am<br>transforming grace. |
| *Choir 2* | Make of me Your dwelling place. |
| *All* | Praise to You, I Am. |
| *Choir 1* | She said,<br>I Am<br>your deepest need. |
| *Choir 2* | I will follow where You lead. |
| *All* | Praise to You, I Am. |

    By M. T. Winter, Crossroad Pub. Co., © 1991 Medical Mission Sisters

| | |
|---|---|
| *Choir 1* | She said,<br>I Am<br>where struggles cease. |
| *Choir 2* | Draw me to Your holy peace. |
| *All* | Praise to You, I Am. |
| *Choir 1* | She said,<br>I Am<br>Who I Will Be. |
| *Choir 2* | I am in You and You in me. |
| *All* | Praise to You, I Am. |

# HAGAR

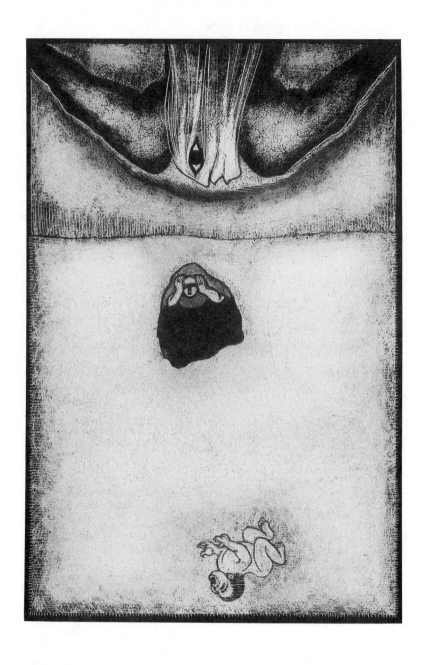

◇ **Scripture Reference**   Gen 16; 17:1, 18–21; 21:1–4, 8–21
Gen 25:5–6, 12–17

◇ **Biography**

Hagar was Sarah's Egyptian slave whom she gave to Abraham as a concubine so that he might have an heir through her. She left their household twice. The first time she ran away because of the situation her pregnancy had created. The second time Sarah sent her away in order to prevent her son from claiming a share of Abraham's inheritance. Both times Hagar fled to the wilderness, both times God's messenger comforted her and intervened to save her life, assuring her that her son Ishmael would become a mighty nation. After she was set free, Hagar made a home for her son in the wilderness of Paran, and when the boy was grown, Hagar went back to her own country to secure a wife for him.

◇ **Context**

It is hard to read Hagar's story with an unbiased eye because the Genesis accounts which favor Isaac as tradition's child of choice put Hagar at a disadvantage. In patriarchy's win-lose redaction, everybody loses. Hagar lost the security of her home and her son lost his share of his father's inheritance. Abraham was forced to relinquish his firstborn son whom he loved, and Sarah is presented in such a way that her interaction with Hagar seems vindictive and she suffers a loss of respect, not only within her family, but with many of us as well. The text states that Sarah treated her pregnant slave so badly that Hagar ran away, and that eventually she banished Hagar over an incident involving their sons. The boys were playing together (the Hebrew word *mitzahek* used here for "playing" has a sexual connotation) when Sarah decided to separate them for good. Ishmael was about sixteen when he faced death in the desert, but to Hagar he was her baby, the firstborn of her womb.

It is hard to know what really happened or what might have been intended solely on the basis of the texts. It is a fact that Sarah had legal jurisdiction over Hagar, her personal slave, which meant that she had the power to order Hagar to have intercourse with her husband and that she also had the right to claim their offspring as her own. The power of position is one thing, but personal achievement is also power. Hagar had accomplished something that her mistress could not do, and in her eyes that had changed her status — she was carrying the master's child. To Sarah she was still her slave, so nothing should have changed. Some of their recorded behavior may have arisen from issues such as these. However, to reduce the Hagar narratives solely to a power struggle between two women is to succumb to the disempowering force of patriarchy and to miss some important points.

The children of both women were children of a promise. God spoke on behalf of both of them. Both Ishmael and Isaac would have descendants too numerous to be counted. Both would become a great nation. The covenant would be transmitted through Sarah's child, but Hagar's son would also be blessed. The texts clearly indicate that Hagar was very special to God and suggest that a covenant was also made between God and Hagar and her descendants. Hagar had an apparition, twice, in which God came to her to comfort and reassure her, and she named the God of her experience "One who sees me." God revealed directly to Hagar the name she should call her son. In both her wilderness sojourns she was led by God to a source of water where she was physically and spiritually refreshed. For these reasons Hagar is listed here among the early matriarchs. Did Sarah banish Hagar? Or did she give Hagar her freedom? Only the women themselves really know.

◇ **Lectionary Reading**

Ten years had passed in the land of Canaan
when Sarai, still childless,
took her Egyptian slave, Hagar,
and gave her to Abram as a wife
so that they might have children through her.
Hagar conceived,
and when she knew she was pregnant,
she treated her mistress with contempt.
Then Sarai said to Abram,
"May this injustice be turned on you.
I handed my slave over to you,
and now that she is pregnant,
she treats me with disdain.
May God be the judge between us."
Then Abram said to Sarai,
"Your slave is at your disposal.
Do with her what you will."
Then Sarai dealt with her so severely
that Hagar ran away from her.
An angel of God found Hagar
by a spring of water
in the wilderness on the way to Shur.
"Hagar," said the angel, "slave of Sarai,
where have you come from
and where are you going?"
"I am running away from my mistress,"
she replied, and the angel said to her,
"Return to Sarai and be obedient to her,
for I will make your descendants
too numerous to be counted.
You have conceived and you will bear a son,
and you shall name him Ishmael,
for God has heard you in your affliction.
A wild ass of a man will he be,

with his hand against everyone
and everyone's hand against him,
in defiance of his kin."
Hagar gave a name to the voice of God.
"You are El-roi," she said.
"Surely here in this place
I have seen the one who sees me."
So Hagar gave birth to a son
and Abram named him Ishmael.
Abram was eighty-six years old
when Hagar bore Ishmael.

◇

When Abram was ninety-nine years old,
God appeared to him and said,
"I am El Shaddai.
I will make a covenant between me and you
and I will greatly increase your numbers."
Abraham said to God,
"O let Ishmael live in your presence!"
God said, "Sarah will bear you a son
and you shall name him Isaac.
I will establish my covenant with him
as an everlasting covenant
with his offspring after him.
And I will grant your request for Ishmael.
I will bless him and make him fruitful
and greatly increase his numbers.
He will be the father of twelve princes
and I will make of him a great nation.
But my covenant I will establish with Isaac,
whom Sarah will bring to birth
at precisely this time next year."

◇

God kept that promise to Sarah.
She conceived and gave birth to Abraham's son
at the time that God had foretold.
Abraham named him Isaac
and circumcised the boy
when he was eight days old,
just as God had commanded.
Isaac grew and Abraham gave a banquet
on the day the boy was weaned.
After watching the son
whom Hagar the Egyptian had borne to Abraham
playing with her son Isaac,
Sarah finally said to Abraham,

"Dismiss this woman and her offspring,
for the son of a slave shall never inherit
along with my son Isaac."
Abraham was deeply distressed, but God said to him,
"Do not be distressed because of the boy
and because of his mother, Hagar.
Do whatever Sarah tells you,
for it is through Isaac that your name will be carried on.
I will also make a nation of Hagar's son,
for he too is your child."
So early in the morning Abraham arose
and took some bread and a skin of water
and gave them to Hagar,
wrapped her arm around their son,
and sent them both away.
Hagar departed and wandered about
in the wilderness of Beer-sheba.
When the water in the skin was gone,
the boy sat down under a bush,
while Hagar sat at a distance,
about a bowshot away, saying,
"I cannot watch my baby die."
Ishmael wailed and she wept.
God heard the voice of the boy
and an angel called to Hagar from heaven.
"What troubles you, Hagar? Do not be afraid.
God has heard your son's cry.
Take him in your arms and comfort him,
for I will make of him a great nation."
Then she saw before her a well of water
and she filled the skin with water
and she gave her son a drink.
God was with the boy.
He grew up in the wilderness, an expert with the bow,
and he made his home in the vicinity of Paran.
Hagar his mother went down to Egypt
and chose a wife for him.

◇

Abraham left his inheritance to Isaac.
He also gave gifts to the sons of his concubines
while he was still alive,
but separated them from his son Isaac
by sending them to settle somewhere in the east.

◇

These are the descendants of Ishmael,
whom Hagar the Egyptian, Sarah's slave,

bore to Abraham.
His sons in the order of their birth:
Nebaioth, Kedar, Adbeel, Mibsam, Mishma, Dumah,
Massa, Hadad, Tema, Jetur, Naphish, and Kedemah.
These are the names of Ishmael's sons
by their villages and their encampments,
twelve princes according to their tribes.
The length of the life of Ishmael
was one hundred and thirty-seven years.

◇ **Points for Shared Reflection**

- The Hagar narratives reveal two strong women and a passive, somewhat powerless male. Find evidence in the text to support or contra-
  dict these images of Hagar, Sarah, and Abraham.

- Has tradition been fair to Hagar? What might God have intended for
  Hagar and her descendants?

- How might Hagar serve as an inspiration and a role model for you?
  Can you retell her story a different way?

- How might things be different globally if both Ishmael and Isaac were
  considered chosen by God?

◇ **A Psalm on Seeing** (see page 42)

◇ **Prayer**

I look to You,
O One Who Sees
through me
and my deceptions.
You look upon my emptiness
and fill me with encouragement
and a deep, sustaining love.
Seek me out in the wilderness
of my struggle for survival,
where my spirit longs for nurture
and my heart for tenderness.
O One Who Sees Me,
look at me
in our solitudes together,
and let me be the one who sees Shalom
when I look at You.
Blessed be Thou, now and forever.
Amen.

## ◊ A PSALM ON SEEING ◊

*All*   I look at You,
O One Who Sees,
and this is what I see:

*Choir 1*   Love eternally present,

*Choir 2*   walking beside me,
dwelling within me,

*Choir 1*   going before me,
coming behind me,

*Choir 2*   Love all around me
above me, below me;

*Choir 1*   Shekinah, a loving Presence,

*Choir 2*   living and loving in me.

*All*   Look at me,
O One Who Sees.
Tell me, what do You see?

*Voice*   I see someone
longing for love,
someone longing for Me.

*All*   I look at You,
O One Who Sees,
and this is what I see:

*Choir 1*   Wisdom eternally present,

*Choir 2*   at the root of my discerning,

*Choir 1*   at the heart of all my yearning,
guiding me, reaching me,

*Choir 2*   touching me, teaching me
how to be understanding;

*Choir 1*   Sophia, compassionate Wisdom,

*Choir 2*   carefully encompassing me.

*All*   Look at me,
O One Who Sees.
Tell me, what do You see?

*Voice*   I see someone
longing for wisdom,
someone longing for Me.

 By M. T. Winter, Crossroad Pub. Co., © 1991 Medical Mission Sisters

*All*    I look at You,
O One Who Sees,
and this is what I see:

*Choir 1*    Peace eternally present,

*Choir 2*    building bridges,
softening perceptions,

*Choir 1*    taking chances,
dispensing justice,

*Choir 2*    seeing the world
from the opposite side;

*Choir 1*    Shalom, the peace of Well-being,

*Choir 2*    being at peace in me.

*All*    Look at me,
O One Who Sees.
Tell me, what do You see?

*Voice*    I see someone
longing for peace,
someone longing for Me.

# REBEKAH

◊ **Scripture Reference**   Gen 22:20–23; 24; 25:19–34
Gen 26:1–11, 17, 23, 34–35; 27
Gen 28:1–5; 49:29, 31

◊ **Biography**

Rebekah, sister of Laban, daughter of Bethuel, granddaughter of Milcah and of Sarah's brother Nahor, left her home in Paddan-aram to become wife to Isaac in the land of Canaan and mother to twins, Esau and Jacob. She is buried beside Isaac, Abraham, and Sarah at Machpelah, which is Hebron.

◊ **Context**

The matriarchal tradition buried beneath the patriarchal reconstruction of the stories in Genesis surfaces in Rebekah. This granddaughter of Milcah confidently and courageously left her family at a young age unaccompanied by any blood relative and migrated to the land of Canaan to

44

begin a new life with a virtual stranger who happened to be her relative. Rebekah's mother played a prominent role in confirming her daughter's betrothal. The girl ran immediately to tell her mother about the stranger's proposal, and in the process of negotiation, her mother accepted gifts from him and tried to delay her daughter's abrupt departure from her life and her tradition. Who but a mother would have asked her daughter whether she wanted to stay or go? And her mother was surely one of those who called down upon Rebekah a blessing of fruitfulness.

Rebekah's story is clearly a matriarchal story and the continuation of Sarah's story. Abraham sent his servant in search of a wife for Isaac immediately after Sarah died, and when Rebekah came to Isaac in the Negeb, he took her into his mother's tent to spend their wedding night. Rebekah's story is Isaac's story, or more significantly, his story is hers. It is striking how prominent a role Rebekah plays in the narratives of the son through whom the covenant promise was to be fulfilled. Five major episodes — the lengthy process of her betrothal and the journey to her marriage; her pregnancy and the birth of their twins; her posing as his sister to the Philistine king Abimelech, just as Sarah had done for Abraham; her conspiring with Jacob to deceive his father to secure his brother's blessing; her getting Isaac to send Jacob to her relatives for a wife and secretly to escape Esau's wrath — these five episodes in the life of Isaac and Rebekah clearly feature Rebekah, indicating the strength of the matriarchal tradition represented by her. They comprise most of the story of Isaac.

There were similarities between Sarah's life and Rebekah's. The Abimelech incident happened to both women, an identical situation in which both wives were sexual hostages to their husbands' passivity. Both women were also barren, Rebekah for twenty years, Sarah until she was ninety. Both women were dominant figures who spoke out and took initiative in making decisions affecting their lives. Rebekah went to great lengths to ensure the precedence of her younger son. Jacob was Rebekah's choice, not Isaac's, and she had no qualms about deceiving her husband so that his blessing and therefore his authority would pass to Jacob and not to Esau. The patriarch from whom the twelve tribes and consequently the nation of Israel would descend was a quiet man who stayed in the tents and was influenced and directed by his mother. Later perspectives have not managed to erase all of the matriarch Rebekah's contribution to tradition.

◇ **Lectionary Reading**

Now it was told to Abraham,
"Milcah has also borne children
to your brother Nahor:
Uz the firstborn,
Buz his brother,

Kemuel the father of Aram,
Chesed, Hazo, Pildash,
Jidlaph, and Bethuel."
Bethuel had a daughter named Rebekah.

◇

Now when Abraham was well advanced in years,
he said to his eldest servant
who had charge of all his possessions,
"Swear by the God of heaven and earth
that you will not choose a wife for my son Isaac
from among the daughters of the Canaanites,
but that you will return to my country
and take a wife from among my relatives."
The servant said to him,
"What if the woman is unwilling
to come back with me to Canaan?
Shall I then take Isaac back again
to the land from which you came?"
Abraham said to him,
"Do not take my son back there.
The God of heaven who led me
out of my father's house
and away from the land of my birth,
who spoke to me and swore to me
that my offspring would be given this land,
this God will send an angel before you
to find a wife there for my son.
But if the woman is unwilling to return with you,
then you will be free from this oath,
only do not take my son back there."
So the servant swore to do this.
Then he took ten camels and many choice gifts
and left for the city of Nahor
which is called Aram-naharaim.
At the outskirts of the city, toward evening,
when the women go forth to draw water,
he settled his camels near the village well
and uttered a fervent prayer,
"O God of my master Abraham,
please grant me success today
and show your steadfast love to my master.
The girl to whom I say,
'Please give me your jar that I may drink,'
and who answers,
'Drink, and I will water your camels' —
let her be the one whom you have chosen

as wife for your servant Isaac.
By this shall I know that you have shown
your steadfast love to my master."
Before he had finished praying,
Rebekah, daughter of Bethuel,
granddaughter of Milcah,
approached with her water jar.
She was lovely to look at, unmarried,
and she went down to the spring to fill her jar.
Just as she was coming up again,
the servant ran to meet her and said,
"Please let me sip a little water from your jar."
"Drink, my lord," she responded,
and she lowered her jar to give him a drink.
And when he had finished she said to him,
"I will draw water for your camels also,
until they have had their fill."
So she emptied her jar into the trough
and ran to draw some more
until she had watered all his camels.
The servant gave her two gold bracelets
and a gold nose ring.
"Tell me whose daughter you are," he asked.
"Is there room in your father's house
for us all to spend the night?"
"I am the daughter of Bethuel
and the granddaughter of Milcah," she said.
"We have plenty of straw and fodder
and a place to spend the night."
The servant bowed and worshiped God, saying,
"Blessed be the God of Abraham,
who has shown a steadfast love
and has been faithful to my master.
For God has led me directly
to the house of my master's relatives."
The girl ran and told her mother's household
about all that had occurred.
Her brother Laban,
seeing the ring and bracelets,
and hearing his sister's excited words,
hurried out to the spring of water.
"Welcome, O blessed servant of God.
Why do you stand outside?
Our house is prepared to receive you."
So Laban led him into the house
and gave him water to wash his feet

and brought water for the men who were with him,
then Laban unloaded the camels
and fed them straw and fodder.
When food was set before Abraham's servant,
he refused to eat until he had spoken of his errand.
Then he recounted to Rebekah's family
every detail of his journey,
the oath, the sign, Rebekah's response,
and inquired of Laban and Bethuel
what they were prepared to do.
"This is of God," they answered.
"There is nothing we can add.
Here is Rebekah, take her and go.
Let her be the wife of your master's son,
as God has clearly spoken."
On hearing their words,
Abraham's servant bowed to the ground.
He took garments and jewelry of silver and gold
and gave these to Rebekah.
He also gave to her mother and her brother
some costly ornaments.
Then he and the men who accompanied him
ate and drank and spent the night,
and when they rose in the morning, he said,
"Send me back to my master."
Her mother and brother pleaded with him.
"Let the girl stay a little longer.
After ten days, she may go."
But the servant said, "Do not delay me,
for God has made my journey successful.
Let me return to my master."
"We will ask the girl," they said to him,
and when Rebekah was asked,
"Will you go with this man?"
she responded, "Yes, I will."
So they sent Rebekah and her personal maid
with Abraham's servant and his men,
and they blessed Rebekah and said to her,
"Sister of ours, may you increase
to thousands and tens of thousands!
May your descendants gain possession
of the gates of their enemies!"
Then Rebekah and her maids mounted the camels
and followed Abraham's servant.
Now Isaac had gone for a walk in the field
just as it was evening.

Looking up he saw camels approaching.
Rebekah, when she saw Isaac,
quickly dismounted the camel and asked,
"Who is the man over there
who is crossing the field to meet us?"
The servant said, "It is my master, Isaac."
So she took her veil and covered her face.
The servant told Isaac all that had happened.
Then Isaac brought Rebekah into the tent
that had belonged to his mother, Sarah,
and he took Rebekah for his wife.
Isaac loved Rebekah,
and his love for her was a comfort to him
after his mother's death.

◊

These are the descendants of Isaac and Rebekah.
Isaac, son of Abraham and Sarah,
was forty years old when he married Rebekah,
granddaughter of Milcah,
daughter of Bethuel of Paddan-aram,
sister of Laban the Aramean.
Rebekah was barren,
but after much prayer,
she discovered that she was pregnant.
Her pains were so fierce
she was close to despair,
so she sought an explanation from God.
And God said to Rebekah,
"Two nations are struggling within your womb.
You will give birth to two rival peoples.
One nation will dominate the other,
and the elder will serve the younger."
When the time came for her to give birth,
there were indeed twins in her womb.
Her firstborn was red and hairy all over,
so they named the baby Esau.
His brother was born clutching Esau's heel,
so they named the second son Jacob.
Now Isaac was sixty years old
when Rebekah gave birth to Esau and Jacob.
When the boys grew up,
Esau was a hunter, a man of the fields,
while Jacob, a quiet man, stayed in the tents.
Isaac was partial to Esau,
because he was fond of game,
but Rebekah loved Jacob.

Once when Jacob was cooking a stew,
Esau came in from the field, famished,
and he said to his brother Jacob,
"Let me eat some of that red soup there,
for I am very hungry."
"You may if you sell me your birthright," Jacob said.
"What use is a birthright if I die of starvation,"
was Esau's quick response.
"Swear to me first," said Jacob.
So Esau swore to sell his birthright,
and Jacob gave him bread and lentil stew.
He ate and drank
and rose up and went away,
without a second thought for his birthright.

◇

There was famine in the land of Canaan,
like in the days of Abraham,
so Isaac, led by the word of God,
went to King Abimelech of the Philistines
in the town of Gerar in the Negeb.
God had appeared to Isaac and said,
"Do not go down into Egypt.
Settle here as an alien,
and I will be with you and will bless you,
for I will give to you and your descendants
all these lands as I promised to Abraham your father.
And I will make you as numerous as the stars of heaven
and all nations of the earth shall be blessed through you,
because Abraham obeyed my voice
and kept all of my commandments."
So Isaac and Rebekah settled in Gerar,
and when the men inquired about Rebekah,
he told them, "She is my sister,"
for he was afraid to say, "my wife,"
for fear that some man might kill him for her,
for Rebekah was very beautiful.
Now after they had been there for quite some time,
King Abimelech looked out of a window
and saw Isaac fondling his wife.
So Abimelech sent for Isaac and said,
"So she is your wife!
Then why did you say, 'She is my sister?'
What if someone had taken her
and brought guilt upon us all?
Why have you done this to us?"
"Because I was afraid," said Isaac.

"I might have been killed because of her."
So Abimelech warned everyone, saying,
"Whoever touches this man or his wife,
he will be put to death."
So Isaac and Rebekah departed from there
and camped for a time in the valley of Gerar
before moving on to Beer-sheba.
Now when Esau was forty years old,
he married Judith,
the daughter of Beeri the Hittite,
and Basemath,
daughter of Elon the Hittite,
and they made life bitter for Rebekah and Isaac.

◇

When Isaac was old and nearly blind,
he summoned his firstborn, Esau, and said,
"The day of my death is approaching.
Take your weapons, go into the fields,
and hunt some game for me.
Then prepare a dish of savory food,
the kind that I enjoy,
so I might eat it and bless you
before I die."
Now Rebekah overheard what Isaac had said,
so she went to Jacob and said to him,
"Your father sent Esau to hunt for game
and to prepare a savory stew for him,
that he might eat and bless him
before he dies.
Now listen to what I say.
Take two choice kids from our own flock
and I will prepare a savory dish,
the kind your father enjoys.
You will take it to your father,
so that he may bless you before he dies."
But Jacob said to his mother,
"My brother Esau is a hairy man,
while my own skin is smooth.
If my father should feel me
and discover our deceit,
he may curse me rather than bless me."
"Let the curse be on me," Rebekah replied.
"Only do as I have said."
So Jacob brought to his mother two choice kids
and she prepared the kind of savory food
that Isaac especially loved.

Then Rebekah wrapped Jacob in Esau's garments,
covered his neck and hands with the skins of the kids,
and gave him the food and the bread she had baked
to take to his father Isaac.
Jacob went in to his father, who asked,
"Who are you, my son?"
"I am your firstborn, Esau," he replied.
"I have done what you requested.
Now eat of the game, and bless me."
But Isaac said to Jacob,
"How could it be that you found the game so quickly?"
"God made me successful," he replied.
Then Isaac said,
"Come here and let me feel you,
to be sure that you are Esau."
So Jacob drew near to Isaac,
who felt his hands and said,
"The voice is the voice of Jacob,
but the hands are the hands of Esau."
Because Jacob's hands were hairy,
Isaac failed to recognize him.
"Are you really my son, Esau?" he asked.
"I am," Jacob responded.
"Then bring me the food
that I might eat
and afterward give my blessing."
So Jacob gave him food and wine,
and when he was finished eating and drinking,
Isaac said to Jacob,
"Come here and kiss me, my son."
So Jacob kissed his father,
who smelled the smell of his garments
and blessed him with these words:
"Ah, the smell of my son
is the smell of a field
which God has graciously blessed.
May God give you the dew of heaven,
and the fatness of the earth,
and grain and wine in abundance.
May others serve you,
and may other nations bow before you.
May your mother's sons bow down to you
and may you rise above your brothers.
Cursed be the one who curses you,
and blessed be those who bless you!"
When Isaac had finished blessing Jacob,

and Jacob had left his presence,
his brother Esau came in from the hunt.
He brought savory food to his father and said,
"Come, eat this game, and then bless me."
"Who are you?" asked Isaac.
"I am your firstborn, Esau," he replied.
Isaac shook visibly and asked with alarm,
"Then who was here before you?
I ate his game and I blessed him.
And the blessing cannot be recalled!"
Esau howled when he heard these words.
"Bless me also, father!" he cried.
But Isaac replied,
"Your brother came in here deceitfully
and he has taken away your blessing."
"Jacob!" shouted Esau.
"How well he is named,
for twice now he has supplanted me.
He took away my birthright
and now he has taken away my blessing!"
Then Esau pleaded with Isaac,
"Have you not reserved a blessing for me?"
Isaac answered Esau.
"I have already made him lord over you,
and I have made his brothers his servants,
and with grain and wine I have sustained him."
"Have you only one blessing, father?
Please, bless me too!"
And Esau wept in despair.
Then Isaac said these words:
"Your home shall be far from the fatness of earth
and away from the dew of heaven.
By your sword you shall live.
You shall serve your brother,
but when you break free,
you shall remove his yoke from your neck."
Now Esau hated Jacob
because he had stolen his father's blessing,
and Esau plotted revenge.
"After we bury my father,
I will kill my brother Jacob," he mused.
But Rebekah learned of Esau's plans
and she sent for Jacob and told him.
"Esau is planning to kill you," she said.
"Flee at once to my family in Haran
and stay with my brother Laban.

When Esau's anger eases,
and he forgets what you have done,
I will send for you and bring you back."
Then Rebekah said to Isaac,
"These Hittite women have made me miserable.
If Jacob should marry one of these,
what good will my life be?"

◇

Then Isaac summoned Jacob and said,
"You shall not marry a Canaanite.
Go to Paddan-aram
to the house of your mother's family,
and take one of Laban's daughters as wife.
May El Shaddai bless you and make you fruitful
and may you become a multitude of people.
May God give the blessing of Abraham and Sarah
to you and to your descendants,
that you may take possession of the land
that God has promised to Abraham and Sarah."
So Jacob left for Paddan-aram,
to Laban the Aramean,
the brother of his mother Rebekah.

◇

When Jacob was about to die,
he said, "Bury me with my ancestors —
in the cave in the field of Ephron the Hittite.
There Abraham and Sarah were buried,
there Isaac and his wife Rebekah were buried . . .
in the cave in the land of Canaan."

## ◇ Points for Shared Reflection

- If Bethuel were Rebekah's mother and not her father (see "Context," page 32), her self-identification would have been, "I am Rebekah daughter of Bethuel daughter of Milcah." Move through the group identifying yourselves in turn as daughter (or son) of _____ granddaughter of _____ great-granddaughter of _____, naming the women as far back as you can remember on your mother's side of the family. You may also want to include the women from whom your father descended.

- How far back were you able to remember? How do you feel about that? What does our truncated memory say about the value we place on genealogy? About the value we place on our matriarchal ancestry? How do we differ from biblical tradition, or do we?

- Rebekah told her son to deceive his father and steal his brother's blessing. How does the tradition justify her action? Can you justify it? What application, if any, can you make to your life?

- When Isaac felt threatened by other men, he used his wife as a shield, just as his father had used his mother, and exposed her to sexual harassment and rape. What does this say about his culture's attitude toward women's bodies? Are men more, or less, respectful of women's bodies today? Be specific in your response.

◇ **Berekah: A Psalm**  (see page 56)

◇ **Prayer**

Blessed are You,
Matriarch of the Universe,
for creating me
and re-creating me
more and more in Your image
as I enter daily
more deeply
into the meaning
and the mystery
of Your unconditional love.
I who am
daughter of earth
daughter of word
daughter of fire and Spirit,
lift my heart and the whole of my being
in prayer and praise to You.
Blessed are You,
Shekinah-Shaddai.
Blessed are You forever.
Amen.

*Choir 1*    Blessed is She, Song of the Universe,
Who sang our world into being,
weaving mystical melodies
out of themes composed of dust.

*Choir 2*    She gathers us into Her cosmic choir
to teach us Her song of love.

*Choir 1*    Blessed is She, Dance of the Universe,
Whose grace-full movement
breaks open our lives
to the twists and turns of Her Spirit.

*Choir 2*    She gathers us into Her circle of friends
to teach us Her dance of trust.

*Choir 1*    Blessed is She, Hope of the Universe,
spilling new possibilities
on the dead dreams of the despairing.

*Choir 2*    She gathers us into Her new creation
to help us begin again.

*Choir 1*    Blessed is She, Heart of the Universe,
beating with passion,
warm with compassion,
holding us all,
enfolding us all
in Her gentle, mystical Presence.

*Choir 2*    She gathers us into Her energy
to show us the strength of Her love.

*Choir 1*    Blessed is She, Soul of the Universe,
feeling the pain of those who grieve
and the joy of those rejoicing.

*Choir 2*    She gathers us into Her Spirit-space
to teach us to be like Her.

*Choir 1*    Blessed is She, Shalom of the Universe,
Holy and wholly present
to the whole of Her cherished creation.

*Choir 2*    She draws us into Her sacred Shalom
until we are one with Her.

# LEAH

◇ **Scripture Reference**   Gen 29:15–36; 30:1–21; 31:4–55
Gen 32:22–24; 33:1–7, 12–14
Gen 34:1; 35:23, 26; 46:8–18; 49:31

◇ **Biography**

Leah was the elder daughter of Laban, Rebekah's brother, who lived in Paddan-aram beyond Canaan. She tricked Jacob into marriage by taking the place of her sister Rachel on Jacob's wedding night. He married Rachel one week later. Leah bore six sons and a daughter, Dinah, and had two more sons through Zilpah her maid whom she gave to Jacob as a concubine. Leah suffered from Jacob's preference for Rachel and continued to hope her own fertility would turn his heart toward her. After her death, Jacob buried Leah in the tomb of his ancestors in Hebron.

Leah slips sideways into the narrative of Jacob's pursuit of Rachel. Having labored seven years in payment of her bridal price, Jacob wed Rachel fully expecting to spend the night with her and woke up beside her sister. Surely there is evidence of textual tampering here. One can imagine deceiving a man through a ceremony but not through the whole of his wedding night. Jacob probably discovered the switch too late and had to go along with it. After spending the required week with Leah, Jacob married Rachel as he had planned, not exactly an affirming beginning to Leah's married life. The marriages of Leah and Rachel to Jacob present a rare instance of sororal polygamy which is accepted without critique. From the beginning, however, biblical writers set up a rivalry between the sisters, consistently discrediting Leah in favor of the sister of choice. Leah's eyes were said to be *rak* (Hebrew for "tender, delicate, soft"). Until recently, scholars translated this as "weak" or "dull." Now some are saying "lovely." Although Leah is depicted as the less attractive and less loved wife, she does have an advantage. She is fertile and produces sons. With each birth Leah hoped to secure Jacob's favor. She may even have succeeded, because as her story progresses, Leah seems less insecure. After six biological sons and two more sons by adoption, Leah finally gave birth to a daughter whom the received text actually names, but there is no word of the mother-daughter bond that must have existed between them. Years later when her daughter Dinah is raped, Leah is not mentioned in the text.

The two sisters dominate the narratives of Jacob and exercise some control over their lives. They decide between them who will sleep with Jacob. They name all of their children. They expect to inherit and are bitterly disappointed when they learn that their father has forfeited what was supposed to have come to them. They discuss and support Jacob's decision to return to the land of Canaan and they choose to go with him. Leah emerges as a strong, positive figure when these points are emphasized. She was not a second-class wife or a secondary sister. As niece of Rebekah and biological mother of half the twelve tribes of Israel, she was a significant matriarch in the mainstream of tradition. Rachel's son Joseph as Pharaoh's aide in Egypt may have figured prominently in the lives of the Hebrew people, but it was from Leah's son Judah that David would descend.

◇ **Lectionary Reading**

When Jacob had been with Laban about a month,
his host said, "Just because you are a relative
does not mean you should serve me for nothing.
What shall I give you for wages?"
Now Laban had two daughters;

the elder daughter was Leah,
the younger one was Rachel.
Leah had lovely eyes.
Rachel was beautiful and graceful.
Jacob loved Rachel.
"I will serve you seven years
for your younger daughter Rachel," he said.
"Stay with me then," said Laban.
"It is better that I should give her to you
than to any other man."
So Jacob served Laban for seven years,
but they seemed to him like a couple of days
because of his love for Rachel.
After seven years, Jacob said to Laban,
"Give me Rachel as my wife,
for my time has been completed."
So Laban prepared a feast,
gathered the people,
and in the evening he brought his daughter to Jacob,
who took her as his wife.
When morning came and Jacob awoke,
he saw that he had slept with Leah!
Jacob went to Laban.
"Why have you done this to me?
Why have you deceived me?
Did I not serve you for Rachel?"
"This is not done in our country," said Laban,
"to give the younger daughter as wife
before the firstborn is married.
Stay a week with Leah,
and I will give you Rachel also,
if you serve me for another seven years."
So Jacob remained a week with Leah,
then took Rachel as his wife.
And Laban gave Zilpah to his daughter Leah
and Bilhah to his daughter Rachel
to serve them as their maids.
Now Jacob loved Rachel more than Leah
and willingly served Laban another seven years.
Leah, unloved, was fertile,
but her sister Rachel was barren.
Leah conceived and gave birth to a son,
and she named her firstborn Reuben, saying,
"God has looked on my affliction.
Surely now my husband will love me."
She conceived again and bore a son.

"Because God has heard how I am hated,
God gave me a second son," she said,
and she named the baby Simeon.
Again she conceived and again bore a son, saying,
"Now my husband will be joined to me,
for I have given him three sons."
She named the third child Levi.
Once more she conceived and when she gave birth,
she named her fourth son Judah, saying,
"This time I will give glory to God."
Then Leah stopped bearing children.

◊

Rachel, unable to give Jacob children,
envied her sister Leah.
One day she said to Jacob,
"Give me children or I shall die!"
Jacob became angry with Rachel and said,
"Do you think that I am God?
It is God who has withheld from you
the fruit of the womb."
Then Rachel said,
"Here is Bilhah, my maid.
Sleep with her, that she may give birth on my lap,
then I too will have children through her."
So Jacob took Bilhah to bed as his wife,
and Bilhah conceived and bore Jacob a son.
Then Rachel said, rejoicing,
"God has heard me and judged me
and given me a son."
Therefore, she named him Dan.
Bilhah conceived a second son.
"I have fought God's fight with my sister and won,"
said Rachel, and she named the newborn Naphtali.
Leah had ceased bearing children,
so she gave Zilpah her maid to Jacob as a wife,
and Zilpah gave Jacob a son.
And Leah said, "Good fortune!"
so she named the baby Gad.
Zilpah bore Jacob a second son,
and Leah said, "Happy am I
for women will call me happy."
She named the new son Asher.
Now during the days of the wheat harvest,
Reuben found mandrakes in a field
and brought them to his mother.
Then Rachel said to Leah,

"Please give me some of your mandrakes."
But Leah responded in anger,
"You have taken away my husband.
Would you take my son's mandrakes as well?"
Then Rachel said to her sister,
"Jacob can sleep with you tonight
if you give me some of your mandrakes."
When Jacob came in from the field that evening,
Leah went to him and said,
"Tonight you must come and sleep with me,
for I have hired you with my son's mandrakes."
So Jacob slept with Leah that night,
and she conceived and gave birth to a fifth son.
"God has paid me my wages in exchange
for giving my maid to my husband," she said,
so she named her new son Issachar.
Leah conceived again,
and when she gave birth to a son, she said,
"God has given me a fine dowry;
now my husband will honor me,
for I have given six sons to him."
She named the baby Zebulun.
Afterwards she bore a daughter,
and she named the little girl Dinah.
Then God remembered Rachel.
God heard her prayer, opened her womb,
and she conceived and bore a son.
"God has taken away my shame," she said,
and she named her child Joseph, saying,
"God, give me another son!"
After Rachel had given birth to Joseph,
Jacob said to Laban,
"Give me leave to return to my own home and my country.
Let me take my wives and my children
for whom I have served you all these many years."

◇

One day Jacob took Rachel and Leah into the field
where his flock was grazing and said,
"Your father no longer looks favorably on me.
But the God of my ancestors has been with me.
You know that I served your father faithfully,
yet he cheated me, changing my wages ten times,
and God kept me from harm.
God has taken away your father's livestock
and given them to me.
Then God's angel said to me in a dream,

'I have seen all that Laban is doing to you.
I am the God of Bethel,
where you once made a monument and a vow to me.
Leave this land immediately
and return to the land of your birth.' "
Then Rachel and Leah responded,
"What inheritance is there for us in our father's house?
Does he not look on us as foreigners?
He sold us and used all the money
that was given to him for us.
All the property that God took away from our father
belongs to us and our children.
Do whatever God has told you."
So Jacob set his wives and his children on camels
and drove out all of his livestock,
took all of his possessions,
all that he had acquired in Paddan-aram,
and left to return to his family home in Canaan.
Now Laban had gone to shear his sheep
and Rachel stole his household gods.
Laban did not know that Jacob was departing,
for Jacob had not told him.
Now Jacob and all his retinue
set out across the Euphrates
toward the hill country of Gilead.
On the third day Laban discovered
that Jacob and his daughters had fled,
so he assembled his kinsfolk and pursued him,
and seven days later overtook him in Gilead.
God warned Laban in a dream that night,
to "say not a word to Jacob."
When Laban entered Jacob's encampment,
he said to him, "What have you done?
Why have you deceived me?
Why have you carried my daughters away
like captives at the point of a sword?
Why did you flee in secret?
I would have sent you away with merriment and song,
with tambourines and lyres.
You should have let me kiss my children
and bid them all farewell.
What you have done is very foolish
and I have the power to harm you,
but your God spoke to me last night, saying,
'Speak neither good nor bad.'
You left because you were longing for home,

but then why did you steal my gods?"
Now Jacob did not know that his wife Rachel
had stolen her father's gods.
So when he answered Laban, he said,
"We left secretly because I was afraid
you would take your daughters away from me.
As for your gods, if you should find them here,
then the one who took them will die."
Laban searched the tent of Jacob,
then Leah's tent and the tents of his daughters' maids,
but he did not find his gods.
Now Rachel had hidden them in the camel's saddle
and she was sitting on them.
When Laban entered Rachel's tent,
she apologized to him.
"Forgive me for not rising to greet you,
but it is now my time of month."
So he searched the tent thoroughly
but he did not find the household gods.
Then Jacob, angry, scolded Laban.
"Exactly what is my offense
that you have so hotly pursued me
and rummaged through all my goods?
What have you found that is yours?
These twenty years I have been with you,
neither ewe nor goat has miscarried.
I did not eat the rams of your flocks.
When any of your herd was destroyed by beasts,
I bore the loss myself.
The heat of the day consumed me
and cold kept me awake at night.
For twenty years I was in your house.
I worked fourteen years for your daughters
and six years for your flock,
and ten times you changed my wages.
If the God of my ancestors had not been on my side,
I would now be empty-handed.
God saw my affliction and the work of my hands
and reprimanded you last night."
Then Laban answered Jacob,
"The daughters are my daughters,
the children are my children,
the flocks are my flocks,
and all that you see is mine.
But what am I to do about these daughters of mine
or their children whom they have borne?

Come, let us make a covenant, you and I,
and let it be a witness between us."
So Jacob took a stone and made a monument;
then he said to his relatives, "Gather stones,"
and they made a mound of stones,
and they ate a meal beside it.
They called the mound Galeed
and they called the pillar Mizpah.
Then Laban said to Jacob,
"May this mound be a witness between you and me,
and may God watch over us when we are apart.
If you should ill-treat my daughters,
or take wives in addition to my daughters,
although no one is present, remember:
God is a witness between us.
This mound and this monument also bear witness
that I will not pass beyond this point
to cause you bodily harm,
nor will you pass beyond this point
in order to do harm to me,
and may God be the judge between us."
Then Jacob made an oath that this would be so
and offered a sacrifice there on the mountain
and invited his whole family to the meal,
and they feasted well into the night.
Then Laban arose early in the morning,
kissed his grandchildren and his daughters
and blessed them,
then departed and went back home.

◇

Jacob took his two wives, his two maids,
and his eleven children,
and crossed the ford of the Jabbok.
He set these and everything else he had
on the other side of the stream,
and while he was alone,
he wrestled with an angel until daybreak.

◇

Now Jacob looked up and saw Esau coming,
and four hundred men were with him.
So he separated his children
among Leah and Rachel and their two maids.
He put the maids with their children in front,
then Leah with her children,
then Rachel and Joseph last of all.
He himself went on ahead of them,

bowing low to the ground seven times,
until he came close to his brother.
But Esau ran to meet him,
and he kissed him and embraced him,
and both Jacob and Esau wept.
When Esau saw the women and children, he asked,
"Who are these who are with you?"
And Jacob said to his brother,
"The children God has graciously given your servant."
Then the maids and their children drew near and bowed,
and Leah and her children approached and bowed,
and finally Rachel and Joseph arrived,
and they too bowed before him.
Then Esau said, "Let us journey together
and I will travel beside you."
Jacob said to his brother,
"The children are frail,
some of the flock and herds are nursing;
if they are overdriven but a single day,
I fear that the flocks will die.
Let my lord pass on ahead of his servant
and I will follow slowly,
according to the pace of the cattle
and the children and their needs,
until we meet in Seir."

[*Leah's story concludes below. For the conclusion of Rachel's story, turn to page 70.*]

◇

The sons of Leah were Reuben, Simeon, Levi,
Judah, Issachar, and Zebulun.
These were the sons of Leah,
whom she bore to Jacob in Paddan-aram,
together with a daughter Dinah;
all her children and grandchildren
numbered thirty-three.
The sons of Zilpah, Leah's maid, were Gad and Asher.
The children and grandchildren of Zilpah and Jacob
numbered sixteen persons in all.

◇ **Points for Shared Reflection**

- We have thought of Rachel as beautiful and Leah as plain or unattractive, even though the meaning of the Hebrew *rak* describing Leah is uncertain. What role does physical beauty play in influencing our attitudes? How does your own religious preference or prejudice bias your perception of others?

- Do you think tradition has misrepresented Leah? What is her significance? Why is Rachel considered the one whom God has favored?

- In what ways might Leah be an inspiration to you? In what ways do you identify with her?

- Briefly consider the meaning of the names Leah gave to her eight biological and adoptive sons. What do these names say about Leah and her relationship to those around her? Why is there no meaning statement accompanying the name of her daughter Dinah?

◇ **A Psalm on Naming God** (see page 67)

◇ **Prayer**

O One Who Is Beyond All Names,
how eager we are to name You
from our limited perspective,
so we can claim You
as Someone we know
because You have been named.
Yet if we have no name for You,
how can we call upon You
in the fullness of our exuberance
and the emptiness of despair?
Give us the word to call You by
and the images by which to know You
as One Who is bonded to us in love,
now and forever.
Amen.

# ◇ A PSALM ON NAMING GOD ◇

*Choir 1*   Encircling One
Who encircles all
in a love that lasts forever:

*Choir 2*   we know You will encircle us
when we call You by Your name.

*Choir 1*   One Who Waits
for those who forget
and for those who walk away:

*Choir 2*   we know You will always wait for us
when we call You by Your name.

*Choir 1*   Breasted One
Who lavishly feeds
all those who hunger for wholeness:

*Choir 2*   we know You will feed and nurture us
when we call You by Your name.

*Choir 1*   Still Voice in a Raging Storm,
the quiet intuition
in the depths of our inner selves:

*Choir 2*   we know You will speak Your truth to us
when we call You by Your name.

*Choir 1*   One Who Longs and Is Longed For,
the ache at the heart of our universe,
the desire of all to be one:

*Choir 2*   we know You will be one with us
when we call You by Your name.

*Choir 1*   One Who Sits with Sorrow,
cradling the pain of generations
in the hollows of Your heart:

*Choir 2*   we know You will sit with us in our pain
when we call You by Your name.

*Choir 1*   Rainbow of Chaotic Color,
encompassing all the variety
of a pluriform universe:

*Choir 2*   we know You will open Your world to us
when we call You by Your name.

By M. T. Winter, Crossroad Pub. Co., © 1991 Medical Mission Sisters    

# RACHEL

◇ **Scripture Reference**    Gen 28:1–5; 29:1–31; 30:1–26; 31:4–55
Gen 32:22–24; 33:1–7, 12–14
Gen 35:16–21, 24–25; 46:19–22; 48:7
Jer 31:15

◇ **Biography**

Rachel was the younger daughter of Laban, Rebekah's brother. When Jacob journeyed to the country of his ancestors to find a wife among his relatives, he fell in love with Rachel and agreed to work seven years for her, but when his service was completed, her father tricked him into marrying her older sister Leah. Rachel became Jacob's second wife for whom he worked another seven years. Rachel, loved by Jacob, was childless, while Leah gave birth to sons. Rachel gave her maid Bilhah to Jacob as a concubine and claimed two sons through her before she herself became pregnant and gave birth to Joseph. She died on the way to Canaan while giving birth to her son Benjamin and was buried near Bethlehem.

When Jacob with his wives and children decided to emigrate to Canaan, Rachel stole her father's *teraphim* — his sacred images or household gods — and took them along with her. She concealed this fact from Jacob and hid the images from her father who came in search of them. Why did she take these religious objects? Was it because she was a believer? Was it because they bestowed spiritual authority and power on the person who possessed them? Did Rachel really steal them from her father or could her mother have given them to her for support in a foreign culture? Rachel's mother is not mentioned in the narrative nor anywhere else in the Bible, perhaps because of her religious influence on the matriarch whom biblical tradition favored. The tradition favored Rachel because Rachel was the mother of Joseph who saved the Hebrew people during the years of devastating famine. But Joseph would also contribute much toward his people's enslavement in Egypt, taking their land for Pharaoh in a desperate exchange for grain that would pull them deeper into bondage and set the scene for the Exodus. Long after Rachel's death, Joseph married the daughter of an Egyptian high priest, a choice his mother might have understood. The episode of the *teraphim* is treated as a minor moment in Rachel's main storyline, but subsequent events suggest it was much more important than that. After settling in the land of Canaan, Jacob insisted that members of his household and others who were with him relinquish their foreign gods, which he buried near Shechem (35:2–4). Then God appeared to Jacob at Bethel to renew the covenant and to change Jacob's name to Israel. Shortly after leaving Bethel, Rachel died in childbirth. She had named her son Ben-oni, but Jacob renamed him Benjamin, wiping out yet another trace of the matriarch's influence.

◇ **Lectionary Reading**

Then Isaac summoned Jacob
and blessed him and said,
"You shall not marry a Canaanite woman.
Go now to Paddan-aram
to the house of Bethuel, your mother's kin,
and take for your wife
one of the daughters of Laban, your mother's brother.
May El Shaddai bless you and make you fruitful
and may you become a multitude of people.
May God give the blessing of Abraham and Sarah
to you and to your descendants,
that you may take possession of this land
that God has promised to Abraham and Sarah."
So Isaac sent Jacob to Paddan-aram,

to Laban the Aramean,
brother of Rebekah,
the mother of Jacob and Esau.

◇

When Jacob had arrived at the end of his journey,
he stopped by a well
where three flocks of sheep and their shepherds
were waiting.
The stone on the mouth of the well was large,
and when all the flocks were gathered there,
the shepherds would remove the stone,
water the sheep, and then put it back in place.
"My brothers, where do you come from?" Jacob asked.
"We are from Haran," they answered.
"Do you know Laban son of Nahor?"
"Yes, we do," they responded.
"Is it well with him?" asked Jacob.
"Yes," they replied,
"and here is his daughter Rachel
coming with the sheep."
Then Jacob said, "It is still quite light,
too early to gather the sheep.
Water your sheep and return them to pasture."
"We must wait until the flocks are gathered," they said.
"Only then is the stone removed from the well
and all the sheep are watered."
While he was still speaking,
Rachel arrived with her father's flock.
Jacob rolled the stone from the mouth of the well,
watered his mother's brother's sheep,
kissed Rachel, and wept.
He told her he was her relative,
that he was Rebekah's son,
and Rachel ran to tell her father.
When Laban heard it was his sister's son,
he ran to Jacob, embraced him, kissed him,
and brought him to his house.
After Jacob had told him all the news, Laban said,
"Surely you are my flesh and bone."

[*Turn to the Lectionary Reading for "Leah," page 58, and continue with Rachel's story, which concludes with the text below.*]

◇

When they began their journey from Bethel
where they had settled for awhile,
Rachel was with child.

When they were still some distance from Ephrath,
Rachel went into labor and her delivery was hard.
The midwife said to Rachel,
"Do not be afraid, you will have another son."
Rachel died giving birth to her baby.
She had named the boy Ben-oni,
but his father called him Benjamin.
Jacob buried Rachel in Bethlehem,
which is on the way to Ephrath,
and he placed a monument on her grave.
It is the monument of Rachel's tomb,
and it stands there to this day.
Now the sons of Rachel were Joseph and Benjamin,
and the sons of Bilhah, Rachel's maid,
were Dan and Naphtali.
The children and grandchildren of Rachel and Jacob
numbered fourteen persons in all.

◇ **Points for Shared Reflection**

- Why does biblical tradition favor Rachel instead of Leah? Compare both sisters, their strengths and weaknesses. Is one more significant than the other? Why?

- What do you suppose was Rachel's relationship to those household gods? What religion did Rachel practice?

- The influence of the goddess traditions and new age spirituality is widespread in contemporary culture. Do you think it is appropriate to incorporate some of their images and traditions into the rites and rituals of biblical religion? If so, to what degree?

- With what particular aspect of Rachel's life do you particularly identify? In what ways is she an inspiration to you?

◇ **A Psalm in the Spirit of Gaia** (see page 73)

◇ **Prayer**

Glory of Gaia,
Creator of Earth,
sensitize us
to the Spirit-filled forces
at work in the womb
of our planet,
healing the wounds inflicted
on humanity's vulnerable sister,
and teach us to hallow
as sanctuary
the ground beneath our feet.

You are the Earth Mother
Gaia serves,
the Birth Mother
of our being,
incorporating all
cosmic energy
into Your wisdom ways.
All planetary harmony
echoes Your name.
In You is the Gaia
to whom we return
and from whom
humanity came.
Through You
Gaia is ever changing
and yet forever the same.
Blessed are You.
Amen.

# ◇ A PSALM IN THE SPIRIT OF GAIA ◇

*Choir 1*   My sister Gaia
wakes with dawn,
flushed with contentment,
praising Shaddai:

*Choir 2*   may the dawn of a new day
break upon us
with blessings for the earth.

*Choir 1*   My sister Gaia
walks in the light
of sun and moon,
praising Shaddai:

*Choir 2*   may the light of wisdom
enlighten us
with blessings for the earth.

*Choir 1*   My sister Gaia
cries in the rain,
writhing in pain
from the rape of her body,
beseeching Shaddai:

*Choir 2*   may the pain of our planet
move us all
toward a healing of the earth.

*Choir 1*   My sister Gaia
sits in the forest
hugging her trees
which were gifts from Shaddai:

*Choir 2*   may all that grows
take root in us
and make us one with the earth.

*Choir 1*   My sister Gaia
swims like a fish,
soars like a bird,
resembles all animals,
for she is all species
loved by Shaddai:

*Choir 2*   may all living creatures
teach us how
to be caretakers of the earth.

By M. T. Winter, Crossroad Pub. Co., © 1991 Medical Mission Sisters   *WomanWisdom* / 73

# MIRIAM

◇ **Scripture Reference**   Ex 2:1–10; 15:19–21; Num 12; 20:1–2
Deut 24:8–9; 1 Chr 6:1–3; Mic 6:3–4

◇ **Biography**

Miriam, daughter of Jochebed and Amram and granddaughter of Kohath who was a son of Levi, was the sister of Moses and Aaron and shared leadership with her brothers during the exodus from Egypt. She led the women in song and spirited dance following the miracle at the Sea of Reeds and was briefly afflicted with a debilitating skin disease after criticizing her brother Moses. Miriam died and was buried in Kadesh in the wilderness of Zin without reaching the promised land.

◇ **Context**

Phyllis Trible's exegesis of the biblical texts that comprise the full narrative of Miriam ("Bringing Miriam Out of the Shadows," *Bible Review*, February 1989) reclaims for us all a strong female leader from the early days of our tradition. The woman who emerges as equal to her brothers, Moses and Aaron, was a woman who had power, prominence, and prestige, an image decidedly minimized by the writers of her texts. We meet Miriam for the first time on the banks of the Nile River where her baby brother, Moses, floats between life and death while his big sister negotiates the terms of his survival. We see her next on the banks of the Sea of Reeds just after the miraculous run for freedom, leading the community in song and energetic dance accompanied by the women. When she dies in the wilderness and is buried in Kadesh, the text notes that there was no water there for the people. The water symbol in the Miriamic texts is a strong liberation motif: she saves Moses from the water, leads the Israelites through the water, and her absence parallels the absence of water, the source of life in the desert.

In the beginning of her story Miriam has no name, yet initiative and courage are characteristic of her even as a child. At the Sea of Reeds she has both a name and a title. She is Miriam the prophet, the first female prophet to appear in the Hebrew scriptures. She also has a role as leader of song and community celebration. Sometime later Miriam was involved in an incident where she and Aaron criticized their brother's leadership style and challenged his authority. Miriam, a prophet, wanted to share in his prophetic leadership. An exhausted Moses had asked for assistance, but God punished Miriam severely, according to the text. From that moment on Miriam is silent. She does not appear again until her death, where the text implies that she was buried in disgrace when, as Trible so aptly put it, her detractors "tabooed her to death" (p. 23).

Miriam was a leader who had the people's support. When she was put outside the camp, the people refused to go forward until she was brought back in again. When she died, the people refused to go on until she was properly buried. The text tries to present her as anonymous, silent, ineffective, excluded, disobedient and justifiably punished. Tradition remembers her for her courage, candor, initiative, spirit, her ability to inspire loyalty, and her quality of leadership, which included musical gifts. Miriam is one of the matriarchs, a heroine of the tradition.

◇ **Lectionary Reading**

The Israelites were fruitful and prolific.
They multiplied and grew powerful
and spread over the land of Egypt.
Pharaoh, king of Egypt, said to the Hebrew midwives,
"When you are called by the Hebrew women
to assist them in giving birth,
be attentive to the delivery.
If a boy is born, kill him.
If you deliver a girl, let her live."
(Ex 1:7, 15–16)
Now a man from the house of Levi
married a Levite woman
who conceived and bore a son.
When she saw how beautiful her baby was,
she hid him for three months.
When she knew she could hide him no longer,
she procured a papyrus basket,
sealed it with bitumen and pitch,
put her baby in the basket
and set it among the reeds
on the edge of the river Nile.
His sister stood by at a distance
to see what would happen to him.
Pharaoh's daughter came to the river to bathe
while her attendants strolled along its banks.
She saw the basket among the reeds
and sent her maid to fetch it.
She opened the basket and saw the child
and he began to cry.
"This must be one of the Hebrew children," she said,
and she took pity on him.
His sister approached Pharaoh's daughter.
"Shall I find a Hebrew woman
who is able to nurse the child for you?"
"Yes," the woman replied.
So the girl went and got her mother
and brought her to Pharaoh's daughter who said,
"Nurse this child for me

and I will see that you are paid."
So the woman took the child and nursed it.
When the boy grew older,
she brought him to Pharaoh's daughter
who treated him like a son.
She named the young boy Moses,
because "I drew him out of the water."
                    ◇
When the horses of Pharaoh
with his chariots and their drivers
went into the midst of the sea,
the waters washed over them,
but God saw to it that the Israelites
passed through the sea on dry ground.
Then the prophet Miriam, Aaron's sister,
took up a tambourine,
and all the women joined in with her
with tambourines and with dancing.
And Miriam led them in this song:
"Sing to God who has gloriously triumphed:
horse and rider are thrown into the sea."
                    ◇
While they were encamped at Hazeroth,
Miriam and Aaron criticized Moses
because of the Cushite woman
whom Moses had married —
for he had indeed married a Cushite.
"Has God spoken only through Moses?" they said.
"Has God not spoken also through us?"
And God heard their complaining.
Now Moses was a very humble man,
one of the humblest on the face of the earth.
Suddenly God spoke directly to Moses, Aaron, and Miriam.
"Come out to the tent of meeting, you three."
So the three of them went,
and God came down in a pillar of cloud
and stood at the entrance to the tent.
Then God called Aaron and Miriam
and the two of them came forward.
"Hear my words," said God.
"When there are prophets among you,
I make myself known to them in visions.
I speak to them in dreams.
Not so with Moses my servant.
He is entrusted with all of my house.
With him I speak face to face —

clearly, not in riddles.
And he beholds the form of God.
Why were you not afraid then
to speak against my servant Moses?"
And the anger of God lashed out against them,
and then God departed.
When the cloud had disappeared from the tent,
Miriam was like a leper.
Her skin was white as snow.
When Aaron saw that Miriam was leprous,
he cried out to Moses,
"I entreat you, my lord, do not punish us
for this sin we have so foolishly committed.
Do not make her hideous like an abnormal birth
whose stillborn flesh is already decayed
as it comes forth from its mother's womb."
And Moses cried to God:
"O God, I beg you, please heal her."
But God said to Moses,
"If her father had spit in her face,
would she not bear this shame for seven days?
Banish her from camp for seven days,
and after that, bring her in again."
So Miriam was banished for seven days,
and the people did not set out on their march
until Miriam had been brought in again.
After that the people set out from Hazeroth
and camped in the wilderness of Paran.

◇

The Israelites came into the wilderness of Zin,
the whole company of them, in the first month,
and the people camped in Kadesh.
Miriam died and was buried there.
Now there was no water for the congregation,
so they rose up against Moses and Aaron.

◇

Hear what God says:
"My people, what have I done to you?
How have I been a burden to you? Answer me!
I brought you out of the land of Egypt
and delivered you from slavery,
and I sent before you to lead you,
Moses, Aaron, and Miriam."

◇

The sons of Levi were:
Gershom, Kohath, and Merari.

The sons of Kohath were:
Amram, Izhar, Hebron, and Uzziel.
The children of Amram were:
Aaron, Moses, and Miriam.

◇ **Points for Shared Reflection**

- List the various ways in which Miriam exercised real leadership and discuss one or two of these points in depth.

- Can you think of a contemporary female figure who was considered a leader by the people and who was disparaged by those in authority?

- What moment in Miriam's life do you find particularly appealing or inspiring? What can you learn from her experience in that event that might be of benefit to you?

- What kind of song did Miriam sing? Was this a sacred or secular song? How does her song fit in with your definition of sacred music? Compare the music-making at the Sea of Reeds with your own tradition's ritual music. Which, if either, is more appropriate, and why?

◇ **Miriam's Psalm**  (see page 80)

◇ **Prayer**

We leave our chains behind
as You deliver us from bondage,
O One Who Parts the Waters.
Never again will we be slaves
to a system or to men.
We are crossing over
into hope
and into a new world order,
singing, dancing,
celebrating
the gift of our liberation
as the daughters
of Shaddai.
Amen.

*All*   Sing to Her with joy,
we are Her sisters and Her daughters.
Our liberation is at hand,
we are coming through the waters.

*Choir 1*   We who were once enslaved
will not let past pain
overtake us.

*Choir 2*   They brought our courage
to its knees,
but they could never break us.

*Choir 1*   We who were so long silent
shout the word
we are discerning.

*Choir 2*   We took the long way out
and we will never be returning.

*All*   Shout to Her with joy,
we are Her sisters and Her daughters.
Our restoration is at hand,
we are coming through the waters.

*Choir 1*   A short while
in the wilderness
will strengthen and prepare us.

*Choir 2*   They tell of the heat
and aridness,
but they will never scare us.

*Choir 1*   We are intimate
with barren wastes,
our very lives
were aborted.

*Choir 2*   Our deserts bloom
from hidden springs
that have yet to be reported.

*All*   Dance for Her with joy,
we are Her sisters and Her daughters.
Our transformation is at hand,
we are coming through the waters.

   By M. T. Winter, Crossroad Pub. Co., © 1991 Medical Mission Sisters

*Choir 1*   We can see into the promised land,
there are giants there
to top us.

*Choir 2*   They may delay
our coming in,
but they will never stop us.

*Choir 1*   We managed to make it
on our own,
but no more isolation.

*Choir 2*   Together we'll turn our world around.
We are a new creation.

*All*   Sing and dance with Her,
we are Her sisters and Her daughters.
Our celebration is at hand,
we are coming through the waters.

# ◇ II ◇
# Wives and Concubines

# CAIN'S WIFE

◇ **Scripture Reference**   Gen 4:1–17

◇ **Biography**

The wife of Cain, who murdered his brother Abel, was the daughter-in-law of Eve, the mother of a son named Enoch, and the grandmother of Irad.

◇ **Context**

Who was this woman, Cain's wife, and where on earth did she come from? The question may well be asked. The passages immediately preceding this narrative imply that Cain's mother Eve was the only woman on earth. One interpretation holds that Adam and Eve were intended to be representative of both genders, and that in the beginning, God created humanity, that is, a number of women and men. It is to these other women that we trace the origins of Cain's wife. There is no information about her, just the notation that Cain had a wife who had a son. Cain married his wife after he was banished and may have found her in the land of Nod (the Hebrew *nad* means "wanderer"), that is, as he wandered about the land. What was life like with the man she married, a professed murderer living in exile? Did he ever repent? Was he able to control his jealous rage? Was she ever abused? Did she ever meet her mother-in-law or come to know Cain's sisters? We can only speculate about Cain's wife.

Now Eve conceived a child by Adam
and gave birth to a son named Cain, meaning,
"I have produced with the help of God."
Soon after, she gave birth to his brother, Abel,
who grew up to be a shepherd,
while Cain cultivated the land.
In the course of time
Cain offered to God the fruit of the earth
and Abel brought the first-born lamb
and an offering of fat from his flock.
God favored Abel's offering,
but had no regard for Cain's,
and Cain was angry and depressed.
"Why are you so upset?" asked God.
"If you are well disposed, lift up your head,
if not, take care to overcome the sin
that is lurking at your door."
Cain said to his brother Abel,
"Come with me to the field."
And when they got there, Cain killed Abel.
Then God said, "Cain, where is Abel?"
"How should I know?" Cain responded.
"Am I my brother's keeper?"
Then God replied, "What have you done?
Listen to the sound of your brother's blood
crying out to me from the ground.
From now on the ground will be a curse to you,
for the land will no longer be fruitful
under your cultivation,
and you will be a fugitive
and wander across the earth."
Then Cain cried out,
"My punishment is greater than I can bear!
I am cut off from the soil,
I must hide from your face,
I must wander aimlessly over the earth,
and whoever meets me may kill me."
God said, "No! Whoever kills Cain
will suffer sevenfold vengeance."
So God put a mark on Cain to ensure
that none who saw him would kill him.
Then Cain went away from the presence of God
and settled east of Eden,

somewhere in the land of Nod.
The wife of Cain conceived a child
and she gave birth to a son named Enoch.
Her husband built a city
and named it Enoch
after his son.

◇ **Points for Shared Reflection**

- Speculate a bit about Cain's wife. Who was she? Where did she come from? What was it like to be married to Cain?

- Cain's wife married a man who had been banished. Have you ever been cut off from all support or felt that you had been? Share something of that experience.

- Women marry men who commit violent acts in the hope that they can change them. Comment on their chances of success and on the lives into which they are marrying. Has this happened to you? To anyone you know?

- If you could ask Cain's wife one question, what would that question be? Form a group with two or three others and speculate together on what her answer to the question might be.

◇ **A Psalm for the Wanderer** (see page 87)

◇ **Prayer**

O God of a Pilgrim People,
journey with us
as we seek the proper path
of our becoming.
From our mother's womb
until the tomb
You mark the passing moments
until we rest in You.
May we not wander
aimlessly
in search of ultimate meaning,
but lead us
gently and firmly
to the oasis
deep within You,
and show us how
to pitch our tents
in the valley of Your love.
Amen.

## ◇ A PSALM FOR THE WANDERER ◇

*Choir 1*    Guide the feet of those who walk
to the four corners of creation.
Make straight and smooth the path
that winds its way
back home to You.

*Choir 2*    Strengthen the hands that place the staff
to support us
on the mountains,
and give firm hand-holds
all the way up
the treacherous peaks of life.

*Choir 1*    Clear the eye that scans the sky
for hope on the far horizon,
and send warm rain
at a delicate pace
to erase the trace of tears.

*Choir 2*    Open wide our pilgrim heart
to the beauty and splendor of being,
and give a taste of that freedom we crave
in the confines of our souls.

*Choir 1*    Remember Your people,
O God of the Exodus,
remember their wilderness wandering,
so that never again
may Your children want
for water or for bread.

*Choir 2*    See to it that the ones You love
always travel downwind from danger,
and the snares
that sneak up on every side
are everywhere
overcome.

*Choir 1*    Praise the God of a pilgrim people
Who guards our coming and going.

*Choir 2*    Praise the God who guides us safely home
without our knowing.

By M. T. Winter, Crossroad Pub. Co., © 1991 Medical Mission Sisters    *WomanWisdom* /

# NOAH'S WIFE

◇ **Scripture Reference**   Gen 6:17–22; 7:1–16; 8:6–20; 9:8–17

◇ **Biography**

Noah's wife is an unknown, unnamed presence at the heart of the Genesis story of the flood. Mother of three sons, Shem, Ham, and Japheth, she was there when the ark was being built and when it was filling up with animals. She rode out the flood in cramped quarters, aware that the rest of the world was perishing and these few alone would live. Within her own small family circle, she created her world all over again after the flood waters receded. Who she was and how she felt as a female survivor, we will probably never know.

◇ **Context**

Legends of a flood exist in many cultural traditions, among the Indians of the Western Hemisphere, the Aborigines of Australia, the islanders of Central and South Pacific, and in various parts of Asia. Versions preserved in the ancient Mesopotamian traditions of Babylonia and Sumeria, in particular the Sumerian Epic of Gilgamesh, come closest to the biblical account. In Genesis God decides to punish humanity for its transgressions by destroying civilization, then gets very detailed about the kind of vessel needed to ride out the storm. The text implies that the building of the ark was a matter solely between Noah and God. It is hard to believe that Noah's wife had nothing to say about it. Noah's wife appears as an unknown, unimportant factor, necessary only as the female half of the human couple needed to continue the race. She is not consulted, she is not addressed, she does not speak a word. Intriguing questions arise and one immediately thinks of the woman. Who did the cooking, the feeding, the cleaning during those forty-plus days on the ark? The text makes clear that the world will survive because "one man alone is acceptable" and he will save his family. Texts, however, are not the sum total of tradition, and one might legitimately suspect that in the oral phase of transmission, particularly in matriarchal societies, the tale had other emphases. In fact the Genesis narrative itself is a synthesis of two independent texts, one with a cosmic emphasis (P source), the other more personal (J source). In both accounts the deluge is a cataclysmic fact and Noah is the favored one. After the flood God made a covenant, promising never again to destroy the world by water, and gave the rainbow as a sign, yet how many of us are aware that God made a covenant not only with Noah but also with Noah's wife and children and the animals and all of God's creation.

◇ **Lectionary Reading**

God said to Noah:
"I will cause a flood to cover the earth;
all flesh, all life
will perish in its waters;
all that inhabits the earth shall die.
But I will establish my covenant with you;
and you, your wife, your sons, their wives
shall come into the ark,
and you shall bring with you
two of all flesh,
two of every living thing,
female and male,
you shall bring with you into the ark
to keep their species alive.
Birds according to their kinds,
animals according to their kinds,
creeping things of every kind
shall come with you into the ark
so that they may be kept alive.

Store up every kind of food
for yourselves
and for the animals.
This Noah did.
He did all that God commanded.

◇

Then God said to Noah,
"Go into the ark with all of your household,
for you alone are acceptable to me
among this generation.
Take seven pairs of all clean animals,
the male with its mate;
and a pair of those animals that are not clean,
the male with its mate;
and seven pairs of the birds of the air,
female and male,
to keep their kind alive on earth.
In seven days I will send the rain;
it will rain for forty days and forty nights,
and every living thing that I have created
I will blot out from the face of the earth."
And Noah did all that God had commanded.
Noah was six hundred years of age
when the flood waters fell upon the earth.
And Noah with his wife
and his children with their spouses
went into the ark to escape the flood.
Of every animal, clean and unclean,
of birds and of all that creep on the ground,
two and two, female and male,
went into the ark with Noah and his wife,
just as God had commanded.
And seven days later,
the flood waters came
and the waters covered the earth.
In the six hundredth year of Noah's life,
on the seventeenth day
of the second month,
the windows of heaven were opened
and the fountains of the deep burst forth.
Rain fell on the earth
forty days and forty nights.
On that day Noah and his three sons,
Shem and Ham and Japheth,
and Noah's wife and his sons' wives
went into the ark

with every wild animal of every kind
and all domestic animals of every kind
and every creeping thing that creeps on earth
and every winged bird that flies from the earth.
They went into the ark with Noah and his wife,
went in as God had commanded.
And God shut the door behind them.

◇

After forty days Noah sent forth a dove
to see if the water had subsided,
but the dove returned to the ark.
Seven days later, a second dove returned with an olive branch.
After seven more days, a third dove went forth and did not return.

◇

On the first day of the first month,
when Noah was six hundred one years old,
the waters receded from the earth.
When Noah removed the covering of the ark
he saw that the ground was drying.
On the twenty-seventh day of the second month,
the earth was completely dry.
Then God said to Noah,
"Go out of the ark, you and your wife,
and take your sons and their wives with you.
Bring out with you every living thing —
every bird, every animal, every creeping thing —
so that they may flourish and fill the earth.
So Noah and his wife and his sons and their wives
and all the animals that inhabit the earth
left the ark in families.
Then Noah built an altar
and sacrificed burnt offerings to God.
Then God said to Noah and to all who were with him:
"I am establishing my covenant with you
and with your descendants after you
and with every living creature that is with you —
birds, domestic animals, every animal of the earth,
as many as came out of the ark.
I establish my covenant with you.
Never again shall all flesh be cut off by the waters.
Never again shall a flood destroy the earth.
This is the sign of the covenant that I make
between me and you and every living creature
for all future generations:
I have set my bow in the clouds,
and it shall be a sign of the covenant

between me and the earth.
When the bow is in the clouds,
I will see it and remember the everlasting covenant
between me and every living creature that inhabits the earth."

## ◇ Points for Shared Reflection

- Imagine for a moment that you are Noah's wife and you have just sealed the door against the rising waters. There you are with your family and representatives of every species on earth. Tell us, how do you feel? What is going through your mind?

- How would you retell the deluge story in a way that makes the woman equal to the man? You might want to act out the retelling.

- The text implies that Noah's wife is needed solely for making babies. Is this an accurate reading of the text? Would you care to comment on the statement in light of past and present attitudes?

- The aftermath of the flood bears some similarity to surviving nuclear annihilation. Imagine it is the morning after, and, like Noah's wife, you and several family members are the last females on earth. Talk about starting over and the sources of your strength.

## ◇ A Psalm for the Deluge (see page 93)

## ◇ Prayer

O One Who Stills the Waters,
Who makes the rising flood recede
after the deluge is over,
give us the strength
to ride out the storm
around us or within us.
Mitigate those violent forces
that can so quickly annihilate
the good we have accomplished,
destroying the world of the spirit,
submerging us in despair.
Be haven of hope
and an anchor
as we struggle against the current,
and sow new seeds of promise
when it is time to begin again.
God of Rain and God of Rainbow,
we trust You
and we love You.
Praise be to You.
Amen.

# ◇ A PSALM FOR THE DELUGE ◇

*Choir 1*  Save us, O God our Help,
for the waters are rising above us
and the waves are washing over us;
we are sinking,
sinking,
in the overwhelming
circumstances
that circumscribe our lives.

*Choir 2*  Help us, O God our Hope,
we are drowning
in the current ways
we deal with life around us,
deluged
with a flood of facts
and fears we cannot manage.

*Choir 1*  Storm-tossed,
we weep
as we see the world we cherish
disappearing,
grasp at uncertain symbols
as we thrash about to compensate
for the loss of security.

*Choir 2*  Set afloat
in a sea of wills,
we search for a clear direction,
trusting there is a haven
somewhere
just beyond
the slim horizon of hope
we can barely see.

*Choir 1*  Build us an ark
sturdy enough
to take us through tomorrow,
then set it a'sail
in the depths of our soul
with a single star
to guide us,
with a single song
to soothe us,
with Your Spirit
to keep us from breaking to bits
on the rock of self-preservation.

*Choir 2*   Fill us up with a double dose
of everything worth saving:
joy and gladness,
love and laughter,
goodness and kindness,
care and compassion,
justice and peace,
healing and hope,
silence and song,
wisdom and inspiration,
and all that has integrity
in the world of our familiar.

*Choir 1*   Send us a sign of encouragement
before we reach the breaking point,
a sign that says,
yes, there is hope,
yes, there is help,
yes, there is a world out there
ripe for the new creation,
where all that is valued
has a chance
to take root
and survive.

*Choir 2*   Spread above us,
around us,
within us,
a rainbow of the promises
Your covenant confirmed,
and let it be sign,
Shekinah,
of Your everlasting Presence
through storm,
struggle,
trial,
denial,
always ready to rescue us
and help us begin again.

   By M. T. Winter, Crossroad Pub. Co., © 1991 Medical Mission Sisters

# LOT'S WIFE

◇ **Scripture Reference**  Gen 19:1–26

◇ **Biography**

Lot's wife no doubt accompanied him on his journeys with Abraham and Sarah in and out of Egypt and up into the Negeb before settling in the city of Sodom in the fertile Jordan plain. She was the mother of two daughters. The story of the destruction of Sodom is the only specific reference to Lot's wife. It concludes with her looking back and being turned into a pillar of salt.

◇ **Context**

The one thing for which Lot's wife has been remembered is that she was turned into a pillar of salt. All kinds of negative associations surround this development. She disobeyed orders. She was overcome with curiosity. She looked back. And the next phrase that usually follows is, "Now wasn't that just like a woman!" What did happen to Lot's wife? No one really knows, but one fact is fairly certain: she did not turn into a pillar of salt. She may have died on the way — from a fall, a heart attack, smoke inhalation, or she may never have made it out of Sodom. She may have decided to remain where she was and consequently died in the conflagration because she could not bring herself to relinquish the familiar yet another time. Or maybe she did not believe her husband or did not want to go with him. After all, he had just offered their virgin daughters to an unruly mob to be raped in order to protect some passing strangers. What kind of God would reveal anything of import to a person such as that? And since God had spoken directly to Lot, not to Lot's wife, there was no question of disobeying God, despite what the commentators say, just a question of distrusting a husband. On the other hand she might have escaped to safety, then died a little while later. There may have been an interlude between arriving at the city of refuge and seeking asylum in a cave. Her death in Zoar may have led her husband and daughters to conclude that God was not yet finished with destruction. That could have sent them fleeing to the hills.

What then of the pillar of salt? It was probably an etiological legend which circulated to explain the origins of natural rock-salt formations in the area of Sodom and Gomorrah. Patriarchy could then have built on this with warnings of similar consequences for others inclined to look back to better days or to disobey the law. Salt does have some negative associations in biblical tradition. The pillar of salt becomes evidence of wickedness, "standing as a monument to an unbelieving soul" (Wis 10:7). It is threat of eternal damnation. "Remember Lot's wife. Those who try to make their life secure will lose it" (Lk 17:32–33). When Abimelech captured Shechem, "he razed the city and sowed it with salt" so it would not survive (Jdg 9:45). Salt was a sign of "the devastation of the land and the afflictions with which God has afflicted it — all its soil burned out by sulfur and salt, nothing planted, nothing sprouting, unable to support any vegetation, like the destruction of Sodom and Gomorrah" (Deut 29:22–23). At prayer one was reminded that God transforms "a fruitful land into a salty waste, because of the wickedness of its inhabitants" (Ps 107:34). However, the positive aspects of salt in biblical tradition and its essential role in Jewish life, ritual, and symbolism far outweigh the negative. This gives rise to a new perspective. For Lot's wife to be identified as having turned to salt may not be as derogatory as it might first appear. In fact, the pillar of salt may well have meant or may yet come to mean a sign of hope for women. The problem with the legend of the pillar of salt is not the story itself but its interpretation. It becomes for women a whole new symbol of meaning and power when taken positively.

In biblical times salt was a basic necessity of life. It had a natural association with food; it was used as a condiment to bring out full flavor, as a preservative to withstand decay. It had medicinal value. Newborn babies were rubbed with salt (Ezek 16:4). It had religious significance. Salt was used to bestow life-giving qualities and to safeguard against demonic influence. Elisha purified the spring at Jericho with salt (2 Kings 2:19–22). God's everlasting covenant was described as a "covenant of salt" (Num 18:19; 2 Chr 13:5). It was among those provisions required for temple use. It was strewn on sacrifices, on both cereal offerings and burnt offerings (Ezek 43:24). In fact it was essential to all sacrifices according to rabbinic interpretation of Lev 2:13; and it was used to season incense (Ex 30:35). Jesus said, "You are the salt of the earth" (Mt 5:13); and, "Have salt in yourselves" (Mk 9:50). The early Christian church continued the metaphor. "Let your speech always be gracious, seasoned with salt, so that you may know how you ought to answer everyone" (Col 4:6). Oscar Cullmann (*Essays on the Lord's Supper,* John Knox, 1958) points out that the Lord's Supper was regularly celebrated with bread and salt in Judaic Christianity (p. 10). He explains that "to take salt with someone" meant "to eat together" and that "to share in the salt" had become, in the Pseudo-Clementine writings, a technical term for "to celebrate the Lord's Supper" (p. 12). Today the Catholic church puts a tiny bit of salt on the candidate's tongue during the baptismal ritual. Salt is used by Jews in the process of making certain foods kosher and by just about everyone in making food more palatable. Cooks count on salt to can, pickle, preserve, and season foods, and hospitals give saline solutions intravenously to correct electrolyte imbalance. Idiomatic phrases in general use today illustrate the positive virtues of salt. Someone of value is "worth their salt," an experienced sailor is "an old salt." So why not remember Lot's wife as one who was a pillar of salt? If a pinch of salt can make such a difference, imagine a pillar of salt. What a powerful symbol, well worth preserving, one that women might justifiably aspire to own.

◇ **Lectionary Reading**

In the evening two angels came to Sodom.
Lot was sitting at Sodom's gate.
As soon as he saw them,
he rose to meet them
and bowed with his face to the ground.
He said, "Please, my lords,
spend the night with me;
you can wash your feet
and in the morning
you can be on your way again."
"We will spend the night in the square," they said.
But he persisted until they went home with him.
He made them a feast,
baked unleavened bread,
and they sat and ate their fill.
Before the guests had gone to bed,
the men of Sodom surrounded the house,
every last male, young and old.
"Where are the men who are with you tonight?"
the mob of Sodomites shouted.
"Hand them over to us
so that we might have sex with them."
Lot stepped out to reason with them
and shut the door behind him.

"I beg of you, my brothers," he said,
"do not do such an evil thing.
Look, I have two daughters who are virgins.
Let me bring them out to you
and you can do to them as you please,
only do not violate these men
who have sought hospitality with me."
But the mob responded, "Move out of the way."
Then they said to one another,
"This man who came here as a foreigner
now sets himself up as a judge!
We will do worse things to him
than we had planned to do to his guests."
Then they pushed Lot back against the door
and began to break it down.
The guests reached out, pulled Lot inside,
and barred the door behind him.
Then those who were pressing forward
were suddenly struck with blindness
and they could not find the door.
The guests said to Lot, "Is anyone else here?
Sons, daughters, sons-in-law, daughters-in-law,
or other relatives in the city?
You must get them out of here.
We are going to destroy this place
because the outcry against its people
has reached the ears of God
and God has sent us to wipe it out."
So Lot went and said to his sons-in-law
who were about to marry his daughters,
"Get up, we must get out of this place,
for God is about to destroy it."
But they thought that he was joking.
When morning came,
the angels urged Lot, saying to him,
"Get your wife and your daughters
and get out of here
or you will be consumed
in the punishment of this city."
But Lot lingered, so the angels seized him
and his wife and his two daughters,
and they took them and led them by the hand
out of the doomed city,
because God was merciful to them.
On the outskirts of Sodom they said to them,
"Run for your life. Do not look back

or stop anywhere in the plain.
Head for the hills or you will be consumed."
And Lot said to the angels,
"Oh no, my lords, you have saved my life
and shown me overwhelming kindness,
but I am afraid to flee to the hills
where the disaster might overtake me
and then I will surely die.
Look, see that small town over there?
It is near enough to flee to
and it is such a little place.
Spare that town — it is only a little one —
and I will go there to escape God's wrath
and there my life will be saved!"
"Very well," said the angels,
"we grant this favor also to you.
We will not destroy that town.
Hurry now, escape there,
for we can do nothing until you are safe."
Now the name of that town is Zoar.
As the sun was rising the following morning,
Lot and his family entered Zoar.
Then God rained fire and sulfur
on the cities of Sodom and Gomorrah
and overthrew the cities and the plain
and the inhabitants of the cities.
Lot's wife looked back,
and she became a pillar of salt.

◇ **Points for Shared Discussion**

- Lot's wife looked back. What's wrong with looking back? Is that reason for punishment? Have you ever looked back? It has been said that we only understand life by looking back. How do you feel about that?

- What do you think really happened to Lot's wife? Why might patriarchy have wanted to disparage her? Why might women praise her?

- Discuss Lot's wife as a pillar of salt in light of the information presented above. Is she a positive or negative figure for you? Have you always felt this way?

- Has history been fair to Lot's wife? As a woman, has life been fair to you? Do you see any connections between the biblical story and its interpretation of Lot's wife and the status of women today? Discuss the points that surface.

◇ **A Psalm Celebrating Salt** (see page 101)

◇ **Prayer**

O Salt of the Earth,
Who created the earth
and solicitously
sustains it,
to You we turn
when times are tasteless
and life has lost its flavor.
We savor Your goodness,
savor Your greatness,
and beg You to preserve us
from danger, damage, evil, pain
and any who would harm us,
now and forever.
Amen.

## ◇ A PSALM CELEBRATING SALT ◇

*All*    O taste and see how good God is!
Savor the One Who saves us!

*Choir 1*    Blessed are they
who are worth their salt,
who are pillars of strength
and integrity,
who are valuable
and valued,
on whom our world depends.

*Choir 2*    Blessed are they
who are salt of the earth,
who never lose perspective,
who carry on
and follow through
and always do
a whole lot more
than what has been intended;
for example,
they go the extra mile;
for example,
they turn the other cheek,
and are examples
to us all.

*All*    O taste and see how good God is!
Savor the One Who saves us!

*Choir 1*    Blessed are they
who are pillars of salt,
symbols of all who take a stand,
signs of life
in a desolate land,
telling us of the need
to look back
in order to understand.

*Choir 2*    Blessed are they
who share the salt
of human sweat
and human tears,
assuming some of the bondage
of the more desperate among us,
shouldering some of the crippling weight
of oppression in our midst.

By M. T. Winter, Crossroad Pub. Co., © 1991 Medical Mission Sisters

| | |
|---|---|
| *All* | O taste and see how good God is!<br>Savor the One Who saves us! |
| *Choir 1* | Blessed are You<br>Who season with salt,<br>O God of All Occasions.<br>You give our sometimes insipid selves<br>a radical new perspective,<br>even as you preserve the best<br>of what we already are. |
| *Choir 2* | Blessed are you,<br>our Protector.<br>Throw salt<br>on our doubts and our demons;<br>let them chase their tails forever.<br>Pour salt<br>on the wounds of all who dare<br>to lift their hand against You.<br>May they wallow in the wasteland<br>of their arrogance<br>and pride. |
| *Choir 1* | Blessed are You!<br>May the covenant of salt<br>between us<br>last forever. |
| *Choir 2* | From the psalter<br>of our conviction<br>we will praise<br>Your holy name. |
| *All* | O taste and see how good God is!<br>Savor the One Who saves us! |

   By M. T. Winter, Crossroad Pub. Co., © 1991 Medical Mission Sisters

# KETURAH

◇ **Scripture Reference**  Gen 25:1–6; 1 Chr 1:32–33

◇ **Biography**

The Bible gives no information at all about Keturah. She is simply listed as Abraham's concubine whom he married after the death of Sarah. She was the mother of six of his sons.

◇ **Context**

Sarah shared in the covenant promised by God through Abraham to their offspring, for Isaac her son was the one from whom God's chosen generations would descend. Hagar, Sarah's maid and Abraham's concubine, was also given a promise. The descendants of her son Ishmael would become a great nation. And then there was Keturah. Abraham took her, at least officially, after the death of Sarah. Was she wife or concubine? She is called both in the texts. A concubine could achieve a certain status if she gave birth to sons. Keturah had six sons, but we have no idea how she fit into Abraham's life or affection. Did he acquire her for a sexual relationship or simply to have more sons? Did he love her? The scriptures do not say. Abraham gave gifts to Keturah's sons, property no doubt, and livestock, but he kept them at a distance from Sarah's son who would inherit all that he had. Keturah's sons were the ancestors of six Arab tribes, the most prominent of which was Midian, the tribe of Jethro, father-in-law of Moses.

Abraham married another wife.
Her name was Keturah.
She bore him Zimran, Jokshan, Medan,
Midian, Ishbak, and Shuah.
Jokshan was the father of Sheba and Dedan.
The sons of Dedan were
Asshurim, Letushim, and Leummim.
The sons of Midian were
Ephah, Epher, Hanoch, Abida, and Eldaah.
All these were the children of Keturah.
Abraham gave all he had to Isaac.
He did give gifts to the sons of his concubines
while he was still alive,
but separated them from his son Isaac
by sending them to settle somewhere in the east.

◇ **Points for Shared Reflection**

- Keturah is a classic example of woman's second-class status. Name other examples from your own experience.

- Keturah gives another perspective of the patriarch Abraham. What new information have you learned about Abraham from his relationship with Keturah?

- Had you ever heard of Keturah? Why is she never mentioned?

- Who are the Keturahs of society today?

◇ **A Psalm to Widen Our Tents** (see page 105)

◇ **Prayer**

God of all cultures,
God of all people,
help us not to label anyone
inferior or second-class.
Help us overcome our attitudes
of superiority and oppression.
May we broaden our vision
and widen our tents
so that plurality and diversity
determine who we are:
people called and committed
to a world united
in justice and peace,
now and forever.
Amen.

## ◇ A PSALM TO WIDEN OUR TENTS ◇

*Choir 1*    Our world is too small.
Our lives are too small.
Our vision is too restricted.

*Choir 2*    May the people of various countries,
various cultures, tribes, and families
find room in our world and our lives.

*All*    Help us to widen our tents, Shaddai,
so that all are welcome among us.

*Choir 1*    Our attitudes are too parochial,
our assumptions too simplistic,
our behavior too predictable.

*Choir 2*    May special people,
may the differently abled,
may minorities of any kind —
of race, class, or gender —
find room in our world and our hearts.

*All*    Help us to widen our tents, Shaddai,
so that all are welcome among us.

*Choir 1*    Our boundaries are too limited,
our preferences too conditioned,
our habits too ingrained.

*Choir 2*    May the aging
and the very young,
may subcultural groups of every kind,
may special interest caucuses
find room in our world and our prayer.

*All*    Help us to widen our tents, Shaddai,
so that all are welcome among us.

*Choir 1*    Our God is too small.
Our rites are too rigid.
Our ways are too exclusive.

*Choir 2*    May people of various religions and rites,
whose name for God
and claim to God
are different from our own,
find room in our world and our love.

*All*    Help us to widen our tents, Shaddai,
so that all are welcome among us.

# ZILPAH AND BILHAH

◇ **Scripture Reference**    Gen 29:24, 29; 30:1–13; 31:17, 33
Gen 32:22–24; 33:1–14; 35:21–22, 25–26
Gen 37:2; 46:18, 23–25

◇ **Biography**

Laban gave Zilpah as maid to his daughter Leah and Bilhah as maid to his daughter Rachel when the women married Jacob. Both sisters gave their maids as wives to their husband in order to conceive children. Rachel, who was barren, experienced motherhood through Bilhah, who gave birth to two sons whom Rachel named Dan and Naphtali. Leah claimed two more sons through Zilpah, who bore Jacob Gad and Asher. Although the women became wives of Jacob and bore children who were his heirs, they retained their status and their function as maids to Leah and Rachel.

◇ **Context**

Zilpah and Bilhah emerge from the shadows of biblical history as archetypal symbols of female servitude. They have second-class status not only in the eyes of men, but also in relationship to women. Their roles are clearly defined — slave, concubine, child-bearer — and their identities are coterminous with their roles. The two women were given to Leah and Rachel as a wedding gift, and Leah and Rachel owned them. As slaves they did all the things that maids do for women, and eventually a whole lot more. When Rachel realized she could not compete with Leah's fertility because she was barren, she gave Bilhah to her husband and conceived vicariously through her, twice, naming the two sons Bilhah bore and claiming them as her own. Leah, in a competitive fit, did the same with her slave Zilpah, claiming two more sons as her own.

What relationship did the slave women have to Jacob? Were they wives or concubines? Or were they simply overnight strategies for making babies for their owners? When Jacob was about to confront his brother Esau with all his household and all his possessions, he lined up his women and children in the order of their value to him in case Esau was out to kill. First in line were Zilpah and Bilhah, followed by their children. His favorite wife came last. The father of Leah and Rachel had given Zilpah and Bilhah to them, and they in turn gave the women to their husband. From man to women to man, passed around like a piece of property — that was the story of women's lives. Women had very little opportunity to exercise control. Did Zilpah and Bilhah want to have sex with Jacob? That really was not an issue. It was probably considered a privilege to carry Jacob's sons. Women who lacked power and control took control of other women in a scramble to stay on top. Slaves were on the bottom. Zilpah and Bilhah were slaves.

◇ **Lectionary Reading**

Laban gave Zilpah to his daughter Leah
and Bilhah to his daughter Rachel
to serve them as their maids.

◇

Rachel, unable to give Jacob children,
envied her sister Leah.
One day she said to Jacob,
"Give me children or I shall die!"
Jacob became angry with Rachel and said,
"Do you think that I am God?
It is God who has withheld from you
the fruit of the womb."
Then Rachel said,

"Here is Bilhah, my maid.
Sleep with her, that she may give birth on my lap,
then I too will have children through her."
So Jacob took Bilhah to bed as his wife,
and Bilhah conceived and bore Jacob a son.
Then Rachel said, rejoicing,
"God has heard me and judged me
and given me a son."
Therefore, she named him Dan.
Bilhah conceived a second son.
"I have fought God's fight with my sister,
and won," said Rachel,
and she named the newborn Naphtali.
Leah had ceased bearing children,
so she gave Zilpah her maid to Jacob as a wife,
and Zilpah gave Jacob a son.
And Leah said, "Good fortune!"
so she named the baby Gad.
Zilpah bore Jacob a second son,
and Leah said, "Happy am I
for women will call me happy."
She named the new son Asher.

◇

Jacob set his wives and his children on camels
and drove out all of his livestock,
took all of his possessions,
all that he had acquired in Paddan-aram,
and left to return to his family home in Canaan.

◇

Then Jacob took his two wives, his two maids,
and his eleven children,
and crossed the ford of the Jabbok.
He set these and everything else he had
on the other side of the stream,
and while he was alone,
he wrestled with an angel until daybreak.

◇

Now Jacob looked up and saw Esau coming,
and four hundred men were with him.
So he separated his children
among Leah and Rachel and their two maids.
He put the maids with their children in front,
then Leah with her children,
then Rachel and Joseph last of all.
He himself went on ahead of them,
bowing low to the ground seven times,

until he came close to his brother.
But Esau ran to meet him,
and he kissed him and embraced him,
and both Jacob and Esau wept.
When Esau saw the women and children, he asked,
"Who are these who are with you?"
And Jacob said to his brother,
"The children God has graciously given your servant."
Then the maids and their children drew near and bowed,
and Leah and her children approached and bowed,
and finally Rachel and Joseph arrived,
and they too bowed before him.
Then Esau said, "Let us journey together
and I will travel beside you."
Jacob said to his brother,
"The children are frail,
some of the flock and herds are nursing;
if they are overdriven but a single day,
I fear that the flocks will die.
Let my lord pass on ahead of his servant
and I will follow slowly,
according to the pace of the cattle
and the children and their needs,
until we meet in Seir."

◇

Jacob pitched his tent beyond the tower of Eder,
and while he was living there,
Reuben slept with Bilhah,
his father's concubine,
and his father learned of it.
Now the sons of Bilhah, Rachel's maid,
were Dan and Naphtali.
The sons of Zilpah, Leah's maid,
were Gad and Asher.
These were the sons of Jacob
who were born to him in Paddan-aram.

◇

The children and grandchildren
of Zilpah and Jacob
numbered sixteen persons in all.
The children and grandchildren
of Bilhah and Jacob
numbered seven persons in all.

◇ **Points for Shared Reflection**

- Women are often treated as objects or possessions by men. Give instances of this in society today. Has this ever been true in your life?

- Although times are slowly changing, married women are still expected to bear children, and a woman who opts to remain childless often has to explain herself. How do you feel about marriages that are childless by choice?

- A woman's use of a female slave to bear her own child is a type of surrogate motherhood. What is your opinion of surrogate motherhood? What does it do for the status of women?

- In what ways has women's status changed since the time of Zilpah and Bilhah and in what ways has it remained the same?

◇ **A Psalm about Children** (see page 111)

◇ **Prayer**

We know You are there
to watch over us,
Mother of All Earth's Children.
We sleep beneath Your shadow
and we wake to the warmth of Your sun.
Protect us from all anxiety
and from every kind of evil
as we walk in the strength
of Your providential care
and feed on Your nourishing word.
Through times of abundance
and days of drought
You lead us, guide us, comfort us
as a Swallow with Her fledgling,
as a Mother with Her child.
We run to Your protection, Shaddai,
now and forever.
Amen.

## ◊ A PSALM ABOUT CHILDREN ◊

*Choir 1*  Children
are God's most sacred surprise,
a light in the eyes,
a lift to the heart,
a storyline's continuation.

*All*  Thank You, Shaddai, for children.

*Choir 2*  Children
mirror Mystery.
Children
are God's preferred way of being,
preferred way of seeing
the world and all its people.

*All*  Teach us, Shaddai, through our children.

*Choir 1*  Our children
are not our children.
They are given to us
and pass through us
into worlds of their own making,
into risks of their own taking,
into futures we will not know.

*All*  Help us, Shaddai, to let go of our children.

*Choir 2*  Our children
are reminders
of what we like best about ourselves,
of when we knew love
that gave birth to ourselves,
of how we can live beyond ourselves.

*All*  Help us, Shaddai, to learn to be ourselves
with our children.

*Choir 1*  When children cry,
when children die,
the whole world is diminished,
for a child's pain
is the earth's pain,
and when an innocent child is abused,
none of us is ever the same again.

*All*  Help us, Shaddai, to protect our children.

By M. T. Winter, Crossroad Pub. Co., © 1991 Medical Mission Sisters

*Choir 2*  When children feel
they are included,
a little hope rises on all horizons,
a new dream dances in our generation
and seeds are sown for a new creation.

*All*  Help us, Shaddai, to grow through our children.

*Choir 1*  When children
are simply children,
filling their day with life
spilling over,
sharing love,
sharing laughter,
grabbing the whole of their
once-upon-a-time,
making us believe in
happy-ever-after,
anything at all is possible.

*All*  We live into hope, Shaddai, through our children.

*Choir 2*  All of us
are children:
children of God,
children of children,
children whose children
are children of children.
Be reconciled
to the child within,
so that love can live on
beyond us
forever.

*All*  We praise You, Shaddai, and we thank You
in the name of all Your children.

   By M. T. Winter, Crossroad Pub. Co., © 1991 Medical Mission Sisters

# ESAU'S WIVES: JUDITH, BASEMATH, MAHALATH, ADAH, OHOLIBAMAH

◇ **Scripture Reference**　Gen 26:34–35; 27:46; 28:8–9
　　　　　　　　　　　　　　Gen 36:2–19, 25, 41–43; 1 Chr 1:51–54

◇ **Biography**

Judith and Basemath, the Hittite women who were Esau's wives, were never accepted by his parents, Rebekah and Isaac, because they were foreigners. His third wife, Mahalath, was Ishmael's daughter and therefore family. Adah and Oholibamah were Canaanites. Adah, Basemath, and Oholibamah are the only ones listed in the Genesis genealogy chronicling Esau's descendants, but here Basemath is considered to be Ishmael's daughter. They bore him five sons. Adah was the mother of Eliphaz, Basemath was the mother of Reuel, and Oholibamah was the mother of Jeush, Jalam, and Korah. A list of sons and grandsons is the only information about these women which has survived.

◇ **Context**

The two main references to Esau's wives frame the narrative that tells us how Esau lost his father's blessing and was left with only a curse. The textual arrangement is not unintentional, for the references to Esau's

**113**

marriage are part of the P redaction. It is the editor's way of explaining the reasons for Esau's misfortune, and the reasons are his wives. Throughout the Hebrew scriptures, three types of women are particularly despicable — the sexually promiscuous (the wife who commits adultery; the harlot), the woman who worships alien gods, and the foreigner. Hebrew men go to great lengths to acquire wives from their own people, particularly from among their relatives. Esau, however, at the age of forty married two Canaanite women. His parents must have been devastated. The text says simply that Esau's wives made life miserable for Rebekah and Isaac. It was probably the other way around, for the firstborn son on whom so much depended had defiled the covenant. Esau was deprived of his father's blessing, a consequence inevitable since the time of his birth, but we are led to believe that the women were the reason for his curse. To strengthen this perception, we read that Jacob, blessed by his father, went off to his ancestral homeland to find a wife for himself, and his parents of course were pleased. Chagrined and somewhat chastened, Esau took another wife, one bound to be legitimate, for she was the daughter of Ishmael. But then he turned to Canaanite women when he decided to marry again. The wives in this narrative function as commentary and four of them symbolize something evil, for their presence in the life of Esau earns him his father's curse. The confusion concerning the name of Ishmael's daughter stems from two separate traditions chronicled in Genesis.

◇ **Lectionary Reading**

When Esau was forty years old,
he married Judith,
daughter of Beeri the Hittite,
and Basemath,
daughter of Elon the Hittite,
and they made life miserable
for Rebekah and Isaac.

◇

Then Rebekah said to Isaac:
"I am weary of my life
because of the Hittite women.
If Jacob marries one of these,
one of the women of the land,
what good will my life be to me?"

◇

When he saw that the Canaanite women
did not please his father Isaac,
Esau went to Ishmael
and took Mahalath his daughter to be his wife
in addition to the wives he already had.

She was the sister of Nebaioth
and the granddaughter of Abraham.

◇

Esau took wives from the Canaanites:
Adah daughter of Elon the Hittite,
and Oholibamah daughter of Anah son of Zibeon the Hivite,
and Basemath, Ishmael's daughter, sister of Nebaioth.
Adah bore Eliphaz to Esau;
Basemath bore Reuel;
and Oholibamah bore Jeush, Jalam, and Korah.
These are the sons of Esau who were born in the land of Canaan.
Esau took his wives, his sons, and his daughters,
all the members of his household,
his cattle, his livestock, and all the property he had acquired
while he lived in the land of Canaan
and moved some distance from his brother Jacob,
for their possessions were too great
for them to live too close together;
the land where they were staying
could not support the extent of their livestock.
So Esau settled in the hill country of Seir.
In fact, Esau is Edom.
These are the descendants of Esau, ancestor of the Edomites.
These were the names of Esau's sons:
Eliphaz son of Adah, Esau's wife;
Reuel son of Basemath, Esau's wife;
and Jeush, Jalam, and Korah,
the sons of Esau's wife Oholibamah.
The sons of Eliphaz were Teman, Omar, Zepho, Gatam, Kenaz,
and also Amalek born of Timna,
who was his concubine.
All these were the sons of Adah, Esau's wife.
These were the sons of Reuel:
Nahath, Zerah, Shammah, and Mizzah.
All these were the sons of Basemath, Esau's wife.
Here are the ancestral clans.
Teman, Omar, Zepho, Kenaz, Korah, Gatam, and Amalek
are the clans of Eliphaz, and these are Adah's sons.
Nahath, Zerah, Shammah, and Mizzah
are all the clans of Reuel,
and these are Basemath's sons.
Jeush, Jalam, and Korah
are the clans born of Oholibamah,
who was the daughter of Anah.
These are the descendants of Edom,
and these are their clans according to their families

and their localities by their names:
Timna, Alvah, Jetheth, Oholibamah,
Elah, Pinon, Kenaz, Teman, Mizbar, Magdiel, and Iram.
These are the clans of Edom according to their settlements
and according to the land they held.

◇ **Points for Shared Reflection**

- Esau married women of different tribes and cultures and different religious perspectives. What are the positive features of having a home environment of such diversity?

- There was no way that Esau's Canaanite wives could ever do right by their in-laws. Have you ever experienced a similar situation of non-acceptance within your own family circle?

- Men still blame women for what is wrong in their lives and in the world. Has this ever happened to you?

- How important is it that a married couple share the same religion? How does one go about resolving the tensions posed by different religious traditions in a marriage and in a family? Is there more than one tradition in your family?

◇ **A Psalm to Shaddai** (see page 117)

◇ **Prayer**

Wide are the windows of Your compassion,
warm are the wings of Your protection,
eternal, maternal Shaddai.
I run to You in my pain and fear
and am comforted to know
You are near
in trial and tribulation,
lifting me up to new heights of hope
in the circle of Your mercy.
As I walk with You
through uncertainty,
I feel at home in the ambience
of Your never-failing love.
May I never fall out of favor.
May I never lose hold of hope.
Keep me close to You, Shaddai,
now and forever.
Amen.

# ◇ A PSALM TO SHADDAI ◇

*All*    Bless Shaddai, O my soul.
May all that is within me
bless Her holy name.

*Choir 1*    She shakes Her canopy of stars
onto the mantle of sister night,

*Choir 2*    bathes herself in reflected light
from the silver pool of moon woman's aura.

*All*    Bless Shaddai, O my soul.
May all that is within me
bless Her holy name.

*Choir 1*    She blushes with delight
at dawn daughter's radiance
in early morning,

*Choir 2*    and walks beside her the rest of the day,
till she sinks with the setting sun.

*All*    Bless Shaddai, O my soul.
May all that is within me
bless Her holy name.

*Choir 1*    I touch Her tree limbs reverently
and Her rustling leaves reassure me,

*Choir 2*    as Her roots reach out for permanence
down deep inside of me.

*All*    Bless Shaddai, O my soul.
May all that is within me
bless Her holy name.

*Choir 1*    Her little girl giggle bounces
from the brook's cascading waters,

*Choir 2*    as Her daughters,
the rivers, oceans, seas
and all creation's waterways
praise spontaneously.

*All*    Bless Shaddai, O my soul.
May all that is within me
bless Her holy name.

By M. T. Winter, Crossroad Pub. Co., © 1991 Medical Mission Sisters

| Choir 1 | She sings Her sensuous madrigals in the birdsong of the morning, |

*Choir 1*  She sings Her sensuous madrigals
in the birdsong of the morning,

*Choir 2*  does Her raindance
over and over
as field and forest applaud.

*All*  Bless Shaddai, O my soul.
May all that is within me
bless Her holy name.

*Choir 1*  Her sister flowers drop sacred seeds
in a lineage of abundance,

*Choir 2*  as valleys, meadows, terraced slopes
perpetuate Her kin.

*All*  Bless Shaddai, O my soul.
May all that is within me
bless Her holy name.

*Choir 1*  Mother of Earth
rocks our mother earth
as she cries in a fit of discomfort,

*Choir 2*  showing us how to care for her
who cares so much for us.

*All*  Bless Shaddai, O my soul.
May all that is within me
bless Her holy name.

*Choir 1*  She slips in and out
of intimacy with me
as Her Spirit remains within me,

*Choir 2*  helping me,
healing me,
holding me close
to Her life-giving,
living love.

*All*  Bless Shaddai, O my soul.
May all that is within me
bless Her holy name.

   By M. T. Winter, Crossroad Pub. Co., © 1991 Medical Mission Sisters

# ASENATH

◇ **Scripture Text**   Gen 41:45–46, 50–52; 46:20

◇ **Biography**

Asenath the daughter of Potiphera the priest of On in Egypt was given by Pharaoh to Joseph as his wife. She had two sons by Joseph, Ephraim and Manasseh.

◇ **Context**

Asenath was the daughter of the priest of On, the Hebrew name for Heliopolis, one of the most important cities of ancient Egypt and a primary cultic center. The site was known as the home of the Heliopolitan theology, a system whose chief deity was Atum-Re, the sun-god. Asenath means "belonging to" or "the servant of the goddess" Neith. Joseph also received a new name when he received his Egyptian wife. While the precise meaning of Zaphenath-paneah is still being debated, the literal translation is "the god speaks and the one who bears the name

**119**

lives." Both the new name of Joseph and the name of his new wife had definite religious associations and were derivatives of Egyptian gods. One can only guess what influence Joseph's wife, his Egyptian name, and his position of power and affluence in Pharaoh's service had on Joseph's religious aspirations. The names he gave the two sons Asenath bore state that he had been able to forget his former hardship and all of his father's house and that he had been made fruitful in his adoptive land. Asenath seems to have been Joseph's only wife. No doubt she continued to worship in the tradition to which her family was dedicated. Asenath was among the first of those foreign wives of Israelite men who worshiped alien gods. Throughout the Hebrew canon these women are the objects of prophetic and editorial wrath and are consistently blamed for the downfall of Israel and for all its evil and sin.

◇ **Lectionary Reading**

Pharaoh gave Joseph the name
Zaphenath-paneah,
and he gave him Asenath as his wife.
She was the daughter of Potiphera,
who was the priest of On.
So Joseph gained authority
over the land of Egypt.
Joseph was thirty years old
when he entered the service
of Pharaoh king of Egypt.
And Joseph went out
from the presence of Pharaoh
and went through all the land of Egypt.
Before the years of famine came,
Joseph had two sons by Asenath,
daughter of Potiphera, the priest of On.
Joseph named the firstborn Manasseh,
"for God has made me forget my hardship
and all of my father's house."
The second he named Ephraim,
"for God has made me fruitful
in the land of my misfortunes."

◇ **Points for Shared Reflection**

• Try to imagine who Asenath was, what she was like, her relationship to Joseph, her religious beliefs. Tell her story from a woman's point of view.

- What does it mean to be alien? What does it mean to be alienated? Aliens are often alienated. Why? Is the word "alien" a legitimate designation in a country such as the United States? Why not?

- Are there aliens in your family? Are there alienated members in your family? Have you ever felt alienated from anything or anyone? What was the reason and how did you feel?

- On what basis does one not only reject but condemn another's religious beliefs? Is such a position tenable in a pluralistic society and a pluralistic world? Refer to Asenath's story as you discuss your views.

◇ **A Psalm of Freedom** (see page 122)

◇ **Prayer**
O Liberating Spirit
hidden deep
in the shackled hearts
of all Your captive creation,
hear the prayer
we women pray,
caught as we are
in a strange kind of freedom,
never completely liberated,
never entirely bound.
Guilt holds us
firmly in place
in the prisons
of our insecurity
and the doubts of our own self-worth.
Free us from all
that hinders us
from the fullness of life
in Your image,
for the path of our liberation
is Your own most perfect praise,
now and forever.
Amen.

# ◇ A PSALM OF FREEDOM ◇

*All*   Liberate us, Free Spirit,
from all that holds us captive within us.
Call us into freedom:

*Choir 1*   freedom to be
and become and belong;

*Choir 2*   freedom to stand
and admit we were wrong;

*Choir 1*   freedom to see
and to say what we know;

*Choir 2*   freedom to fail
and freedom to grow;

*Choir 1*   freedom to feel
and be grateful for feeling;

*Choir 2*   freedom to heal
and to help with our healing;

*Choir 1*   freedom to laugh
and freedom to cry;

*Choir 2*   and perhaps above all,
the freedom to try.

*All*   Free us, Liberating Spirit,
from all that holds us captive around us.
Give to us our freedom:

*Choir 1*   freedom from systems that do not include us;

*Choir 2*   freedom from structures that do not support us;

*Choir 1*   freedom from practices meant to enslave us;

*Choir 2*   freedom from rules that exist to deny us;

*Choir 1*   freedom from values that only destroy us;

*Choir 2*   freedom from people who refuse to affirm us;

*Choir 1*   freedom from guilt around and within us;

*Choir 2*   freedom from fear and its power to deter us.

*All*   Empower us, Spirit Power,
for a prophetic use of our freedom:

*Choir 1*   freedom for freeing women to be;

*Choir 2*   freedom for setting all people free;

   By M. T. Winter, Crossroad Pub. Co., © 1991 Medical Mission Sisters

| | |
|---|---|
| *Choir 1* | freedom for finding the best way to pray |
| *Choir 2* | and for coming to God in our own unique way; |
| *Choir 1* | freedom for making courageous decisions |
| *Choir 2* | to live by the justice the Spirit envisions; |
| *Choir 1* | freedom for assuring the climate is free |
| *Choir 2* | for you to be you<br>and for me to be me. |
| *All* | Come, Spirit of Freedom.<br>Come, set us free. |

# ZIPPORAH

◇ **Scripture Reference**    Ex 2:5–22; 4:18–20, 24–26; 18:1–7

◇ **Biography**

Zipporah was one of seven daughters of Jethro, the priest of Midian. She married Moses after he fled from Egypt and bore two sons, Gershom and Eliezer. Zipporah accompanied her husband on his return to Egypt, and at some point before or after the Exodus, she and her sons left him and returned to her father's home. Jethro brought her and the boys back to Moses when the Israelites were encamped in the wilderness near Mount Sinai.

◇ **Context**

Zipporah was the daughter of a priest whom scripture refers to as Reuel or Hobab or the more prevalent name, Jethro, according to the tradition of the biblical writer. In Exodus he is identified as a Midianite, in Judges as a Kenite. Zipporah married Moses in Midian, where she gave birth to at least one of their two sons, Gershom. The name of her second son, Eliezer, which meant, "The God of my father was my help and delivered me from the sword of Pharaoh" (Ex 18:4) suggests that he may have been born in Egypt, although the text says two sons accompanied Moses when he returned to assume leadership of the Israelites and responsibility for their liberation. On their way to Egypt, Zipporah intervened to save her husband during an acute, life-threatening illness through what may have been a healing ritual rooted in the religious practices of the ancient Near

East. The only other scriptural reference to Zipporah records her return to Moses when he and the Israelites were encamped in the wilderness near Mount Sinai. She was accompanied by her father and her sons. It is in this context that we learn that Moses had previously sent her away. When and where that occurred we do not know. Because of the danger and uncertainty of her husband's mission, she may not have gone all the way into Egypt with him but may have returned to her family home. It seems strange that Moses would bring his family into a situation of oppression only to join others in a run for freedom away from that situation. Or if he did, he may have sent her away during the onslaught of the plagues. Or he may have dismissed her for religious reasons because of the rite she performed when he was acutely ill. Clearly she was not with Moses in the wilderness until after she arrived there with her father.

◇ **Lectionary Reading**

One day after Moses had grown up,
he went out among his people
and saw the extreme hardships of their life.
He encountered an Egyptian beating a Hebrew
who was a relative of his.
He looked around,
and seeing no one,
he killed the Egyptian
and buried him in the sand.
The next day when he saw two Hebrews fighting,
he went over to them and said to the aggressor,
"Why do you strike your countryman?"
He replied, "Who made you a ruler and judge over us?
Do you intend to kill me as you killed that Egyptian?"
Then Moses was frightened and thought to himself,
"Surely the word is out."
When Pharaoh heard what Moses had done,
he searched for him to kill him.
Moses fled from Pharaoh
and settled in the land of Midian.
One day he was sitting by a well
when the seven daughters
of the priest of Midian
came to the well to draw water.
They came together with their father's flock
and filled the troughs to water the sheep,
but some shepherds drove them away.
Moses came to their defense,
and even watered their flock.
When they returned home their father said,

*"How come you are back so soon?"
"An Egyptian helped us chase the shepherds,
and drew water for us,
and watered the flock," they said,
and their father responded,
"Where is he?
Why did you leave him there?
You should have invited him back for a meal."
So Moses came and he stayed with the man,
who gave him his daughter Zipporah in marriage.
When Zipporah gave birth to a son,
Moses named him Gershom, saying,
"I have been living as an alien in a foreign land."

◇

Moses went to his father-in-law Jethro.
"Please let me return to my relatives in Egypt
to see if they are still alive."
And Jethro said, "Go in peace."
God said to Moses in Midian,
"Return to Egypt,
for all who were seeking your life are dead."
So Moses took his wife and sons,
put them on a donkey,
and went back to the land of Egypt.
And all the way Moses carried the staff of God in his hand.
On the way at a place where they spent the night,
God came to meet Moses
and tried to kill him.
But Zipporah took a flint,
cut off her son's foreskin,
and touched the genitals of Moses with it, saying,
"Truly, you are a bridegroom of blood to me!"
And God let Moses live.

◇

Jethro, the priest of Midian
and the father-in-law of Moses,
heard of all that God had done for Moses
and for the people of Israel,
how God had brought Israel out of Egypt.
After Moses had sent Zipporah away,
his father-in-law Jethro took her back,
together with her two sons.
The name of the one was Gershom, for he said,
"I have been an alien in a foreign land,"
and the name of the other was Eliezer, for he said,
"The God of my ancestors was my help,

God delivered me from the sword of Pharaoh."
Jethro came into the wilderness
where Moses was encamped by the mountain of God,
bringing Moses' wife and sons to him.
He sent word ahead to Moses,
"I, Jethro, your father-in-law, am coming to you
and I am bringing your wife and children."
Moses went out to meet him,
and he bowed before him and kissed him,
and each asked about the other's welfare,
then together went into the tent.

◇ **Points for Shared Reflection**

- Zipporah married a man of a different culture, creed, and social class. How do you feel about cross-cultural, interreligious, interracial marriages? What is the chance of their succeeding?

- Zipporah was like a piece of property in relation to the men in her life. Her father "gave her" to Moses in marriage, Moses "sent her away," her father "took her back" and then "brought her back" to Moses. Comment on the way it was with women in the past and the way it is now.

- Zipporah married a man who had been delivered from bondage as a baby and would deliver his people from bondage as an adult. Was she ever liberated from her own bondage? Are you?

- Moses never entered the promised land. Did Zipporah? Speaking metaphorically, what would the "promised land" be like for you?

◇ **A Psalm about the Promised Land** (see page 128)

◇ **Prayer**

Promise us,
O God of the Exodus,
promise You will keep
Your promise,
for the land we seek
seems far from us
and the road we travel
is long.
Promise we will come
to the promised land
while we can still remember
the vision and the traditions
to which we once belonged.
Amen.

# ◇ A PSALM ABOUT THE PROMISED LAND ◇

*Choir 1*  Lead me into the promised land.
I am sick unto death of bondage,
burdened by doubt and debt
and all those things
by which we are bound.

*Choir 2*  Give me a taste of milk and honey
in a cup that is running over.
It is time to replace the salted tears
that season my daily bread.

*Choir 1*  Lift up Your hand, O Mover of Mountains.
You can divide the waters
to let a whole new generation
pass over from slavery.

*Choir 2*  My heart is ready, O God,
my heart is ready with song and laughter,
ready to lead the victory dance
on the safe side of the sea.

*Choir 1*  Narrow the stream that divides what is
from the blessings that have been promised.

*Choir 2*  Shallow the rivulet separating us
from all that we might be.

*Choir 1*  On that day the lion and lamb
will be at peace within us.

*Choir 2*  On that day, all good people
will climb the mountain of God.

*Choir 1*  Every home will have security,
every heart will have an advantage,

*Choir 2*  and no one will want for anything
in the household of our God.

*Choir 1*  We will sing and bring to birth in each other
the fruits of the new creation.

*Choir 2*  We will sow the seeds of Shalom
among all the survivors of rape and war.

*Choir 1*  Praise be to You, Shekinah-Shaddai,
for You are the Source of the promise.

*Choir 2*  In You we come home to freedom.
You are the Promised Land.

 By M. T. Winter, Crossroad Pub. Co., © 1991 Medical Mission Sisters

# CUSHITE WOMAN

◇ **Scripture Reference**　Num 12:1

◇ **Biography**

The label "Cushite woman" refers to the woman Moses married, a fact attested to by his sister and his brother. Since *Cush* is the Hebrew term for Ethiopia or Nubia, some say that this woman was black. She was definitely not an Israelite. There is no other reference to her, no biographical or narrative evidence to bring her to life for us.

◇ **Context**

The brief biblical reference to the Cushite woman whom Moses supposedly married is cryptic and controversial. It occurs in a moment of intense confrontation between Moses, Miriam, and Aaron and lands explosively, like an expletive, in the midst of a complaint about Moses' leadership. It was meant to be derogatory. Cush was foreign territory, a fairly extensive area in Northeast Africa, and there is a longstanding tradition that Cushites were black. The whole of East Africa was called *Cush* by the Greeks, and *Cushi* is a modern Hebrew term for one who is black. Did Moses marry a black woman? If so, when and where did he marry her? It could have been in Egypt before he ever went into exile. He may have met her in the royal palace. She may have been one of the slaves or part of the royal harem and he may have escaped with her. Or it may have been his first marriage after settling in Midian. He may have dismissed her after he married Zipporah. Or she may have been with him all along but not mentioned by the biblical writers simply because she was black. Or perhaps he married her on his return to Egypt after Zipporah had gone to Midian to live in her father's house. Or she may not have existed at all. The term may have been meant for Zipporah, because she was a foreigner. In marrying a Midianite Moses married outside Hebrew culture and religion and made foreigners of his sons. It was a word said in anger, for Miriam and Aaron were angry with Moses, and the text says that God punished Miriam as a result of the exchange. Since there is no extant information about the Cushite woman, one guess is as legitimate as another. She is indeed elusive, but that is not sufficient reason to conclude she did not exist.

◇ **Lectionary Reading**

While they were encamped at Hazeroth,
Miriam and Aaron criticized Moses
because of the Cushite woman
whom Moses had married —
for he had indeed married a Cushite.

◇ **Points for Shared Reflection**

- Do you think Moses had a second wife? Was she black?

- Relate the story of black people in America to the Exodus story.

- The Cushite woman's story has been lost. Reflect on the lives of other black females whose stories have not been recorded.

- Our social, religious, and political structures are essentially racist. In what ways is your religious community racist? In what ways are you?

◇ **A Psalm Praising Our Ebony God** (see page 131)

◇ **Prayer**

Hold us close, our Ebony God,
and enfold us in the shadow
of Your proud, protective wing.
We are tired, oh, so tired
of prejudice and suffering,
tired of having to struggle
so that all might have an equal chance.
In You everyone is somebody
and nobody needs to worry
about quotas and fitting in.
Be with us in the struggle
so we can be with You in the rapture
forever and ever. Amen.

# ◇ A PSALM PRAISING OUR EBONY GOD ◇

*Leader*   My soul praises our Ebony God.
How good it is that She is black
and oh, so beautiful!

*All*   Sing, all the earth, to our Ebony God.
She is black and She is beautiful.

*Choir 1*   I rejoice in Her deep, dark Presence,
and I sense Her love encompassing me
in the velvet folds of night.

*Choir 2*   I look for Her in the evening
and run to the shade of Her outstretched hand
and the shadow of Her wing.

*Choir 1*   She was there in the holds
of the slave ships,
chained to our sisters
as they were dragged away
from their African homes.

*Choir 2*   She fell beneath the whip and the lash,
felt the sting of the epithet,
worked the big plantations
and wept with the enslaved.

*Choir 1*   She was there at the crucifixion
of a proud, illustrious race.

*Choir 2*   The scars of prejudice still are etched
on Her beautiful Bantu face.

*Choir 1*   She rocked, shouted, clapped, danced
to the rhythms
of determination
in praise houses,
in safe houses,
in the sheds and in the fields.

*Choir 2*   And She sang Her songs
full-throated,
spirituals
and Gospel
filled with improvisation,
with pathos, and celebration,
and if you listen on a moonless night,
you can hear Her sing the Blues.

| | |
|---|---|
| *Choir 1* | She was there in the run for freedom, wading through the water, Ground of Being gone underground in a desperate bid to keep hope alive. |
| *Choir 2* | She is still in search of freedom, an unconditional freedom of spirit in a fully human enterprise. |
| *Choir 1* | I praise Your name, O Ebony God, and seek a sign of Your favor in the eclipse of the sun. |
| *Choir 2* | We rejoice in You, our Ebony God, and cherish Your image reflected in every dark-complected one. |
| *Choir 1* | The charcoal thumbprint of Your blessing marks Your dwelling place. |
| *Choir 2* | The silhouette of Your bold black beauty brings amazing grace. |

 By M. T. Winter, Crossroad Pub. Co., © 1991 Medical Mission Sisters

# ELISHEBA

◇ **Scripture Text**    Ex 6:23, 25

◇ **Biography**

Elisheba was Aaron's wife and mother of his four sons. She was the daughter of Amminadab and the sister of Nahshon, leader of the tribe of Judah and ancestor of David.

◇ **Context**

Aside from her identification as daughter, sister, wife, and mother and the recording of her name, there is absolutely no information about Elisheba. Many biblical chapters try to tell the story of her husband, Aaron, elder brother of Moses, a leader of the Exodus, and in later priestly sources the founder of an everlasting priesthood. No one writes of Elisheba. Aaron himself never mentions her. She is one among a multitude of invisible women. We are left to imagine what it might have been like to experience the plagues in Egypt, to run in terror from Pharaoh's troops, to risk the lives of four young children as she passed through an opening in the midst of the sea, and to raise those children to adulthood during the long, difficult years in the wilderness. Elisheba's name means "my God is fullness." Surely she lived on the strength of her name.

133

◇ **Lectionary Reading**

Aaron married Elisheba,
daughter of Amminadab and sister of Nahshon,
and she gave birth to Nadab, Abihu, Eleazar, and Ithamar.
Their son Eleazar married one of the daughters of Putiel,
who gave birth to Phinehas.

◇ **Points for Shared Reflection**

- If you were Elisheba and you were telling your story, what are some of the things you would say?

- Name three very famous men who are living today and are often in the news. Then say something about their wives.

- Five hundred years from now, someone opens a book in which your name and your story have been briefly recorded. State in a single sentence what you hope that entry might say.

- Do you think recorded history would be different if it had been written by women? In what way? Critique your shared recollection of an event of the recent past. What kind of information is missing which you would have liked to know?

◇ **A Psalm on Aging**  (see page 135)

◇ **Prayer**

Through advancing age
and grey hair
You promised to be with us,
O Keeper of the Seasons.
We call on You now
to keep Your promise
into everlasting life.
Lift us up on Eagle's wings,
give us the strength of Artemis,
the wisdom of Sophia,
the creativity of Gaia,
the gentleness of a little child
and the ability to be ourselves.
From our first until our final breath
Your Spirit breathes within us.
From Your Womb we came
and to Your Womb we gratefully return.
Be with us, in us, and proclaim through us
our faith in all Your promises,
now and forever.
Amen.

*Choir 1*  Blessed be the days
of diminished strength,
for the strength of Shaddai
will inhabit us
and make us strong forever.

*Choir 2*  Blessed be the years
of augmented hope,
when we are no longer preoccupied
with what we will do
or who we will be
or who we are becoming,
but live fully expecting
that the fullness is at hand.

*All*  Seasons change,
we change,
Shaddai's love never changes.
Her Spirit of everlasting life
is with us and in us forever.

*Choir 1*  Blessed be the time of life
when we have time
to be for others.

*Choir 2*  Blessed be the time
when we have time
for God
and for ourselves.

*All*  Seasons change,
we change,
Shaddai's love never changes.
Her Spirit of everlasting life
is with us and in us forever.

*Choir 1*  When hair falls
or changes shade,
when skin withers,
strength weakens,
and the final sparks
of fire fade,
angels dance in anticipation:
a child is coming home;

By M. T. Winter, Crossroad Pub. Co., © 1991 Medical Mission Sisters

*Choir 2*    and a little girl runs
through a field of flowers,
a little boy chases
a red balloon
in the silent shells
that image God,
and all the saints say
soon, soon.

*All*    Seasons change,
we change,
Shaddai's love never changes.
Her Spirit of everlasting life
is with us and in us forever.

*Choir 1*    Blessed is she
or he
or we
who wear the years
with honor
as others sip
from our wisdom cup.

*Choir 2*    There is no one
more engaging
than one who is
gracefully aging.
Such courage
lifts us up.

*All*    Seasons change,
we change,
Shaddai's love never changes.
Her Spirit of everlasting life
is with us and in us forever.

    By M. T. Winter, Crossroad Pub. Co., © 1991 Medical Mission Sisters

# COZBI

◇ **Scripture Reference**    Num 25:1–9, 14–17

137

Cozbi, daughter of Zur, a Midianite who was head of an ancestral clan, was among those local women of Shittim accused of luring Israelite men into a sexual relationship and the sacrificial worship of Baal and other gods. She and the Israelite to whom she was betrothed were slaughtered shortly after he brought her into the camp and into his family.

◇ **Context**

Cozbi's story raises a series of critical questions from a feminist perspective about justice and religious justification. Her narrative presents the final rebellion of the Exodus generation prior to their entry into the promised land. The men of Israel entered into sexual relationships with the women of Moab and Midian in the wilderness at Shittim where they were encamped. The text states that the women also seduced them into worshiping their gods, Baal of Peor (a mountain in Moab), and probably certain fertility gods which may have involved them in the practice of cult prostitution. They were even entering into marriage. The idea of physical and religious intercourse being legalized through intermarriage is said to have outraged the God of Israel. This rage erupted on the Israelite Zimri and the Midianite Cozbi when Phinehas killed them both.

It is hard to differentiate the perspective of God from that of the biblical writer. For his so-called meritorious act on behalf of the word and will of God, Phinehas was rewarded with a perpetual priesthood for himself and for his family. The text says that a total of twenty-four thousand people, foreign women and Israelite men, were slaughtered there in the wilderness because the women of Moab and Midian had led the Israelite men into apostasy through physical prostitution. This is a very difficult pericope. Unavoidable questions lead one to conclude that traditional interpretations need to be reassessed. Commentaries state that the great sin here was the worship of foreign gods, an offense so heinous that the wholesale slaughter ordered by the God of Israel was entirely justified.

However, one cannot help but wonder if, from the perspective of the present, there was not a greater sin. How could the slaughter of anyone for religious purposes ever be justified? Why punish the women for the sins of the men when they were not bound by the same laws that the men were? Why kill because of intermarriage with someone of a different culture and a different creed? Specifically, why kill Cozbi, or for that matter, the man she married? She was a woman of some social status, as the text takes care to point out, and so was he. She joined her husband's family and was prepared to leave her former life behind to go with him to the promised land. Were they killed because they entered the tent of meeting, which would have been blasphemy? There is another intriguing question. What about Zipporah? She was a Midianite and the wife of Moses. The Exodus text (18:1–7) makes clear that she had rejoined Moses in the wilderness, so it is likely that she was there in the camp when the general order was given to massacre all the foreign women, the women of Moab and of Midian. Was she also slaughtered? If not, why not? Finally, what kind of priesthood would one establish in perpetuity on the basis of a double murder? There was a time in our religious history when these questions would never arise, but times have definitely changed.

◊ **Lectionary Reading**

While Israel was encamped at Shittim,
the men entered into sexual relationships
with the women of Moab,
who invited them to attend sacrifices to their gods.
Consequently, Israelites ate sacrificial meals
and bowed down before Semitic gods;
and God's anger flared against Israel
because it had yoked itself to the Baal of Peor.
Then God said to Moses,
"Take all the leaders of these men
and impale them in the sun,
so that the burning anger of God against Israel
might be assuaged."
So Moses said to the judges of Israel,
"Every one of you must put to death
all those among your people
who have committed themselves to the Baal of Peor."
At that moment one of the Israelites appeared
in the sight of Moses and of all the people
as they wept at the entrance to the tent of meeting.
With him was the Midianite woman
he was bringing into his family.
When Phinehas son of Eleazar,
son of Aaron the priest, saw this,
he got up and left the assembly.
Taking a spear, he followed the two of them into the tent
and stabbed them both to death,
the Midianite woman and the Israelite man.
The name of the slain Israelite man
was Zimri son of Salu,
head of an ancestral house belonging to the Simeonites.
The name of the Midianite woman who was killed
was Cozbi, daughter of Zur,
who was the head of a clan,
an ancestral house in Midian.
So the plague within Israel was stopped.
Twenty-four thousand Israelites died.
Then God said to Moses,

"Harass the Midianites and defeat them,
for they have harassed you
by the way they deceived you
regarding the affair of Peor.
Cozbi, the daughter of a Midianite leader
and a sister of the Midianite people
was slaughtered on the day of the plague
as a consequence of Peor."

◇ **Points for Shared Reflection**

- Pretend you are one of the Moabite or Midianite women. Interpret the narrative from their point of view. Is it possible to be sympathetic to their cause? Was their punishment justified?

- Was an injustice done to Cozbi? Name other instances when we have reacted violently against women, making them victims of our prejudice and our rage.

- We have fought religious wars, conquered cultures, even committed genocide, and felt justified in doing so, because our adversaries were of a different religion and we were convinced that God was on our side. How do you feel about this kind of behavior and what it implies about God?

- When the Midianite women were murdered, did they also kill Zipporah? If not, what do you think became of Moses' wife?

◇ **A Psalm Lamenting the Victims** (see page 141)

◇ **Prayer**

We are here
to ask Your forgiveness,
O Source of Love and of Mercy,
for we are aware as never before
of the horror of our sins.
We have put to death
Your call to life
in every generation,
carelessly slaughtering
the innocent
to keep our rites
sacrosanct.
Forgive our past misdirection
and our present indiscretion,
and help us to see
with a clear eye
Your love for everyone. Amen.

Choir 1   Rain falls in torrents,
          spilling its elegy,
          fulfilling a ritual cleansing
          for the dead.

Choir 2   Corpses
          in Soweto,
          in Chicago,
          in the Middle East
          and the Far East
          and east of the legendary Eden
          cry out for vindication;
          the blood of Abel cries
          because the daughter of Zur dies
          and those of us here
          feel justified.

Choir 1   Rain falls
          in a flood of tears,
          but no amount of weeping
          can wash the blood
          from the horns of our altars
          or remove the stain of fear.

Choir 2   Who do we choose to sacrifice
          on the tables of contrition?
          The others,
          the aliens,
          the vulnerable,
          the female,
          and of course barbaric unbelievers.
          Oh God, have mercy on them.
          Oh God, have mercy on us.

Choir 1   Rain falls,
          funereal balm,
          calming, quieting, caressing.
          Rain is an ancient blessing
          and replete with promises.

Choir 2   For the times we have acted
          in haste
          with hate,
          forgive us, O Giver of Mercy.
          Forgive our unforgivable sins.

By M. T. Winter, Crossroad Pub. Co., © 1991 Medical Mission Sisters

# THE LEVITE'S CONCUBINE

◇ **Scripture Reference**   Judg 19:1–30

◇ **Biography**

The central figure of this narrative is a woman from Bethlehem known only as the Levite's concubine. She is brutally gang raped and murdered, and her dissected remains are dispersed throughout the land of Israel.

◇ **Context**

This is a violent narrative, probably the most devastating for and about women in all of scripture. The concubine's story in itself is a tragedy, but seen in relation to its larger setting, it is a tragedy of global proportion (see "Context" on page 149). The slaughter of one defenseless woman escalates into the slaughter of hundreds of defenseless women in a power-hungry thirst for revenge and the fulfillment of patriarchy's structural plan. This story offers not a comforting word but a warning: humanity is capable of falling quite far from the grace of God. Male superiority, power, brutality, betrayal, rape, murder, dismemberment, revenge stand over against female inferiority and powerlessness. The men all speak and they speak to one another. The women remain silent. The men are out to save themselves. No one can save the women. The men are property owners concerned about dividing up what they own. The women are property owned by the men. The concubine's body was hacked to pieces and sent as a bargaining chip to the propertied clans throughout Israel, just as Saul one day would distribute pieces of oxen to the fighting men of Israel as sign of a call to arms.

Who killed the concubine? We cannot definitively say. The Greek Bible records that she died at the hands of her attackers. The Hebrew Bible allows the possibility of her having survived the night of horrors and perhaps even the journey home. Could the Levite himself have killed her in a fit of revulsion or rage? After all, his concubine was damaged property and of no further sexual use to him. If she had not originally left him, this never would have happened. Men who do what he did have a catalogue of excuses for blaming the victim and not themselves. No matter how she died, by the blade of a knife or as a result of her sadistic attack, it was the Levite, her master, who killed her. Deaf to her screams, immune to her pain, he stayed safe and secure just a thin wall away from where she was raped and tortured while knowing that no one, not even the one who supposedly loved her, would come to rescue her. The full scope of the horror of this episode can only be understood in relation to the story of the wives of the Benjaminites (which appears on page 150).

◇ **Lectionary Reading**

In the days before there was a king in Israel,
a Levite who lived in Ephraim
took a woman from Bethlehem of Judah
as his concubine.
One day, in anger, she left him
and returned to her father's house.
After four months had passed,
her master set out to bring her back.
He planned to speak tenderly to her heart.
His servant and several donkeys
accompanied him on the journey.
His father-in-law greeted him joyfully
and he stayed three days with him.
They ate and drank together,
and on the fourth day he prepared to go,
but his father-in-law insisted
that he stay a little longer.

So they ate and drank
and his father-in-law said,
"Enjoy yourself. Spend the night."
He kept insisting, and eventually
the Levite gave in and stayed the night.
The fourth day passed
and the fifth day was passing,
for his host had detained him again.
Finally, toward evening,
determined to delay no longer,
the Levite set out on his journey
with his servant and his donkeys
and his concubine.
As they drew near to Jerusalem,
it was getting dark and the servant said,
"Master, let us spend the night."
"Not here in a town of foreigners," he replied.
"Continue on to Gibeah or Ramah.
We will stay among Israelites."
Gibeah belonged to the tribe of Benjamin
and was not very far away.
They reached Gibeah as the sun was setting,
but no one offered them hospitality,
so they sat in the public square.
An old man returning from the fields,
not a native of Gibeah
but a sojourner from Ephraim
who had settled in the town,
saw the travelers and stopped to inquire,
"Where have you come from?
Where are you going?"
The Levite answered him.
"We are on our way from Bethlehem in Judah
to Ephraim, my home,
but no one has offered us shelter for the night.
We have enough provisions,
straw for the donkeys and bread and wine."
The old man responded,
"Shalom! Come with me.
I will see to all your needs.
You cannot spend the night in the square."
So he took them home and he fed their donkeys.
They washed their feet and ate and drank.
As they were relaxing,
men from the town, abusive and perverse,
surrounded the house and beat on the door,

demanding that the guest be given to them
that they might have sex with him.
The old man pleaded, "My brothers, no!
Do not act like this. The man is my guest.
Do not persist in this wickedness.
Here is my virgin daughter,
and here is his concubine.
Let me bring them out to you.
Enjoy them, ravish them, do what you will,
but do not mistreat this man."
The men would not listen,
they were out of control,
so the Levite took his concubine
and brought her out to them.
They raped her savagely,
again and again,
and abused her until morning.
At the break of dawn, they let her go,
and she fell at the door of the old man's house
where her husband was,
and lay there.
When her husband got up, he opened the door,
ready to continue his journey.
There was his concubine, sprawled at the door
with her hands across the threshold.
"Get up," he said to her, "we are going,"
but his concubine did not answer.
He picked her up,
laid her body across the donkey
and continued his journey home.
When he reached his house,
he took a knife
and dissected his concubine,
limb by limb.
He cut her into twelve pieces
and sent her mutilated body
throughout all of Israel.
He instructed the men whom he sent, saying,
"Announce to all the Israelites,
'Has something like this ever happened
since the day we came out of Egypt,
from the exodus until now?'
Seek counsel, reflect, and speak out."

*(If you wish to set this narrative within its broader context, please turn to
page 150 and continue with the lectionary reading.)*

- Enter into the concubine's story. Tell it again from her point of view. How does it make you feel? What new perspective emerges?

- Why do you suppose the concubine left her master in the first place? Do you sometimes get a premonition about someone or something that later proves to be true? Give an example.

- In what ways does the concubine's story reflect the story of every woman, either factually or symbolically? In what ways does it reflect your story?

- Talk about the network of support for and among the males in this narrative. What support is there for the women? Do you have a network of female support to turn to in times of need?

◇ **A Lament**  (see page 147)

◇ **Prayer**

O Mother of Sorrows,
weep with us
as we mourn the death of our daughters
from AIDS
and drugs
and suicide,
from rape
and violence at another's hand,
and from religious gendercide
by those who would destroy us
for reasons we do not understand.
We turn to You, our Provider,
for protection and compassion.
May our cultic acts
never distract
from You or Your intentions,
never divert our energies
from the need to work for justice
for women
and for everyone.
Amen.

## ◇ A LAMENT ◇

*Choir 1*   O desecrated daughter of Bethlehem,
the priestly class abandoned you,
tossed you out to ravenous beasts,
handed you over to a rampaging mob
to be struck
and stripped
and raped
and mocked
and raped again
and ridiculed,
but God has not abandoned you,
for you have now an everlasting dwelling
among the stars.

*Choir 2*   O desperate daughter of contemporary times —
you, me, my female friends —
religion has disempowered you,
hardened its heart to your cry of pain,
refused to rescue your battered soul
from the guilt of disengagement,
but God has not abandoned you,
for you are held securely
in Her promises to us.

*All*   How the women have fallen prey
to discouragement and disillusion!

*Choir 1*   Howl, you who have been abused
by authority you trusted.

*Choir 2*   Weep, canons that kill the spirit
by canonizing human words.

*All*   Weep for the women who have fallen away
from faith in a caring God.

*Choir 1*   O desolate daughter of Bethlehem,
your future is cut to pieces
as shards of your sacred reality
bleed on the callous consciences
of all who molested you.
We your sisters re-member you.
The pain of your degradation
cries out for restitution.
We raise our voice for justice,
so that you may rest in peace.

| | |
|---|---|
| *Choir 2* | Cry, dismembered daughters.<br>Cry, broken, mutilated body<br>of our dispersed sisterhood.<br>They have cut us all to pieces<br>and sent our shattered vision in rage<br>to an alienated brotherhood,<br>saying, what do you make of this?<br>saying, has anything like this been seen before<br>from the beginning until now? |
| *All* | How the women have been abused<br>by a disbelieving power. |
| *Choir 1* | Weep, words that let go of life<br>in order to cling to paper. |
| *Choir 2* | Weep for the women who look for life<br>on the margins of tradition. |
| *All* | Cry, the beloved tradition!<br>Cry for the women who have had to die.<br>O One Who Weeps, we turn to You.<br>Hear our bitter cry. |

 By M. T. Winter, Crossroad Pub. Co., © 1991 Medical Mission Sisters

# WIVES OF THE BENJAMINITES

◇ **Scripture Text**   Judg 20:1–17, 35–37, 46–48; 21

◇ **Biography**

All the women of the tribe of Benjamin were massacred along with their husbands and children. Only six hundred males survived. To save the tribe of Benjamin from extinction, women were abducted from other areas to serve as wives for them, four hundred virgins from Jabesh-gilead and two hundred virgins from Shiloh. They settled in Benjaminite territory, helped rebuild the cities, and gave their husbands heirs.

◇ **Context**

To fully understand this narrative, turn to "Context" and "Lectionary Reading" on pages 142–145. The Levite's ritual dissection of his concubine and the dissemination of her segmented parts throughout Israel achieved its intended effect. The tribes of Israel punished the Benjaminites for Gibeah's desecration of the concubine because this was an offense against all of Israel. They slaughtered men, women, and children and set fire to Benjamin's cities and towns. When the carnage was over, six hundred men had managed to flee into the wilderness. The victors decided not to pursue them. Israelites had begun to feel remorse over the permanent loss of one of their tribes, but since they had vowed not to give their daughters in marriage to the men of Benjamin, they had to devise an acceptable way to ensure that the male survivors would have heirs to rebuild the tribe. A second oath justified their depleting Jabesh-gilead of its virgin daughters, for the town was earmarked for destruction, since none of its men had participated in the punishment of Benjamin. However, all the virgins of Jabesh-gilead were still not enough for every Benjaminite to have a wife. So the remaining two hundred male survivors lay in ambush at Shiloh and snatched the young festal dancers and took them home with them. The former wives fell to the sword and perished in the flames, but the youthful dreams of future wives died in the fires of arrogance and lust.

What a strange set of values. To avenge the torture and death of one concubine, they slaughtered all the women of Benjamin and the married women of Jabesh-gilead. To make up for one woman being handed over unwillingly to Benjaminites who desired her and used her, six hundred women were handed over against their will to be used to perpetuate the tribe of the abusers. They avenged a violated woman by violating six hundred more. Like the concubine, these silent, anonymous victims were passed around like pieces of property, and we have nothing more to remember them by than their moment of degradation and shame. This episode of the punishment of Benjamin and the destruction of Gibeah brings to a close both the period and the book of the judges. The final irony is yet to come. We read in the book of Samuel that Saul, the first king of Israel, was a Benjaminite, and his capital was in Gibeah.

◇ **Lectionary Reading**

From Dan to Beer-sheba the Israelites came,
they even came from Gilead,
assembling as a community
in the presence of God at Mizpah,
the chiefs of the tribes of Israel
and four hundred thousand armed soldiers.
Benjamin was not represented.
"How did this criminal act come about?"
the Israelites asked the Levite,
and the master of the woman who was murdered replied,
"I came to Gibeah which belongs to Benjamin,
I and my concubine.

We planned to spend the night.
A mob from Gibeah came looking for me
with every intention to kill me.
They surrounded the house,
and then they raped my concubine
and abused her until she died.
So I took my concubine
and cut her up into twelve separate pieces
and sent her mutilated body
throughout the entire land
because these men have committed an outrage in Israel.
So now, Israelites, all of you give advice and counsel here."
All the people stood up as one.
"We will not return to our tents or our homes.
We will march against Gibeah.
Here is our plan. We will cast lots,
taking ten men out of every hundred
from each of the tribes of Israel,
and a hundred out of a thousand,
and a thousand from ten thousand,
and they will bring food for the army
that will repay Gibeah of Benjamin
for the disgrace to Israel."
And the men of Israel stood united against Gibeah.
Then men from the tribes of Israel went
throughout the tribe of Benjamin, saying,
"A crime has been committed among you.
Hand over the guilty ones from Gibeah
so that we may put them to death
and purge Israel of this evil."
But the Benjaminites would not listen.
They came out in support of Gibeah,
and they gathered there prepared to do battle
against the Israelites.
They mustered twenty-six thousand armed men,
plus the inhabitants of Gibeah.
Seven hundred men were left-handed,
every one of them able to sling a stone
and never miss, not even by a hair.
Israel had four hundred thousand warriors,
every one of them armed.
With God's help, Israel defeated Benjamin.
The troops invaded Gibeah
and the city fell to the sword.
The Israelites destroyed Gibeah —
the city, the people, the animals,

and everything else that remained.
After setting fire to Gibeah,
they burned all the remaining towns.
All who fell of Benjamin that day
were twenty-five thousand arms-bearing men,
all of them courageous fighters.
But six hundred fled to the wilderness
and took refuge at the rock of Rimmon.

◇

Now the Israelites had sworn at Mizpah,
"Not one of us
shall give his daughter in marriage to Benjamin."
And the people wept before God at Bethel, saying,
"O God of Israel,
how has it come to pass
that Israel should lose a tribe?"
The next day they arose early
and built an altar
and offered burnt offerings
and sacrifices of well-being.
They began to feel compassion
for the tribe of Benjamin, saying,
"If this tribe is not to be cut off forever,
what should we do about finding wives
for the few men who are left?
For we swore under oath that we would not give them
any of our daughters as wives."
Then it was asked,
"Is there any group from the tribes of Israel
which did not assemble with us?"
For they had sworn an oath at Mizpah
to put any such group to death.
When the roll was called,
no one from Jabesh-gilead was there.
So twelve thousand soldiers were sent
to slay the inhabitants of Jabesh-gilead,
including the women and children,
that is, women who were no longer virgins.
Four hundred young women
who had never slept with a man
were brought back to the camp,
and a declaration of peace was sent
to the remaining Benjaminites,
along with the female survivors
of the carnage at Jabesh-gilead;
but there was not enough women for them.

So the elders of the assembly said,
"What shall we do about wives for the others,
since there are no women left in Benjamin?
There must be heirs for the survivors,
so that the tribe of Benjamin will not disappear,
yet we cannot give our daughters."
Then they came up with a plan.
"The yearly festival is now taking place
at Shiloh, north of Bethel," they said.
"It is east of the highway to Shechem
and south of Lebonah."
Then they said to the Benjaminites,
"Go hide yourselves in the vineyards and wait.
Watch for when the young women of Shiloh
come out to do their dances,
then leave the vineyards
and each of you
carry off a wife for yourself
from the young women of Shiloh
and return to your tribal land.
If their fathers or brothers complain to us,
we will say to them,
'Be generous;
allow us to have your women,
because we did not capture enough women in battle
to give a wife to every man.
This way you do not incur guilt
by giving your daughters to them.'"
The Benjaminites did as they were told.
Each of them took a wife for himself
from the dancers they abducted.
Then they returned to their own territory
and rebuilt their towns
and lived in them,
and all the Israelites went home.
In those days there was no king in Israel.
All the people did what they felt was right.

◇ **Points for Shared Reflection**

- Give instances where the keeping of religious rules were/are far more important than the well-being of women.

- Give one example of how your religious tradition seems to use you to achieve its own ends.

- The narrative is particularly appalling in its wanton destruction of human life. What influence have these kinds of texts had on our own indifference to the lives of people of other cultures or other faiths?

- Note the importance of virginity in the women who are chosen to be wives. No such criterion exists for the male. Discuss your reaction to the double standard in biblical tradition and in the present.

◇ **A Psalm for the Captives** (see page 155)

◇ **Prayer**
Break the chains
that bind our hearts
and hold our spirits captive,
O One Who Sets Us Free.
Too long have we been prisoners
of the past
and all its precedents,
sacrificing a brave new world
to maintain what used to be.
Restore the song
and the tambourines
to all Your dancing daughters,
and lead us in a victory dance
to set the captives free.
Amen.

*Choir 1*   The daughters danced
in the vineyards,
and the men rose up
like a horde of locusts
and carried them all away.

*All*   First we were daughters,
then we were wives.
Liberate us, O Pillar of Fire,
from our captivity.

*Choir 2*   The daughters danced
in papaya groves,
and the traders came
with a fleet of ships
and spirited them away.

*All*   First we were daughters,
then we were slaves.
Liberate us, O *Nyame*,
from our captivity.

*Choir 1*   The daughters danced
among the maize,
and the cavalry charged
their sacred groves
and took their freedom away.

*All*   First we were daughters,
then we were chattel.
Liberate us, O Great Spirit,
from our captivity.

*Choir 2*   The daughters danced
in the sacred rites,
but patriarchy buried
our originating myths
and took our identity away.

*All*   First we were daughters,
then we were robots.
Liberate us, Sophia,
from our captivity.

# SAMSON'S WIFE

◇ **Scripture Reference**   Judg 14; 15:1–8

◇ **Biography**

Samson's wife was a Philistine who lived in the city of Timnah. He saw her there one day, liked what he saw, and decided to marry her despite his parents' disapproval. During their seven-day wedding celebration, Samson's wife betrayed her husband in a trivial matter out of loyalty to her own people. He flew into a murderous rage and left her, so she was given in marriage to his best man. When he eventually tried to return to her, her father would not allow it, and Samson again went beserk. To retaliate, the Philistines burned his wife to death.

◇ **Context**

Samson had a predilection for Philistine women. His wife, a prostitute, and a mistress — all Philistines — were central to his life and mission. Samson's wife surely had no idea what she was getting into when she married this unknown Israelite. He had seen her once when he had come to her city, and a little while later his parents came to her home to arrange a marriage. There was trouble right from the beginning. Her new husband was a stranger among her relatives and friends, and the seven-day celebration was attended by all her people. Even the traditional wedding companions for the groom were Philistines. Samson antagonized them by posing a riddle they could not solve and he upset his new wife by refusing to confide in her when she asked him for the answer. This was no way to begin a marriage. She had to get him to tell her, not only because her people were pushing her to do it, but as a test of the strength of their relationship. He told her, she told them — what harm could it do? That was the end of their marriage. Samson's wife is a tragic figure, a pawn of all the men in her life. It was due to these men, all of them, that she died such a horrible death.

◇ **Lectionary Reading**

Samson went down to Timnah one day
where he saw a Philistine woman,
and he went and told his father and mother,
"I saw a Philistine woman at Timnah.
Get her for me as my wife."
But his father and mother said to him,
"Is there not a woman among your clan
or among all of our own people,
that you must go and take a wife
from the uncircumcised Philistines?"
Samson said to his father,
"Get her for me. She pleases me."
His father and mother were unaware
that this situation was the will of God
who was seeking an excuse
to assault the Philistines
who had Israel in their power.
So Samson went to Timnah
with his father and his mother.
When he came to the vineyards of Timnah,
a young lion attacked him.
Filled with the Spirit,
he seized the lion
and tore it to pieces with his bare hands,
but he did not tell his parents.
He talked with the woman,
she pleased him,
so he returned to her to marry her.
On his way to the woman,

he saw there on the side of the road
the carcass of the lion he had torn apart.
A swarm of bees was in the body of the lion,
so he scraped out some honey into his hands
and ate it along the way.
He gave some to his father and mother,
but he did not tell them he took the honey
from the carcass of a lion.
His father went down to the Philistine woman
and Samson prepared a celebration
that would last for seven days
as was the custom at that time.
When the people saw him,
they selected thirty companions
to spend the time with him.
Samson said to them,
"Let me put a riddle to you.
Explain it to me within seven days
and I will give you thirty linen garments
and thirty festal robes.
But if you fail, then you will give me
thirty garments and thirty robes."
So his companions said to him,
"Tell us your riddle."
And Samson said to them,
"Out of the eater came something to eat.
Out of the strong came something sweet."
They struggled with that for three days
but could not come up with the answer.
On the fourth day they said to Samson's wife,
"Have you called us here to make fun of us?
Convince your husband to explain the riddle
or we will set fire to your father's house
and burn you to death as well."
So Samson's wife went to him in tears.
"You do not really love me.
You have asked my people a riddle
and you have not explained it to me.
Obviously, you hate me."
Samson said to her,
"I have not told my father or my mother.
Why should I tell you?"
She wept before him all seven days
of their marriage celebration.
Finally, on the seventh day,
because she was so persistent,

Samson explained the riddle.
She gave the answer to her people,
and before the sun set on the seventh day,
the local men told Samson,
"What is sweeter than honey?
What is stronger than a lion?"
And Samson said to them,
"If you had not plowed with my heifer,
you would not have found out my riddle."
Then the spirit of God seized Samson
and he rushed down to Ashkelon,
killed thirty men,
took what they wore,
and gave the festal garments
to those who explained the riddle.
In a rage he returned to his father's house,
and his wife was given to the companion
who had served as his best man.

◇

After a while, at the time of the wheat harvest,
Samson went back to see his wife,
and he brought a kid for her.
"Let me visit my wife in her room," he said,
but her father would not allow it.
"I was sure you had rejected her,
so I gave her to your companion," he said.
"Consider her younger sister instead.
Look, she is prettier than her."
Then Samson said to all who were present,
"When I do damage to the Philistines,
this time I will be without blame."
So Samson caught three hundred foxes
and tied the foxes tail to tail
and put a torch between each pair of tails.
He set fire to the torches,
sent the foxes into the standing grain,
and burned up the shocks, the grain,
the vineyards, and the olive groves.
When the Philistines asked, "Who did this?"
They said, "Samson, son-in-law of the Timnite,
because he has taken Samson's wife
and given her to his companion."
So the Philistines came and took Samson's wife
and burned her and her father.
Samson said, "Because of this,
I swear to you I will not rest

until I have taken revenge on you."
He struck them down and slaughtered them,
then hid in a cave in Etam.

◇ **Points for Shared Reflection**

- Why would Samson's wife have needed to know the answer to the riddle and why would she have revealed it to the others?

- Are we any good at keeping a secret today? How good are you at keeping something confidential? What information is legitimate to reveal and to whom? What would be privileged information?

- Samson said to his wife when she asked him to confide in her: "I did not tell my father and mother, why should I tell you?" How would you react if your spouse said that to you?

- From the beginning the marriage had all the signs of a lifetime of domestic violence. What were those signs? Apply this question to your own situation, if relevant, or to that of someone you know.

◇ **A Psalm for Freedom from Violence**  (see page 161)

◇ **Prayer**

O gentle, loving, maternal God,
cradle all the bruised
and bleeding hearts
of Your violated children.
Kiss away the wounds of war
with blessings beyond our telling,
and let the scars of all who hurt
be guarantee of reward.
Hold us all so close to You
that violence dissolves forever
in a never-ending peace.
We praise You, God our Comforter.
Amen.

# ◇ A PSALM FOR FREEDOM FROM VIOLENCE ◇

*All* O One Who soothes the savage seas
and calms the troubled waters,
protect me from the violence around me
and within me.

*Choir 1* Deliver me from the violent ways
of a world bent on destruction,
from global threats
and all those wars
that are fought on our city streets.

*Choir 2* Protect me from those weapons wielded
by our sons and daughters,
from arms, crack, verbal assault,
and gangs hanging out on corners.

*All* O One Who soothes the savage seas
and calms the troubled waters,
protect me from the violence around me
and within me.

*Choir 1* Deliver me from domestic quarrels
that escalate into battles
with a temporary truce,
some lame excuse,
and wounds that last forever.

*Choir 2* Protect me from domestic violence
and all forms of abusive behavior
and every shred of complicity
in the war to break one's will.

*All* O One Who soothes the savage seas
and calms the troubled waters,
protect me from the violence around me
and within me.

*Choir 1* Deliver me from those violent flashes of anger
that sometimes scare me,
unleashing a guilt that is out of control,
throwing my heart off balance.

*Choir 2* Protect me from being violated
in body, mind, or spirit.
Send my guardian angel
to watch over me
and gentle me
and shield me.

By M. T. Winter, Crossroad Pub. Co., © 1991 Medical Mission Sisters  *WomanWisdom* / **161**

*All*   O One Who soothes the savage seas
and calms the troubled waters,
protect me from the violence around me
and within me.

*Choir 1*   Deliver me from demonic forces
everywhere around me.

*Choir 2*   Protect me from avenging notions
latent deep within me.

*All*   O One Who soothes the savage seas
and calms the troubled waters,
protect me from the violence around me
and within me.

 By M. T. Winter, Crossroad Pub. Co., © 1991 Medical Mission Sisters

# HANNAH

◇ **Scripture Reference**   1 Sam 1; 2:1–11, 18–21

◇ **Biography**

Hannah, wife of Elkanah, lived in Ramah with her husband and his other wife, Penninah, and Penninah's sons and daughters. Hannah herself was childless. After an intense period of prayer, she conceived and gave birth to Samuel, whom she consecrated to God. When the boy was weaned, she left him at the sanctuary in Shiloh to be a minister there and gave birth to other children, two daughters and three sons.

◇ **Context**

Many great men of biblical tradition — Isaac, Jacob, Joseph, Samson, and now Samuel — were born of women who were supposedly barren. Hannah's story is reminiscent of Rachel, who was also a beloved wife. She too suffered much because she was childless while her husband Jacob's other wife, her sister Leah, had borne him children. The sons who, by the grace of God, broke through the barrenness of both Rachel and Hannah figured prominently in the continuity of the tradition, Joseph son of Rachel and Samuel son of Hannah. Samuel ushered in the monarchy and oversaw its favorable transition to God's anointed, David. Hannah's song of praise rings with the phraseology of a later *Magnificat*, for both canticles are derived from stock material of Jewish musicology. Her song, however, may well be an editorial insertion here.

163

Hannah's story reveals an extroverted woman of deep faith, fervent piety, and intense feeling. She got irritated and depressed, wept bitterly, complained, cried aloud to God in her distress, and was exuberant in her joy. On the other hand, the miraculous nature of the birth of Samuel was a matter between Hannah and God, for she alone knew what she had asked of God and also what she had promised. The child's conception was not extraordinary, for she had intercourse with her husband, but the timing surely was. Hannah also knew the meaning of sacrifice. The child for whom she so poignantly longed was given away when he was weaned. God gave Hannah the child she asked for and Hannah gave him back to God. She had named her firstborn Samuel, which meant "because from God I have asked him," and God rewarded her with other children without her having to ask. A significant twist to Hannah's story is that she, not her husband, was the one in charge of the decisions regarding Samuel. It was her prayer, her promise, her son. She was the one who named him, who decided when he would leave her, who brought him in person to Shiloh. Hannah took the initiatives, spoke out, acted decisively. Her story needs to be told.

◇ **Lectionary Reading**

There was a man
from the hills of Ephraim
whose name was Elkanah
son of Jeroham
son of Elihu
son of Tohu
son of Zuph.
He had two wives,
Hannah and Penninah.
His wife Penninah had children.
His wife Hannah did not.
Each year on the day
when Elkanah would worship
and sacrifice to God at Shiloh,
he gave portions to his wife Penninah
and to all her sons and daughters.
To Hannah who was barren
he gave a double portion
because of his love for her.
Penninah, her rival, would taunt Hannah
to irritate and provoke her
because God had closed her womb.
So it continued, year after year.
Whenever they went to the house of God,
Penninah would provoke her.

Hannah would weep and refuse to eat.
"Hannah, why do you weep?"
her husband Elkanah would ask her.
"Why is your heart so sad?
Am I not more to you
than ten sons of your womb?"
Then one year at Shiloh,
after they were finished eating,
Hannah presented herself to God.
Deeply distressed, she prayed to God,
weeping bitterly.
Then Hannah made a vow.
"If you will remember me, O God,
if you will look on my affliction,
if you will give me a son,
I will give him back to you
all the days of his life."
Now Eli the priest was sitting there
at the entrance to the house of God.
Observing Hannah, he thought she was drunk,
for her lips moved but she made no sound,
so he said, "Put away your wine!"
Hannah replied, "I assure you,
I have had neither wine
nor intoxicating drink,
but I am deeply troubled.
I poured out my soul to God.
I am not a worthless woman.
I have prayed out of deep anxiety
and vexation all this time."
Then Eli said, "Go in peace,
and may God grant your desire."
And she said, "May I find favor with you,"
and she left and returned to her husband.
They ate and drank together,
and Hannah was no longer sad.
In the morning they rose and worshiped God,
then returned to their home in Ramah,
where Hannah conceived
and gave birth to a son
and named her baby Samuel, saying,
"I have asked for him from God."
When Elkanah and his household
went on their yearly pilgrimage
to Shiloh to worship God,
Hannah did not go.

"As soon as the boy is weaned,"
she said to her husband Elkanah,
"I will bring him to Shiloh,
to the presence of God,
and leave him there forever."
Her husband Elkanah said to her,
"Do what seems best to you.
Wait until you have weaned him,
and may God's word be done."
So Hannah stayed home and nursed her son,
and when at last the boy was weaned,
she took him, along with a three-year old bull,
some flour and some wine,
and brought him to Shiloh
to the house of God,
where they slaughtered the bull
and brought the boy to Eli
who was the priest.
The child was very young.
Hannah said, "As you live, my lord,
I am the woman who stood here
in your presence, praying to God.
This is the child for whom I prayed
and God granted my petition.
Therefore I give him back to God
for as long as he shall live."

◇

Hannah left Samuel in Shiloh and prayed:

•

### HANNAH'S PSALM

My heart is filled with the fullness of God,
my whole being is elated.

I look to the Holy One Who is my Rock,
in Whose power my spirit rejoices.

The living God is a God of knowledge
in Whom every action is weighed.

The weapons of warriors are broken,
and the weak are empowered with strength.

Those who were full now work for their bread
and the famished no longer hunger.

God restores to life again,
reaches down and raises up,

impoverishes and enriches,
humbles and also exalts.

God lifts the destitute from the dust
and the needy out of the ashes,
giving places of preeminence
to the outcasts of every age.

For God Who created the pillars of earth
sets the world there and sustains it,

guarding the feet of the faithful,
ensuring that evil will not prevail,
the demonic will not conquer.

God judges to the ends of the earth
and supports those who are anointed
to a covenant of peace.

The one who was barren has borne a child,
but the mother of many is desolate.

My heart is filled with the fullness of God,
my whole being is elated.

•

Then Hannah went home to Ramah
and the boy remained in Shiloh
in the presence of Eli the priest.
Now Samuel wore a linen robe
as he ministered before God,
for his mother would make him a tiny robe
and take it to him every year
when she went with her husband to worship.
Eli would bless Elkanah and Hannah
and say to the two of them,
"May God repay this woman with children
for the gift she has made to God."
And then they would return to their home.
God remembered Hannah.
She conceived and bore three sons,
and Hannah also had two daughters.

◇ **Points for Shared Reflection**

- In what way might Hannah's story after the birth of her baby serve as a source of strength to birth mothers considering adoption today?
- In what ways might Hannah's story serve as a source of inspiration to you?

- The priest misread Hannah and accused her of inappropriate behavior. Has religious authority ever misunderstood your actions or your intentions and wrongly judged you?

- Talk about Hannah and Elkanah's marriage. What qualities in their relationship to and treatment of each other make them an appropriate model for married couples today?

◇ **A Psalm for Keeping Faith**  (see page 169)

◇ **Prayer**

Help us,
O Keeper of Faith,
to keep the faith entrusted to us,
faith in a world worth saving,
faith in a dream worth sharing,
faith in a heritage worth keeping
even as we reinvigorate it
to have meaning for us now.
Help us keep faith in You,
and help us not lose faith in ourselves,
for faith is the substance of our hope,
and hope, the assurance of love.
Praise to You, O Faithful One,
now and forever.
Amen.

#### ◇ A PSALM FOR KEEPING FAITH ◇

*Choir 1*   How can I keep faith
when deliverance has been so long
in coming?

*Choir 2*   How can I keep confidence
when there is no sign
that You are near?

*Choir 1*   What is there left
to believe in,
when all that I held sacred once
has blown away
with the winds of change?

*Choir 2*   Who is there left
to believe in,
when modern day heroes
and heroines
have shown their feet of clay?

*Choir 1*   How can I keep faith?
How long must I wait
to bring to birth?

*Choir 2*   How can I keep faith?
How many initiatives
must be stillborn?

*Choir 1*   Will our children have hope?

*Choir 2*   They will have hope,
but only if our hope has children.

*Choir 1*   Will our faith have meaning?

*Choir 2*   It will have meaning,
but only if meaning is rooted in faith
so that fear is meaningless.

*Choir 1*   Will our love have mattered?

*Choir 2*   It will have mattered,
but only if we who love
do not lose faith in the power of loving.

*All*   Shaddai, it is hard to keep faith
unless we see the signs of Your faithfulness
around us
and within us.
Do not lose faith in us.

By M. T. Winter, Crossroad Pub. Co., © 1991 Medical Mission Sisters     *WomanWisdom* / **169**

# RIZPAH

◇ **Scripture Reference**   2 Sam 3:6–11; 21:1–14

◇ **Biography**

Rizpah, daughter of Aiah, was Saul's concubine and the mother of Ar-moni and Mephibosheth, two of the sons David captured and delivered to the Gibeonites to atone for the sin of Saul. Seven of Saul's sons and grandsons were executed — their bodies were impaled — and Rizpah kept vigil night and day to protect their bodies from being ravaged by wild animals or birds.

◇ **Context**

We meet Rizpah, Saul's concubine, after she has already been widowed. In both pericopes she is caught in the middle of a power stuggle between men. It is not clear whether the alleged rape by Abner ever happened, but from that moment of accusation, Abner definitively shifted alle-giance from the house of Saul to an alliance with David. The accusation itself indicates that his ambivalence had already been detected, since to take another man's woman was tantamount to attacking the man. David's negotiation with the Gibeonites to seek a probable cause for the extended famine provided a convenient political opportunity to further decimate his rival. He took Saul's two sons, Rizpah's sons, and five of Saul's grandsons and impaled any further threat to him or to his heirs. In both narratives, no consideration whatsoever was given to the woman. The desecration of her body, the destruction of her flesh and blood were immaterial alongside the issues of power and control.

Rizpah reflects all the stereotypical characteristics patriarchy inflicts on women. She was silent, powerless, submissive. Her status was negligible. She was a concubine, a widow, a mother minus her sons. In the society of her times, this made her a non-person, triply insignificant. Yet she had within her a feminist determination that led her to a courageous act of defiance. Out of her silent strength she took control of the only area over which she had any control, herself, and she kept vigil beside the bodies of her mutilated sons for approximately five months, the time between the beginning of the barley harvest and the arrival of the rains. She protected her children from further violation and in the process became a powerful symbol of mother-love, a mother of sorrows, which so humiliated the king that he finally saw to the proper burial of Saul and his sons. In Hebrew Rizpah's name means "glowing coal," daughter of "falcon."

## Lectionary Reading

The war was long and bitter
between the house of Saul
and the house of David.
Abner, Saul's commander,
controlled the house of Saul.
Now Saul had a concubine
whose name was Rizpah.
She was the daughter of Aiah.
Saul's son, Ishbaal, approached Abner
and made this accusation.
"Why have you slept with Rizpah,
my father's concubine?"
These words sent Abner into a rage.
"Am I a dog?" he shouted.
"I have been loyal to the house of Saul,
to his brothers and his friends,
and have kept you from the hand of David,
and yet you dare to accuse me
of a crime such as this?
So may God do to Abner,

and may God add to it,
if what God has sworn to David,
I do not help to accomplish:
to transfer the kingdom from the house of Saul
and establish the throne of David
over Israel and over Judah
from Dan down to Beer-sheba."
And Ishbaal could say nothing to Abner,
because he feared him so.

◇

Now there was a famine in the days of David.
After it had lasted for three full years,
David inquired of God, who said,
"There is blood-guilt on Saul and on his house
for slaughtering the Gibeonites."
The Gibeonites were not part of Israel
but a remnant of the Amorites,
and Israel had sworn to spare them,
but Saul had tried to wipe them out
in his zeal for Israel and Judah.
So David called the Gibeonites
and said to them,
"What shall I do for you?
How shall I make expiation,
so that you may bless the heritage of God?"
The Gibeonites said to him,
"It is not a matter of silver or gold
between us and Saul and his house.
Neither is it up to us
to put anyone in Israel to death."
But David again insisted,
"What do you want me to do for you?"
Then they said this to the king,
"The man who attacked us
and tried to destroy us,
so that we should have no place here
in the territory of Israel —
let seven of his sons be delivered to us
and we will impale them at Gibeon
on the mountain of God."
David said, "I will deliver them to you."
But David spared Mephibosheth,
the son of Saul's son Jonathan,
because of the oath that had been sworn
between David and Jonathan.
David took into custody

the two sons of Rizpah,
Armoni and Mephibosheth,
whom she had borne to Saul;
and the five sons of Merab, Saul's daughter,
whom she had borne to Adriel the son of Barzillai;
and he delivered them to the Gibeonites
and they impaled them on the mountain
in the presence of God.
The seven perished together.
They were put to death at harvest time,
at the start of the barley harvest.
Then Rizpah, daughter of Aiah,
took sackcloth and spread it on a rock,
and sat there from the beginning of harvest
until rain fell from the heavens.
And she did not allow the birds of the air
to touch the bodies by day
or wild animals to come near them
at any time during the night.
When David was told what Rizpah,
Saul's concubine, had done,
he went and collected the bones of Saul
and the bones of Jonathan, his son,
from the people of Jabesh-gilead
who had stolen them from the public square
where the Philistines had hung them
when they killed Saul on Gilboa.
He collected the bones of Jonathan and Saul
and the bones of the seven who had been impaled
and made sure of their burial.
They buried Saul and Jonathan
in Zela in the land of Benjamin,
in the tomb of his father, Kish.
After they had finished doing
all that the king had commanded,
God heeded supplications
offered on behalf of the land.

◇ **Points for Shared Reflection**

- Rizpah knew how to wait and simply let things happen. Would you have had the patience to do what Rizpah did? Do you know how to wait?

- Can you recall an incident in your life when you had no other choice but to wait on God, and you were not disappointed?

- Compare Rizpah with the *madres* and *abuelas* (mothers and grand-mothers) of the missing in Argentina who kept vigil in the public plaza to protest the torture and disappearance of their children. Tell their story. What were the consequences of their action?

- A theme in biblical tradition proclaims that God's power is made manifest in powerlessness. How is that a comforting word for you? Have you felt God's power in a moment of powerlessness in your own life? Tell about it.

◇ **A Psalm for Keeping Vigil** (see page 175)

◇ **Prayer**

O One Who Waits Forever,
keeping guard
at the gates of life,
patiently awaiting
the heart's return,
no matter how long,
no matter how late,
we beg You to keep watch over us.
Guard us when we are sleeping,
guide us when we are awake,
and gently lead us
home to You
now and forever.
Amen.

# ◇ A PSALM FOR KEEPING VIGIL ◇

*Choir 1*   Mothers
keep vigil
when their babies are born
and when they die,
pulling them
from the arms of God
to hold them close
until it is time
to return them again to Her.

*All*   Be vigilant. Keep watch.
Otherwise some itinerant whim
will steal your life away.

*Choir 2*   Lovers
keep vigil
when their time together
is at an end,
either because
life must go on
or it cannot go on this way.

*All*   Be vigilant. Keep watch.
Otherwise some itinerant word
will steal your love away.

*Choir 1*   Stars
keep vigil
when the harvest moon
is dying.
They stand at the door
of the universe
as the aeons come and go.

*All*   Be vigilant. Keep watch.
Otherwise someone is sure to come
and steal your stars away.

*Choir 2*   Dawn
keeps vigil
on the threshold
of day
in a swiftly changing environment,
and still takes time to pray.

By M. T. Winter, Crossroad Pub. Co., © 1991 Medical Mission Sisters   *WomanWisdom* / 175

*All*  Be vigilant. Keep watch.
Otherwise some itinerant storm
will steal your light away.

*Choir 1*  Children
keep vigil
beside and within
their make believes
and let's pretends,
making friends
with growing up
and going out
and moving far away.

*All*  Be vigilant. Keep watch.
Otherwise some itinerant war
will steal your child away.

*Choir 2*  Women
keep vigil
beside the dreams
that die stillborn,
mourning their impossibility
until the time of harvest.

*All*  Be vigilant. Keep watch.
Otherwise some itinerant doubt
will steal your dream away.

*Choir 1*  Shaddai
keeps vigil
beside the child
She brings to birth,
watching her grow
into fullness of life
as She reveals its meaning.

*All*  Be vigilant. Keep watch.
Otherwise some itinerant rule
will steal Shaddai away.

*Choir 2*  Shalom
keeps vigil
within the turbulence
of our hearts.

*All*  Be vigilant. Keep watch.
Otherwise some itinerant fear
will steal Shalom away.

   By M. T. Winter, Crossroad Pub. Co., © 1991 Medical Mission Sisters

# DAVID'S WIVES: AHINOAM, MAACAH, HAGGITH, ABITAL, EGLAH, etc. (and MICHAL, ABIGAIL, and BATHSHEBA) and DAVID'S CONCUBINES

◇ **Scripture Reference**   1 Sam 14:49; 18:20–29; 19:11–17
1 Sam 25:1–44; 27:1–4; 30:1–5, 10, 17–18
2 Sam 2:1–4; 3:2–5, 12–16; 5:13–16
2 Sam 6:12–23; 11:2–27; 12:1–24
2 Sam 15:14, 16; 16:21–22
2 Sam 19:5; 20:3; 1 Kings 1:5, 11–40
1 Kings 2:13–25; 1 Chr 3:1–9; 14:3–7; 15:29

◇ **Biography**
David had eight named wives and ten identified concubines. He took many more unidentified wives and concubines during his thirty-three

177

year reign in Jerusalem. Michal, Saul's younger daughter and David's first wife who was taken away from him and then retrieved by him, was the only named wife who was childless. She loved David and then despised him. Abigail, widow of Nabal of Carmel, and Bathsheba, widow of Uriah, figure prominently in the chronicles of David. References to Ahinoam of Jezreel also recur. Maacah, Haggith, Abital, and Eglah are mentioned only as mothers of his children. David's wives and concubines had many children, both sons and daughters, although only one daughter is identified by name. Bathsheba saw to it that her son Solomon succeeded David to the throne.

◇ **Context**

The wives and concubines reveal another side of David. There is no way their own story can emerge except in relationship to his. Michal, Saul's daughter, was David's first wife. Although she loved him and saved his life, his feelings for her are unclear. Her father took her away from David who retrieved her when he was king, but by then Michal hated him. There is no clear explanation for her change of heart except a suspicion that she must have known something about David that the writers refused to say. Around the time when Michal was taken from him, David married Abigail and Ahinoam. It is not clear whether he married them before or after Michal went away. If before, jealousy and rejection could be factors in her turning against David, but what if Ahinoam of Jezreel was also the daughter of Ahimaaz, who was Saul's wife and Michal's mother? The records are silent about both women. It would explain why Saul took Michal away and why she hated David.

David's marriages seemed to have been politically expedient: Michal daughter of Saul king of Judah; Abigail of the clans of Carmel; Maacah daughter of Talmai king of the Aramean territory of Geshur; Ahinoam of Jezreel either to secure another territorial alliance or as a direct challenge to the house of Saul. David had married all but one of his named wives by the time he was made king in Hebron. He married Bathsheba and supposedly other women during his lengthy reign in Jerusalem, where he also acquired more concubines. He promised Bathsheba that his throne would be given to her son Solomon and she made him keep his promise. His wives gave birth to sons and they also gave birth to daughters, but the only female we know anything about is Maacah's daughter Tamar.

Much of David's remaining narrative is focused on three of his first four sons — Ahinoam's son Amnon, his firstborn and heir, Maacah's son Absalom, and Haggith's son Adonijah. The records are silent about Abigail's Daniel, also known as Chileab. After the rape of their sister Tamar, Absalom killed Amnon and then mounted an attack to take the throne, raping ten of his father's concubines before he was finally slain. In David's last days Haggith's son Adonijah as next in line felt he was the rightful heir and tried to stage his coronation, but Bathsheba invervened and Solomon was crowned king. Solomon killed Adonijah to secure his accession to the throne.

So many unasked and unanswered questions arise in relation to these wives and concubines. Who were they really? How did they feel about their dubious royal status? Where were they as mothers when their sons were being slain, when Tamar was being raped? What about Michal and the ten concubines who were virtually imprisoned in the palace, deprived of a sexual relationship with the man who kept them there and, consequently, deprived of children? What did they really think of David, the man behind the power and the throne? So much history lies buried in the lost lives of these women. The view from the royal harem could cause historians to reevaluate a lot of what they think they know. The stories of Michal, Abigail, and Abishag, who was David's young female attendant just before he died, are told more fully under Memorable Women later in this volume. The story of Bathsheba is featured in the companion volume *WomanWitness*.

◇ **Lectionary Reading**

The names of Saul's two daughters were:
Merab, the name of the firstborn,
and Michal, the name of the younger.

◇

Now Saul's daughter Michal loved David,
and Saul was told, and it pleased him.
Saul speculated to himself,
"Let me give her to him.
Let Michal be a snare for him,
that the Philistines might overcome him."
So Saul said to David a second time,
"You shall now be my son-in-law."
Then Saul commanded his servants,
"Speak to David in private. Say to him,
'See, the king is delighted with you
and all his servants love you.
Now then, become the king's son-in-law.' "
So Saul's servants spoke to David
and David said to them,
"Does it seem such a simple thing to you
for a man who is poor and insignificant
to become the king's son-in-law?"
The servants told Saul what David had said.
"Say this to David," he told them.
"The king desires no marriage gift;
just bring him a hundred foreskins
of his enemies, the Philistines,

that he may be avenged."
Now Saul planned that David would fall
by the hand of the Philistines.
When David was told the words of Saul,
he was pleased to be the king's son-in-law.
He got up, went out, assembled his men,
and killed one hundred Philistines
and brought one hundred foreskins to Saul
that he might become the king's son-in-law.
Saul gave him his daughter Michal as a wife.
But when Saul realized that God was with David
and that his own daughter Michal loved him,
he was even more afraid of David.
So Saul was David's enemy from that moment on.

◇

Now Saul sent messengers to David's house
to keep him under guard that night,
for he planned to kill him in the morning.
David's wife Michal said to him,
"If you do not save your life tonight,
tomorrow you will be killed."
So Michal let David down through a window
and he escaped into the night.
Michal took an idol, covered it with clothes,
put a net of goat's hair on its head,
and laid it on David's bed.
When Saul sent messengers to take David,
Michal said, "He is sick."
Then Saul sent the messengers to see for themselves.
He said, "Bring him here to me in his bed,
so that I might see him and kill him."
When they saw the idol in David's bed,
they brought word back to Saul
and Saul sent for Michal.
"Why have you deceived me like this?
Why have you let my enemy go?
Why has he escaped?"
Michal said to her father,
"He said to me, 'Michal, let me go,
otherwise I will kill you.'"

◇

[For Abigail's story, see page 348 or read the following summary passage.]

A delegation came to Abigail and said,
"David wants you as his wife."
Abigail rose and bowed to the ground, saying,

"Your servant is a slave
prepared to wash the feet of his servants."
Abigail got up quickly
and rode away on her donkey,
her five maids accompanying her.
She rode behind David's messengers,
and she became David's wife.
David also married Ahinoam of Jezreel;
both of them became his wives.
Saul had given Michal, David's wife,
to Palti, son of Laish, who was from Gallim.

◇

One day David said to himself,
"I shall surely perish by the hand of Saul.
Let me leave for the land of the Philistines
and I will escape his wrath."
So David set out and crossed over,
he and six hundred men and their households,
to Achish king of Gath.
David and his two wives,
Ahinoam of Jezreel and Abigail of Carmel,
his troops and all their households,
settled there at Gath.
When Saul was told that David had fled,
he no longer searched for him.

◇

The Amalekites raided Ziklag;
they sacked it and burned it down,
capturing all who were in it,
women and children, young and old,
and carried them all away.
When David and his men returned to the city,
they found the city destroyed
and their families taken captive.
They wept until they could weep no more.
David was in danger of being stoned,
for people were very bitter
at the loss of their wives and children.
David's two wives had also been taken,
Ahinoam of Jezreel and Abigail of Carmel.
So David set out with six hundred men,
but two hundred dropped out at Wadi Besor,
too exhausted to go on.
They entered the Philistine camp;
and David and his troops attacked and fought
from twilight to the following evening.

Only four hundred young men mounted on camels
managed to escape.
David recovered everything
and rescued all the captives,
including his two wives.

◇

Sometime later, David asked God,
"Shall I settle in the cities of Judah?"
God said to him, "Yes, go."
"To which shall I go?" asked David.
And God replied, "To Hebron."
So David went up to Hebron
with his wives Ahinoam and Abigail,
and brought all the men who were with him,
and everyone in his house.
They settled in the towns of Hebron.
The people of Judah came to him,
and there they anointed David as king
over the house of Judah.

◇

Sons were born to David at Hebron.
His firstborn was Amnon, son of Ahinoam;
his second was Daniel (Chileab), Abigail's child;
the third was Absalom son of Maacah,
daughter of King Talmai of Geshur;
the fourth, Adonijah son of Haggith;
the fifth, Shephatiah son of Abital;
and the sixth, Ithream of David's wife Eglah.
These were born to David in Hebron,
where he reigned for seven years and three months.

◇

Abner sent messengers to David at Hebron, saying,
"To whom does the land belong?
Make your covenant with me
and I will support you
and give all of Israel over to you."
David said, "Good, I will covenant with you,
but one thing first I require:
bring Saul's daughter Michal with you
when you come to see me again."
Then David sent word to Saul's son Ishbaal.
"Give me my wife Michal
for whom I paid one hundred Philistine foreskins."
Ishbaal took her from her husband Palti the son of Laish,
but her husband went with her,
weeping, and walking behind her

all the way to Bahurim.
Then Abner said to him, "Go back home!"
so he went back home without her.

◊

David took more wives
and more concubines in Jerusalem,
where he reigned for thirty-three years,
and there he became the father of more sons
and daughters.
These are the names of the children
born to David in Jerusalem:
Shammua, Shobab, Nathan, and Solomon,
four sons by Bathsheba;
then nine more: Ibhar, Elishama, Eliphelet,
Nogah, Nepheg, Japhia,
Elishama, Eliada, and Eliphelet.
All these were David's sons,
besides the sons of the concubines;
and Tamar was their sister.

◊

David went and brought up the ark of God
to Jerusalem with rejoicing.
When those who were bearing the ark of God
had gone six paces,
he sacrificed an ox and a fattened sheep.
David danced with all his might
before the ark of God.
He was clad with a linen vestment.
So David and all the house of Israel
brought up the ark to Jerusalem
with shouting and with trumpets.
As the ark came into the city of David,
Michal looked out of the window
and she saw King David
leaping and dancing with joy before his God,
and she hated him in her heart.
They set the ark inside the tent
that David had prepared for it,
and David offered burnt offerings
and offerings of well-being
and blessed the people in the name of God.
He distributed food among all the people,
a cake of bread, a portion of meat,
and a cake of raisins to all assembled,
both women and men of Israel.
Then the people returned to their homes.

David went to bless his household,
but Michal the daughter of Saul, David's wife,
came to meet her husband and said,
"What a spectacle you made of yourself today,
you the king of Israel,
exposing yourself to the eyes of young maids,
as vulgar men might shamelessly do!"
David said to Michal,
"I danced before God who chose me
in place of your father and his household,
who appointed me prince over Israel,
to rule the people of God.
I will make myself yet more contemptible than this
and abase myself in my own eyes,
but as for the maids of whom you have spoken,
these hold me in high esteem."
And Michal the daughter of Saul
was childless to the day of her death.

◊

It happened late one afternoon
that David was walking on the palace roof
when he saw a woman bathing.
The woman was very beautiful.
When David inquired about her,
he was told, "She is Bathsheba,
daughter of Eliam and wife of Uriah the Hittite."
David sent for the woman.
She came and he made love to her
before she went back home.
Bathsheba, who had just finished her period
and had been purifying herself
when she was seen from the palace roof,
soon discovered she was pregnant,
and she let David know.
David sent word to Joab,
"Put Uriah on the front line.
When the fighting is fierce, let him die."
As Joab was beseiging the city,
he assigned Uriah to the front line
where the valiant warriors were.
Some of David's servants died.
Uriah was killed as well.
When Bathsheba heard that Uriah was dead,
she lamented for her husband.
When the time of mourning was over,
David sent for her and made her his wife

and she gave birth to a son.
But the deed that David had done to Uriah
was really displeasing to God.

◇

David's child by Uriah's wife
suddenly became very ill.
David pleaded with God for the child;
he fasted and lay all night on the ground.
The elders stood beside him, urging him to rise;
but he would not, nor would he eat with them.
On the seventh day the child died,
and his servants were afraid to tell him.
"If he would not listen while the child was alive,
what now that the child is dead?
He may even try to harm himself."
When David saw them whispering,
he knew that his child was dead.
"Is the child dead?" David asked them.
"He is dead," his servants replied.
Then David got up, went and bathed
and anointed himself, and changed his clothes
and went before God to worship,
and then he returned to his own house,
asked for food, and ate.
Bewildered, his servants said to him,
"How are you behaving?
You fasted and wept when the child was alive
and you eat now that it is dead."
And David explained to his servants,
"While the child was alive, I fasted and wept,
saying, 'Who knows?
God may be gracious.
Maybe the child will live.'
But now he is dead, why should I fast?
Can I bring him back again?
More likely it is I who will join him,
but he will not return to me."
Then David consoled Bathsheba, his wife,
and he made love to her,
and she in time gave birth to a son
and David named him Solomon.
God loved the child and made this known
through the word of Nathan the prophet
who named him Jedidiah,
which means, Beloved of God.

◇

David said to all his officials
who were with him in Jerusalem,
"Get up! Flee! We must escape from Absalom.
Hurry, or he will soon overtake us,
and bring disaster upon us
and attack the city with the edge of his sword."
So the king left, with all his household,
except for ten concubines whom he left behind
to look after the house.

◇

Ahithophel said to Absalom,
"Rape your father's concubines,
the ones he left to look after the house;
and all Israel will hear
that you have made yourself despicable to your father,
and the hands of all who are with you
will be strengthened."
So they pitched a tent for Absalom
there on the roof of the palace,
and Absalom had intercourse with his father's concubines
in the sight of all Israel.

◇

David returned to his house in Jerusalem.
The king took the ten concubines
whom he had left to look after the house
and put them in a house under guard
and he provided for them,
but he did not sleep with them again.
So they were shut up until the day of their death,
living as if in widowhood.

◇

King David was old and advanced in years
when Nathan said to Bathsheba,
"Adonijah son of Haggith has been made king
and David does not know it.
Now let me give you some advice
so you may save the life of Solomon your son
and your own life as well.
Go in at once to David and say,
'Did you not swear to your servant, saying:
Solomon your son shall succeed me as king
and shall sit upon my throne.
Why then is Adonijah king?'
Then while you are there still speaking with the king,
I will come in and confirm your words."
So Bathsheba went to the king in his room.

Now the king was very old;
Abishag was attending to him.
Bathsheba bowed to the king and he said,
"What is it you wish?"
She repeated Nathan's words,
adding some more of her own.
"Adonijah has prepared a lavish feast
and invited all but Solomon.
The eyes of all are on you, my lord.
Tell them who will succeed you.
Otherwise on the day you die,
my son and I will be outcasts."
Then Nathan came in, bowed to the ground,
and repeated the words of Bathsheba, adding,
"Everyone including the priest Abiathar
is saying, 'Long live King Adonijah!'
But they did not invite me, or Zadok the priest,
or Solomon, or Benaiah.
Has all this been done by you, my lord,
and have you neglected to tell us
who will follow you to the throne?"
Then King David answered,
"Bring Bathsheba to me."
She came into his presence,
and the king swore an oath, saying,
"As God lives who has saved me from all adversity,
as I swore to you by the God of Israel,
'Your son Solomon shall succeed me as king,
and he shall sit on my throne after me,'
so will I do this day."
Then Bathsheba bowed to the ground and said,
"May King David live forever!"
David said, "Summon before me
Zadok the priest, Nathan the prophet,
and Benaiah son of Jehoida."
When they had arrived, he said to them,
"Take my servants with you,
have Solomon ride on my own mule,
and bring him down to Gihon.
There let the priest and the prophet
anoint him king over Israel;
then blow the trumpet and say to all,
'Long live King Solomon!'
Let him enter and sit upon my throne.
He shall be king in my place,
for I have appointed him ruler over Israel and over Judah."

Benaiah answered the king,
"Amen! May God so ordain it.
As God has been with my lord the king,
may God also be with Solomon,
and make his throne even greater
than the throne of King David my lord."
So Zadok the priest, Nathan the prophet,
and Benaiah son of Jehoida,
and the Cherethites and the Pelethites,
led Solomon down to Gihon astride King David's mule.
And there they anointed Solomon,
then blew the trumpet as the people shouted,
"Long live King Solomon!"
And all the people followed him,
playing the pipes with gladness
and making a joyful noise.

◊ **Points for Shared Reflection**

• Comment on the portrait of David presented by the women in his life. In what ways, if any, has your opinion of David changed?

• Reflect on David's wives and concubines, individually and collectively. How might their story, had it been told, made a difference in your understanding of biblical tradition?

• In what ways has history been unfair to David's wives and concubines? In what ways do we continue to be unfair to the women married to men of heroic stature?

• What would you, as a woman, look for in a husband? What do males look for in women? What do you expect from a marriage?

◊ **A Psalm Celebrating God's Providence** (see page 189)

◊ **Prayer**

It would have been enough
if You had simply given life to us,
O Genesis of Our Being,
but You also gave us meaning
and liberty
and love.
How shall we respond
to such an outpouring of blessing,
except to give back life for Life
and love for unending Love.
Amen.

# ◇ A PSALM CELEBRATING GOD'S PROVIDENCE ◇

*Choir 1*  It would have been enough
if You had lifted us from nothingness
into humanity,

*Choir 2*  but You made us in Your image.

*All*  We thank You, Shekinah-Shaddai.

*Choir 1*  It would have been enough
if You had made a simple covenant
limited to our lifetime,

*Choir 2*  but you wove the generations
into one long benediction.

*All*  We praise You, Shekinah-Shaddai.

*Choir 1*  It would have been enough
if You had led us out of slavery,

*Choir 2*  but You continue to share our bondage
until we are fully free.

*All*  We bless You, Shekinah-Shaddai.

*Choir 1*  It would have been enough
if You had championed the cause of justice
for all who are oppressed,

*Choir 2*  but You heal the broken-hearted,
and You bind up all our wounds.

*All*  We need You, Shekinah-Shaddai.

*Choir 1*  It would have been enough
if You had simply shared Your vision
through the prophets of the past,

*Choir 2*  but You speak prophetic words to us
and through us, even now.

*All*  We hear You, Shekinah-Shaddai.

*Choir 1*  It would have been enough
if You had sojourned briefly among us,

*Choir 2*  but You stayed with us and within us.

*All*  We live by Your Holy Spirit
and we rejoice, Shekinah-Shaddai.

By M. T. Winter, Crossroad Pub. Co., © 1991 Medical Mission Sisters *WomanWisdom* /

# SOLOMON'S WIVES
# AND CONCUBINES

◇ **Scripture Reference**     1 Kings 3:1; 7:1, 8; 9:15–24; 11:1–8
1 Kings 14:21, 31; 2 Chr 8:11; 12:13–14

◇ **Biography**

Solomon had one thousand wives — seven hundred princesses and three hundred concubines — according to what scripture tells us. Many were foreign women. Pharaoh's daughter and a number of Canaanites were among the women he married. Naamah, his Ammonite wife, is the only one we know by name, no doubt because her son Rehoboam succeeded Solomon to the throne.

◇ **Context**

Solomon was a legendary lover and everything about him was extravagant, so the claim of one thousand wives may be somewhat exaggerated.

However, there is no reason to doubt that his sexual conquests were many and his royal harem of astounding proportions. Many of his marriages were politically motivated and proved an effective form of diplomacy in the establishment of his empire. He married the sisters and daughters of kings to seal alliances of arms and commerce. His wives were Moabites, Ammonites, Edomites, Hittites, Sidonians, and the Egyptian Pharaoh's daughter. Her father gave Solomon the city of Gezer as her dowry. He built her a palace of her own in Jerusalem. At least some of Solomon's concubines had to be political hostages or the pleasurable spoils of war.

All of these anonymous women were the property of one man. Except for Pharaoh's daughter and Naamah, mother of Rehoboam, we have no idea who they were. We do not know what they thought or how they felt about their circumstances. Were they jealous of one another, or did they form strong bonds of sisterhood in their common captivity? Was it hard to be one among so many, or did the cultural richness of such diverse experience in close proximity bring blessings of its own? Many of these women brought to Jerusalem their own religious traditions and evidently influenced their husband to some accommodation to their ways. We tell of Solomon's temple, the house which he built for God, yet never mention that this man of God claimed one thousand women as wives and worshiped other gods.


## Lectionary Reading

Solomon made a marriage alliance
with Pharaoh king of Egypt.
He took Pharaoh's daughter
and brought her into the city of David,
until he had finished building
his own house and the house of God
and the walls around Jerusalem.

◇

Solomon was building his own palace
and it took thirteen years before he finished it all.
The house in which he himself would reside,
the one in the court in back of the hall,
was covered with cedar from floor to floor.
Solomon also made a house like this for Pharaoh's daughter,
whom he had taken in marriage.

◇

This is the account of the forced labor
that Solomon conscripted to build the temple
and his own palace, the millo, and the walls of Jerusalem,
as well as Hazor, Megiddo, and Gezer.
Now Pharaoh king of Egypt had captured Gezer,

burned the city to the ground,
and killed all the Canaanites who lived there,
and he gave it as a dowry to his daughter,
Solomon's wife; so Solomon rebuilt Gezer.
The forced labor also built Lower Beth-horon,
Baalath, Tamar in the wilderness,
and sites within the land,
as well as all of Solomon's storage cities,
the cities for his chariots,
the cities for his cavalry,
and whatever Solomon desired to build,
in Jerusalem, in Lebanon,
and in all the land of his dominion.
Amorites, Hittites, Perizzites, Hivites,
and the Jebusites,
all who were left in the land,
all whom the Israelites were unable to destroy,
all who were not Israelites,
Solomon conscripted for slave labor,
but of Israelites Solomon made no slaves.
They were the soldiers
and they were his officials —
his commanders, captains, and chiefs
of his chariotry and cavalry.
Five hundred fifty had charge of the people
who carried on Solomon's work.
These were the chief officers
who supervised the building.
Pharaoh's daughter — Solomon's wife —
went from the city of David
to the house that Solomon had built for her,
her own palace in Jerusalem.

◊

Solomon brought Pharaoh's daughter
from the city of David
to the house that he had built for her,
for he said,
"My wife shall not live in the house
of King David of Israel,
for the places to which the ark of God
have come are holy."

◊

King Solomon loved many foreign women
along with the daughter of Pharaoh:
Moabite, Ammonite, Edomite, Sidonian,
and Hittite women,

women from those nations
about which God had said to the Israelites,
"You shall not enter into marriage with them,
neither shall they with you,
for they will surely incline your heart
toward following their gods as well."
Solomon clung to these women in love.
Among Solomon's wives were
seven hundred princesses
and three hundred concubines;
and his wives turned his heart away
from the God of Israel.
For when Solomon was old,
his wives turned his heart away
toward other gods,
and his heart was not true
to the God of Israel,
as was the heart of his father David.
For Solomon followed Astarte
the goddess of the Sidonians,
and Milcom the Ammonite deity.
So Solomon did evil in the sight of God
and did not faithfully follow God
as his father David had done.
Then Solomon built a place of worship
for Chemosh the deity of Moab,
and for Molech the deity of the Ammonites,
on the mountain east of Jerusalem.
He did the same for all his foreign wives,
who offered incense and sacrifice
to their gods.

◇

Rehoboam son of Solomon
was forty-one years old
when he began to reign in Judah,
and he reigned seventeen years in Jerusalem,
the city that God had chosen
out of all the tribes of Israel.
His mother's name was Naamah the Ammonite.


◇ **Points for Shared Reflection**

- Why did Solomon build a house for Pharaoh's daughter? Because she was special? Because she was different? You may wish to consult the text and share how you feel about what you find.

- Have you ever reached out to a woman of another culture? What did you learn from her?

- Do you find it hard to be yourself in a crowd? Do you have a problem sharing? Reveal something about yourself in your response.

- Try for a moment to imagine yourself in a room with one thousand women of various nations, cultures, and religions. How would you go about establishing a common bond with them?

◇ **A Psalm of Many Nations** (see page 195)

◇ **Prayer**

O Maker of Worlds
beyond us,
help us to live
in the world we know
in peace with one another,
a kaleidoscope of nations,
a patchwork quilt of ways and wills
that rise from the depth of cultures
created by Your love.
Open us up to the richness
of one another's vision
and the good we can accomplish
when we share one another's views.
We pray this prayer of unity and peace
in the hope of Shalom.
Amen.

## ◇ A PSALM OF MANY NATIONS ◇

*Choir 1*   We come from canyons
of painted stone
and scarlet sage
and flint-fingered shadows
slowly climbing
westward to the sun.
We praise Shaddai in the canyons.

*Choir 2*   We come from jungled labyrinths
of luxuriant green
so overgrown
the paths we traveled disappeared
with our grandmother's generation.
We walk with Shaddai through the jungles.

*All*   We are the women* of the nations of earth
who give birth to the men who rule us.

*Choir 1*   We come from high sierra plateaus
where melting snows
in rushing troughs
fall from spectacular vistas
and dance on the plains below us.
We dance with Shaddai in the mountains.

*Choir 2*   We come from frozen tundras
where everything wears
wedding white
and ice caps crack
like whips heralding
the changing of the seasons.
We remember Shaddai in the snow-covered north.

*All*   We are the women of the nations of earth
who give birth to the men who rule us.

*Choir 1*   We come from wind-swept grasslands
where the fleet of foot
race unrestrained
to the song of the savannah,
and the clear of heart
can raise her eyes and see into forever.
We sing to Shaddai in the grasses.

---

*For inclusive settings: We praise the women . . .

By M. T. Winter, Crossroad Pub. Co., © 1991 Medical Mission Sisters *WomanWisdom* / **195**

*Choir 2*   We come from islands
in the sun
where seas break rhythm
on our beaches,
surfacing ancient wisdom.
We worship Shaddai in the ocean.

*All*   We are the women of the nations of earth
who give birth to the men who rule us.

*Choir 1*   We come from deserts
of blinding heat
where dry wadis
cut a swath
across the arid, shifting sands.
We touch Shaddai in the desert.

*Choir 2*   We come from meadows
of singing birds
and larkspur
and rippling brooks
that hug the roots of giant oaks
and willows
green and gracious.
We know Shaddai in the meadows.

*All*   We are the women of the nations of earth
who give birth to the men who rule us.

*Choir 1*   We come from villages
strewn with huts
of thatched roofs
and thick red mud,
from towns of corrugated iron
buried deep in the tribal lands
of our ancestral matriarchs.
We chant to Shaddai in the village.

*Choir 2*   We come from cities
of glass and steel
and concrete cages
multilayered
in a teeming, pulsating
metropolis.
We seek Shaddai in our cities.

*All*   We are the women of the nations of earth
who give birth to the men who rule us.

# WIFE OF JEROBOAM

◇ **Scripture Reference**   1 Kings 11:14–22; 14:1–18

◇ **Biography**

The wife of Jeroboam may have been the sister of the Egyptian Queen Tahpenes and therefore sister-in-law of Shishak the Egyptian Pharaoh. She was the mother of a son, Abijah, who died as a child. Ordered to go in disguise to the prophet Ahijah at Shiloh for a word concerning the child's recovery, she received the full brunt of the prophetic oracle condemning the house of her husband for his infidelity to God and the overthrow of his reign as king of Israel. In her narratives she is silent and obscure, emerging only as sister, wife, and mother.

◇ **Context**

After the reign of David and Solomon, Jeroboam's revolt split Israel into two kingdoms, that of Israel in the north and Judah in Jerusalem. Jeroboam reigned over the Northern Kingdom for twenty-two years. While there are conflicting traditions tracing Jeroboam's rise to power, it was essentially the result of a rebellion against the extreme hardships inflicted on the people by the king of Judah, either Solomon or his son Rehoboam who succeeded him. After becoming king, Jeroboam reintroduced the worship of golden calves and made other cultic changes that resulted in his condemnation by the prophet Ahijah who had once supported him. Because of such actions he was made the paradigm of the evil king in later writings.

It is quite possible that Jeroboam married into the royal family during the time he sought temporary refuge in Egypt before becoming king. The text concerning the sojourn of the Edomite Hadad in Egypt may well preserve a fragment of the Jeroboam tradition. The passage appears in both the masoretic and Septuagint manuscripts. While Hadad is a personal name in the Bible, it is also a Semitic storm god and could conceivably be a metaphor for Jeroboam. His wife remains an enigma. In the later passage she is silent and submissive before her husband, before the prophet, before a scenario of divine retribution, a victim of what seems to be undeserved punishment by a supposedly angry God. When we connect the two narratives, a different picture emerges. According to internal evidence in both pericopes, the child born and weaned in Egypt dies as a boy in Israel, suggesting that his mother has only recently been uprooted from home and culture and relocated in a foreign country. Her silence and the loss of her only child should be placed in this transitional context. The prophet saw through her disguise, perhaps even to an integrity within her. There was something about the child of her womb that was pleasing to God, said Ahijah, and indications are that whatever that was did not come from her husband.

◇ **Lectionary Reading**

God raised up an adversary against Solomon,
Hadad the Edomite,
who was of the royal house in Edom.
When David was in Edom,
Joab commander of his army
killed every male in Edom
but the young boy Hadad
who escaped to Egypt
with some servants of his father.
Pharaoh king of Egypt
gave him a house
and food and land.
Hadad found favor with Pharaoh
who gave him his sister-in-law for a wife.
She was the sister of Queen Tahpenes.
The sister of Tahpenes
conceived a child by Hadad
and gave birth to a son, Genubath,
whom Tahpenes weaned in Pharaoh's house.
Genubath played in Pharaoh's house
among the children of Pharaoh.
When Hadad heard in Egypt that David had died
and that Joab commander of the army was dead,

he said to Pharaoh, "Let me depart,
that I may go to my own country."
But Pharaoh said, "What do you lack with me
that you would now return to your own land?"
And he answered, "Let me go."

◇

Now Abijah the son of Jeroboam became ill
and Jeroboam said to his wife,
"Disguise yourself so that no one will know
that you are the wife of Jeroboam.
I want you to go to Shiloh.
Take with you ten loaves, some cakes,
and a jar of honey,
and consult the prophet Ahijah
who is residing there.
He is the one who said of me
that I would be king of these people.
He will tell you what will happen to our child."
So Jeroboam's wife set out for Shiloh
and arrived at the house of Ahijah.
Now Ahijah could not see very well,
for his sight was impaired by advancing age.
But God informed Ahijah,
"The wife of Jeroboam is coming to you
to inquire about her son who is ill.
Say thus and so to her."
On approaching the prophet,
she pretended to be another woman,
but when Ahijah heard the sound of her feet
as she came in the door, he said,
"Come in, wife of Jeroboam.
Why do you disguise yourself?
I have been charged to speak a difficult word
to you and your husband.
Go tell Jeroboam, 'Thus says God:
I exalted you among the people
and made you leader over Israel;
I removed the kingdom from the house of David
and handed it over to you;
yet you have not been like my servant David
who followed me wholeheartedly,
who kept my commandments
and did only what was right.
But you have done evil over and above
all those who have gone before you;
you have made for yourself other gods;

you have cast images, provoking me to anger
and have thrust me behind your back.
Therefore disaster will come upon
the house of Jeroboam.
I will slay every male,
both slave and free,
consuming the house of Jeroboam
as one burns dung until it is gone.
Any who belong to Jeroboam
who die in the city
shall be eaten by dogs;
and any who die in the open country
shall be food for the birds of the air.
For thus God has spoken.'
Therefore now, go back to your house.
As your feet enter the city gate,
your young son will die.
All Israel will mourn for him.
He alone of your husband's family
will be buried in a grave,
because something in him is pleasing to God
in the house of Jeroboam.
Moreover, God will raise up a king
to rule over Israel
who will cut off the house of Jeroboam
from this very day.
God is about to strike Israel.
As a reed in the water sways and is gone,
so God will uproot Israel
out of their cherished ancestral land
and fling them beyond the Euphrates,
because they have made their sacred poles
and angered the living God.
Israel will be delivered up
because of the sins of Jeroboam,
those which he himself has committed
and those he caused Israel to do."
Then Jeroboam's wife got up and left.
When she reached Tirzah,
her child died,
just as she entered the house.
All Israel buried him and mourned for him,
according to the word of the prophet Ahijah
which he received from God.

◇ **Points for Shared Reflection**

- Why was it necessary for Jeroboam's wife to disguise herself before seeking counsel from the prophet at Shiloh?

- Can you recall a time when you pretended to be somebody else, either seriously or just for fun? Who did you pretend to be and why?

- When masks disguise what the world perceives as our real selves, the spirit is often freed up to reveal the real inner truth about us. On the other hand, the results of our actions sometimes mask our good intentions. Have you had either of these experiences?

- Jeroboam's wife appears to us to be silent and submissive. Does this image reflect you as a woman? as a wife? as a mother? as a participant in organized religion?

◇ **A Psalm for Shedding Pretenses** (see page 202)

◇ **Prayer**

O God of a Thousand Faces,
Who sees through all our pretenses
to that silent,
secret space within
where our true spirit sojourns,
prune away the duplicities
that mask our best intentions
and all those quick defenses
that disguise who we really are.
Open us up to You
and to all who would touch
the truth of our being,
so all may see
the integrity
of lives given over to You,
now and forever.
Amen.

# ◇ A PSALM FOR SHEDDING PRETENSES ◇

*Choir 1*   Happy are we when we can be ourselves
and be thoroughly accepted,
when our identity and personality
are appreciated and affirmed.

*Choir 2*   How sad are we when we choose to pretend
that we are somebody other
than the person God created
or the child a mother knows.

*Choir 1*   Happy are we who need not mask
the feelings that flow within us and through us
and out into the world around us,
warming the hearts of our friends.

*Choir 2*   How sad when we are locked up tight
inside a stoic appearance
that masks forces
bound to erupt inexplicably
in some way.

*Choir 1*   Help us, O Tower of Fortitude,
to drop the lifelong defenses
that prevent us from revealing to any at all
the self we would wish to be.

*Choir 2*   Help us, Unmediated Revelation,
to shed the raft of pretenses
that orchestrate a substitute image
for everyone else to see.

*Choir 1*   In the presence of Thou Who made us,
we are who we are
and who we have been
and who we are yet to be.

*Choir 2*   In the presence of those who love us
into the fullness of our being,
we can live with integrity.

*Choir 1*   So much of our lives is by the way,
so much of us, in between,

*Choir 2*   enslaved
until someone who loves us
sees us,
and suddenly
we are a queen.

   By M. T. Winter, Crossroad Pub. Co., © 1991 Medical Mission Sisters

# THE PROPHET

◇ **Scripture Reference**   Is 8:1–4

◇ **Biography**

The prophet about whom no personal detail survives was the wife of the major prophet Isaiah, and she lived in the latter half of the eighth century B.C.E. Scripture gives no indication as to whether she herself was also a seer, only that her husband referred to her that way. She gave birth to a child whose name was meant to validate an oracle revealed by God through her husband concerning the downfall of Syria and Ephraim.

◇ **Context**

It is generally accepted that the Book of Isaiah was not written entirely by one author. Only chapters 1–39 contain material dating back to the time of the prophet Isaiah ben Amoz. Material in the remaining chapters belongs to a later period, chapters 40–55 to the sixth century B.C.E. and chapters 56–66 perhaps even later. There is a tradition that the chapters which form sections two and three of the prophetic book may have been written over time by an ongoing circle of disciples or supporters of Isaiah who applied the prophet's words to later situations and added prophetic statements of their own. Given this general background about authorship, it is tempting to speculate about Isaiah's wife, whom he cryptically calls "the prophet." Was she indeed a prophet? It would seem so given the title bestowed by so eminent a prophetic voice as Isaiah. Did she utter any oracles? Did she leave any writings? Were any of the passages in her husband's book really hers? Or were any of the thoughts or images hers, particularly those incorporated into the later chapters?

The strikingly female images toward the end of the book might appropriately come from a woman's hand. Perhaps she did prophesy. Perhaps her writings remained unpublished or unpopular because she was female or because her husband's words overshadowed hers. Perhaps they were appropriated later by an admiring circle of supporters who either knew they were hers or suspected they were his when they incorporated them into Isaiah's book. Read the final chapters of Isaiah with this in mind and form your own opinion.

◇ **Lectionary Reading**

God said to me,
Take a scroll and write
in common characters:
"Maher-shalal-hash-baz,"
[meaning, "swift the spoiling, prompt the plundering"]
and have it attested by reliable witnesses,
by the priest Uriah
and by Zechariah son of Jeberechiah.
I went to the prophet
and she conceived
and she gave birth to a son.
Then God said to me,
Name the child Maher-shalal-hash-baz,
for before the child learns
to call you "my father"
or to say "my mother,"
the king of Assyria will come
and confiscate the wealth of Damascus
and the spoil of Samaria
and carry it all away.

◇ **Points for Shared Reflection**

- Why do you suppose we have heard absolutely nothing about the woman known as "the prophet," Isaiah's wife?

- Given the general anonymity of women in biblical tradition, is it possible that some of the passages in the book of Isaiah actually originated with Isaiah's wife?

- In your experience, are women generally less insistent or less careful about claiming credit for their spoken or written words? Do you think the problem of undocumented sources is still prevalent in female circles?

- In the Book of Isaiah there are images of God as a midwife (66:9), a nursing mother (49:14–15), a woman in labor, and again a nursing mother (66:7–13). Take time to read and discuss these passages. What do they say about God? What do they say about their author?

◇ **A Psalm in the Spirit of Isaiah's Wife** (see page 206)

◇ **Prayer**

Creator of Earth
and of all earth's children,
Creator of soil and sea and sky
and the tapestries of stars,
we turn to You for guidance
as we look on our mutilated planet,
and pray it is not too late for us
to rescue our wounded world.
We have been so careless.
We have failed to nurture the fragile life
You entrusted to our keeping.
We beg You for forgiveness
and we ask Your grace to begin again.
Be with us in our commitment to earth.
Let all the earth say: Amen.

### ◇ A PSALM IN THE SPIRIT OF ISAIAH'S WIFE ◇

*Choir 1*   Rejoice, planet earth,
and all you who love her.
Rejoice and be glad,
all you who weep
at her environmental distress.

*Choir 2*   For God Shaddai has heard her cry
and will respond to your supplication.

*Choir 1*   Eternally Present
in the womb of the world,
Shekinah has spoken Her comforting word,

*Choir 2*   assuring us of Her
maternal Presence
to all of creation
forever.

*Choir 1*   Thus says Shaddai:
Did I not labor
to bring forth a universe?
Did I not deliver this planet?
The world you inhabit
and love fiercely,
is it not the child of My womb?

*Choir 2*   Thus says Shaddai:
Should human reasoning pass away
and common sense falter,
I will never forsake you.
I will draw you to Me so tenderly —
earth, animals, seas, forests,
and people who love the earth and the animals,
who love the seas and the forests —
and I will speak to your heart.

*Choir 1*   Thus says Shekinah:
I will cleanse your polluted waterways
and restore your virgin forests.
I will replace your clay
with fertile soil
and your deserts with oases.

*Choir 2*   Thus says Shekinah:
I will clear the air so you can see
the stars I have created,
and once again your grasslands

   By M. T. Winter, Crossroad Pub. Co., © 1991 Medical Mission Sisters

will hear the hoofbeats of freedom,
and the air above will split with the cry of eagles
on the wing.

Choir 1   Thus says Sophia:
I will fill your dreams with wisdom.
You will discern
what is good for life
and beneficial for the planet
before you build your cities
or damn cascading waters
or mine the gems of earth.

Choir 2   Thus says Sophia:
I will teach you to ask forgiveness
for all endangered species,
for the loss of primeval innocence
in the disappearing rain forests
which I so dearly love.

Choir 1   And I, Shaddai,
will teach you
an elegy for creation
which Gaia and her children
will chant along with you.

Choir 2   And I, Shaddai,
will comfort you
as a Mother comforts Her children
when they know they have done wrong,
and peace will flow
from the River of Life
and thrill you with its song.

# GOMER

◇ **Scripture Reference**    Hos 1:2–9; 2; 3; 4:1, 5–6, 10

◇ **Biography**

Gomer was the prostitute who married the prophet Hosea. She was also a metaphor for Israel in her husband's prophetic oracles during the final days of the Northern Kingdom. The marriage, divorce, and remarriage of Gomer and Hosea, the naming of their children — Jezreel, "Unloved," and "Not My People" — and the indictments with regard to Gomer's promiscuous behavior symbolize the relationship between Israel and God. For this reason it is impossible to determine how much of what is said about Gomer is fact and how much is prophetic function.

◇ **Context**

Hosea ben-Beeri was one of the eighth-century B.C.E. prophets who believed that only the word of God, however devastating, could save the nation of Israel from internal and external destruction. His prophetic utterances as they occur in the Book of Hosea are not presented in finished form but rather as an amalgamation of reflections, soliloquies, direct addresses, metaphoric imagery, and bits of personal and family history. The end result is extremely confusing. The integrating image of Hosea's ministry involves both his prophetic call and his family, but it is hard to tell where oracle ends and life itself emerges. The call to marry a promiscuous woman is unique in the Bible. The story of his marriage and the birth of his children become for Hosea an allegory depicting God's relationship to Israel. Theological images arise out of his struggle to keep his marriage intact, and its status is reflected in the naming of his children. It is impossible to separate the story of Hosea and Gomer from the story of God and Israel because they are so intertwined. Their interconnections cannot be taken literally, however, nor can they be lightly dismissed. The full extent of their meaning still eludes us, although interpretations abound.

Gomer eventually left her husband but Hosea brought her back. To Hosea, losing Gomer meant losing God. So where does that leave Gomer? Probably in very difficult circumstances. It is not easy to be the object of someone's fanatic fantasy, even if it has a prophetic basis, or to be all tangled up in a spouse's religious fervor. It is hard to leave one's past behind when it is brought up at every turn. Gomer could not have felt very good about herself or about her husband in the midst of all the condemnations and the constant comparison between her and a faithless, whoring nation. Perhaps this was why she left her husband. Hosea sometimes speaks in tender terms, but he is so patronizing, and his mind seems more on God than on Gomer. Prostitution may have been Gomer's way of simply looking for love.

◊ **Lectionary Reading**

When God first spoke through Hosea,
God said to Hosea,
"Take a whore for a wife
and have the prostitute's children,
for the land commits prostitution
when it forsakes its God."
So he married Gomer daughter of Diblaim,
and she conceived and gave birth to a son.
And God said, "Name him Jezreel;
for in a little while
I will punish the house of Jehu
for the blood of Jezreel,
and I will put an end to the kingdom
of the house of Israel.
On that day I will break the bow of Israel
in the valley of Jezreel."

Gomer conceived again
and she gave birth to a daughter.
"Name her Lo-ruhamah," said God,
"for I will have no more pity on the house of Israel,
I will have no more forgiveness.
But I will have pity on the house of Judah,
yes, I their God will save them."
When Gomer had weaned Lo-ruhamah
[the name means Not Pitied or Unloved],
she conceived again and bore a son.
God said, "Name him Lo-ammi
[which means No-People-of-Mine],
for you are not my people
and I am not your God."

◇

Say to your brother Ammi
and to Ruhamah your sister:
plead with your mother,
plead with her —
for she is not my wife
and I am not her husband —
that she put prostitution
away from her face
and adultery from between her breasts,
or I will strip her naked
and expose her as on the day she was born
and make her like a wilderness,
and turn her into a parched land,
and kill her with burning thirst.
Neither will I have pity on her children
because they are the children of whores.
Their mother has played the whore;
she has acted shamefully.
She said, "I will stay with my lovers;
they give me my bread and my water,
my wool, my flax, my oil, my drink."
Therefore I will surround her with thorns
and build a wall against her,
so she cannot find her paths.
She shall pursue her lovers,
but never overtake them,
seek them but never find them.
Then she will say, "I will go
and return to my first husband,
for that was better for me than now."
She did not know it was I who gave her

the grain, the wine, the oil;
it was I who lavished silver upon her
and gold that was used for Baal.
Therefore I will take back my grain in its time
and my wine in the midst of its season;
I will take away my wool and my flax
which had covered her nakedness.
Now I will uncover her shame
in the sight of all her lovers
and there will be none to rescue her
from my avenging hand.
I will put an end to all her merriment,
to all her appointed festivals,
her new moons and her sabbaths.
I will destroy her vines and her fig trees
of which she had said,
"These are my compensation.
My lovers gave these to me."
I will make them into a forest;
wild animals will devour them.
I will punish her for the festivals
and the incense offered to Baal,
when she adorned herself with jewelry,
seeking lovers, forgetting me.
Therefore now I will lure her
and lead her into the wilderness
and speak tenderly to her heart.
I will give her back her vineyards
and make the valley a door of hope.
And there she will respond to me
as she did when she came out of Egypt,
as she did when she was young.
On that day — it is God who speaks —
she will call me, "My husband,"
she will no longer call me "Baal."
I will wipe the names of Baal from her lips
and they will be named no more.
I will make a covenant for her that day
with animals and birds and all of creation;
and I will abolish the bow and the sword
and all of the weapons of war,
and she will lie down in safety;
she will rest secure.
I will betroth her to me forever,
with integrity and justice,
with tenderness and love,

betroth her to me with faithfulness,
and she shall know her God.
On that day I will answer, says God,
I will answer the heavens
and they will answer the earth;
and the earth will answer
the grain, the wine, the oil,
and they will answer Jezreel;
I will sow him for myself in the land.
I will have pity on Lo-ruhamah,
and I will say to Lo-ammi,
"You are my people,"
and he shall say,
"You are my God."

◇

God said to me again,
"Go love a woman who has a lover
and is an adulteress,
just as God loves Israel
though they turn to other gods."
So I bought her for fifteen shekels of silver,
some barley and a measure of wine.
I said to her, "Stay home with me.
Do not sleep with another man.
Neither will I sleep with you
for a certain number of days."
For Israel shall remain without king or prince,
without sacrifice or pillar,
without vestment or cultic figurine.
Then Israel will return and seek their God
and turn to David their king;
and they shall come gratefully to their God
and God's goodness in those latter days.

◇

Hear the word of God, O people of Israel;
hear God's indictment against you.
There is no faithfulness or loyalty,
no knowledge of God in the land.
Day and night you stumble along
and the prophet stumbles with you.
I will destroy your mother,
and I will forget your children.
They shall eat but not be satisfied,
make love, but not multiply,
because they have chosen promiscuity,
because they have forsaken their God.

◇ **Points for Shared Reflection**

- What is your religious community's attitude toward prostitutes? What is yours?

- Was Hosea's treatment of Gomer patronizing? In what way? Is the religious community's treatment of women patronizing? In what ways?

- Given Gomer's circumstances, how would you assess her sense of herself? How would you relate to life in similar circumstances?

- What image do you get of God, and of God's relationship to women, from the prophecies of Hosea?

◇ **A Psalm for the Outcast** (see page 214)

◇ **Prayer**

God of Compassion,
God of People,
do not forsake the ones
cast out
from the center
of the circle.
Move closer
to the core of them
as others move away.
Cast Your circle wider
than our small circumference,
so that all who are out
are in
and blessed
in Your own loving way.
Amen.

# ◇ A PSALM FOR THE OUTCAST ◇

*Choir 1*   Do not cry, little daughter.
For I have prepared a home for you
where there will be no more tears.

*Choir 2*   Your pain will no longer ravage you.
Your sorrow will pass away.

*Choir 1*   Do not be sad, little daughter.
For I, Shaddai, understand you.
I see beyond your outer shell.
I see deep into your heart.

*Choir 2*   There will be no misunderstanding.
You will never be sad again.

*Choir 1*   Do not cringe, little daughter.
The name I call you is our secret name.
I look on you with love.

*Choir 2*   Never again will you want for love.
You will never be taunted again.

*Choir 1*   Do not be afraid, little daughter.
I will be with you whenever you are
in need of nurturing.

*Choir 2*   Never again will you live in fear
of anyone or anything.

*Choir 1*   Come to Me, all My daughters.
I will weave My web of blessing upon you
and shower you with shalom.

*Choir 2*   Come to Her Who comforts us
and makes us feel at home.

 By M. T. Winter, Crossroad Pub. Co., © 1991 Medical Mission Sisters

# SARAH, WIFE OF TOBIAS

◇ **Scripture Reference**    Tob 3:7–17; 6:10–18; 7; 8
Tob 9:6; 10:7–12; 11:1–3, 15–17
Tob 12:3, 6, 12–15, 22; 14:12

◇ **Biography**

Sarah, the only child of Edna and Raguel who lived in Ecbatana, was possessed by a demon, Asmodeus, who was responsible for the deaths of her seven bridegrooms on their wedding nights, before they had slept with her. Sarah was depressed and close to suicide when Tobias came to claim her by his right of next-of-kin. His companion, the angel Raphael, helped him dispel the demon. He survived and Sarah was liberated. She left with Tobias for his family's home in Nineveh, and after her in-laws died, she and her husband and children returned to Ecbatana.

◊ **Context**

The Book of Tobit (or Tobias), an apocryphal work that is part of the
Roman Catholic canon, is considered the most artistic story of the
Apocrypha and survives in many Greek versions, several Hebrew adap-
tations, and on some fragments in Hebrew and in Aramaic found among
the Qumran scrolls. It tells about life among the Jewish exiles in diaspora
after the fall of the Northern Kingdom of Israel. Set in eighth-century
B.C.E. Nineveh, the story has elements of both fiction and fact, and while
the demon-lover and angel-in-disguise were common themes in folk-
lore, it is quite possible that members of the two main families actually
existed.

The separate stories of Tobit and of Sarah are woven together through
the exploits of Tobias, Tobit's son and Sarah's husband, and the assistance of Raphael, the healing angel. Sarah's story is one of tragedy and
triumph. An only child in a culture constructed around a male heir, she
had married seven men and was still a virgin, having buried every one of
them on her wedding nights. She was humiliated by her maid, ridiculed
in the community, severely depressed, and suicidal, until Tobias came
along and everything changed. How much of her story really happened?
It would only take the death of a single husband on their wedding night
to start the rumor going that Sarah was possessed. The number seven
suggests that no one at all could possibly marry her and expect to survive.
Many aspects of her story are historically conceivable.


◊ **Lectionary Reading**

At Ecbatana in Media,
Sarah, daughter of Raguel,
was reproached by one of her father's maids.
Sarah had married seven husbands,
but each of them died on their wedding night
without having slept with her.
The maid shouted at Sarah,
"Killer of husbands, that's what you are!
Seven already and not a one
has given his name to you.
So why strike out at us?
Because your husbands are dead?
May you join them!
May we never see
a son or daughter of yours!"
Grief-stricken, Sarah withdrew and wept.
She went to her father's upper room
intending to hang herself.
But then she thought it over and said,

"No, they shall never pity my father
and say to him in reproach,
'You had but one beloved daughter
who hung herself in distress.'
Such sorrow in his old age
would surely kill my father.
It is better not to hang myself
but to pray that I might die,
so I won't have to listen
to these reproaches anymore."
With hands outstretched, Sarah prayed:
"Blessed are you, merciful God.
Blessed is your name forever.
Let your works forever praise you.
I turn my face to you, my God,
and raise my eyes toward you.
Release me from earth
so that I might not hear
these reproaches anymore.
You know that I am innocent.
I have not disgraced my name
or the name of my family in exile.
I am my parents' only child.
There is no other child or heir,
and no close relative to marry me.
Already I have had seven husbands,
and every one of them died.
Why am I still living?
If it should please you, take my life,
if not, remove my disgrace."
At that very moment,
the prayers of both Sarah and Tobit
were heard in the presence of God,
and God sent Raphael to heal them both:
Tobit, by removing the films from his eyes
so that he might see God's light;
and Sarah, daughter of Raguel,
by giving her in marriage to Tobit's son, Tobias,
and by freeing her from her demon.
Tobias was entitled to have Sarah
before all other men
who might desire to marry her.

The two men entered Media and were near Ecbatana,
when Raphael said to Tobias,
"We must stay this night in the home of Raguel.

He has a daughter named Sarah
and he is your relative.
He has no other child but Sarah,
and you are her next-of-kin.
You have a hereditary claim on her
before all other men.
It is fitting that you should be the one
to inherit her father's possessions.
Moreover, the girl is sensible
and beautiful and brave
and her father is an honorable man.
Since you have the right to marry her,
I will speak to her father tonight,
so that she might be your bride.
Raguel cannot keep her from you
without incurring the penalty of death
according to the law of Moses."
Then Tobias said to Raphael,
"She has had seven husbands
who died in the bridal chamber.
They were all killed by a demon.
This is what I have heard.
It does not harm her
but kills all those
who desire to make love to her.
I am afraid that I too will die,
and I am an only child.
My mother and father would perish with grief
if something happened to me,
and then who would bury them?"
But Raphael said to Tobias,
"Do you not recall your father's orders
to take a wife from your father's house?
Forget about the demon.
Take her for your wife.
I know that this very night
she will be given to you in marriage.
When you enter the bridal chamber,
take some of this fish's liver and heart
[which they had caught along the way]
and put them on embers of incense.
This will produce an odor.
The demon will smell it and flee
and will never trouble her again.
Then when you are about to take her to bed,
both of you first stand up and pray,

imploring God that mercy and safety
may be graciously granted you.
Do not be afraid,
for she was set apart for you
before the world was made.
You will save Sarah,
and she will go with you
and you will no doubt have children
who will be very close to you.
Come now, and say no more."
When Tobias heard the words of Raphael
and learned that he was related to Sarah,
he loved her very much,
and his heart was drawn to her.

When they entered Ecbatana,
Tobias said to Raphael,
"Take me straight to Raguel's house."
So he did and they found Raguel sitting
beside the courtyard door.
After exchanging greetings,
Raguel took them inside the house
and said to Edna his wife,
"How much he resembles Tobit!"
Before long they learned that their visitor
was Tobias, the son of Tobit,
and that they were relatives.
Raguel kissed him, blessed him, and wept.
When they heard of Tobit's blindness,
Raguel and Edna wept again,
and their daughter wept as well.
Raguel slaughtered a ram from the flock,
and they bathed and washed
and reclined at table
and Tobias whispered to Raphael,
"Ask Raguel to give me my kinswoman Sarah."
But Raguel overheard it.
"Eat, drink, and be merry tonight,"
Raguel said to Tobias,
"for you are my nearest relative
and no one but you has the right by law
to marry my daughter Sarah.
But let me speak truthfully to you.
I have given her to seven men,
all of them our relatives,
and all of them died on their wedding night.

But now, my son, just eat and drink,
for I am sure that God will intervene
on behalf of both of you."
"I will not eat or drink," said Tobias,
"until this thing is settled."
So Raguel said, "She is given to you
in accord with the law of Moses.
She is given to you today and forever.
It has been decreed from heaven.
May God protect you both this night
and grant you mercy and peace."
Then Raguel summoned his daughter Sarah.
He took her and gave her to Tobias, saying,
"Take her to be your wife
in accordance with the law of Moses.
Take her and bring her safely home.
And may God bless your journey with peace."
Then he asked her mother for writing material
and he wrote a marriage contract.
And then they ate and drank.
Later, Raguel said to Edna,
"Prepare the other room
and take our daughter there."
So she went and prepared the bridal bed
and brought her daughter there.
Wiping away her tears, she said,
"Be brave, my daughter, be brave.
The God of heaven grant you joy
in place of all your sorrow."
Then Edna departed and left Sarah alone
in the bridal chamber.

When they had finished eating and drinking
and were ready to retire,
they escorted Tobias to the room
where Sarah his bride was waiting.
Tobias remembered Raphael's words.
He took the fish's liver and heart
and put them on embers of incense.
The odor so repelled the demon
that he fled to the ends of Egypt
where Raphael, having followed him there,
bound him hand and foot.
When Raguel and Edna had left the room
and shut the door behind them,
Tobias said to Sarah,

"My sister, get up and let us pray,
imploring God for mercy
and for safety through the night."
So Sarah got up
and together they prayed,
and these were the words of Tobias,
"Blessed are you, O God of our ancestors,
and blessed is your name
throughout all generations
now and forever.
Let the heavens bless you forever.
Let all creation bless you forever.
You made Adam and Eve
and the two of them
gave birth to the human race.
You said, 'It is not good to be alone;
let me make them for each other.'
I take tonight this kinswoman of mine,
not out of lust, but sincerity.
Grant us both your mercy,
that we may grow old together."
And both of them said, "Amen."
Then they went to sleep for the night.
But Raguel that night summoned his servants
to go out and dig a grave.
"It is possible he will die," he said,
"and we will be marked for derision
and for ridicule by everyone."
When the grave was dug, Raguel called for Edna.
"Send a maid to look in on them," he said,
"to see if he is alive.
But if he is dead, let us bury him
without anyone knowing of it."
So they sent a maid who lit a lamp
and opened the bedroom door.
She went in and found the two of them
sound asleep together.
She came out and informed them
that nothing was wrong,
that Tobias was alive.
So they blessed God and Raguel prayed,
"Blessed are you, O God;
let all your chosen children bless you;
let us bless your name forever.
Blessed are you for making me glad.
It has not happened as I expected,

for you have shown your mercy.
Blessed are you who have had compassion
on these two only children,
the only child of Edna's womb
and the only child of Anna's.
Be merciful to them and keep them safe
and bring their lives to fulfillment
in happiness and peace."
Then he ordered his servants to fill in the grave
immediately, before daybreak.
Edna baked many loaves of bread
while Raguel slaughtered rams and steer
as they began their preparations.
When Tobias awoke,
Raguel swore an oath to him in these words,
"You shall not leave for fourteen days
but shall eat and drink with me.
You shall cheer up my daughter
who has been depressed.
Half of what I own you may take with you
when you return to your father;
the other half will come to you
after Edna and I have died.
Take courage, my son, Edna and I,
we are your mother and father.
We belong to you as well as your wife,
this day and forever."

In the morning Raphael rose early
at the house of Gabael, a relative,
and they went to the wedding celebration.
[Raphael had gone to collect the money
entrusted to Gabael by Tobit,
the father of Tobias.]

When the fourteen days of the wedding celebration
which Raguel had sworn to observe for his daughter
had come to an end, Tobias said,
"Let me go home,
for I know that my mother and father are certain
they will not see me again.
I beg of you, let me go,
so that I might return to them."
But Raguel said to Tobias,
"Stay but a little longer, my son.
I will send messengers to your parents

who will tell them all about you."
Tobias refused, so Raguel gave him
Sarah his wife
and half of all his property:
slaves, sheep, oxen, donkeys, camels,
clothing, money, and goods.
He embraced Tobias and said to him,
"Farewell, my son; have a safe journey.
May God prosper you and Sarah, your wife,
and may I see children before I die."
Then he kissed his daughter Sarah and said,
"Honor your father-in-law and your mother-in-law,
for now they are as much your parents
as the ones who gave you birth.
Go in peace, my daughter,
and may I hear only good about you
for as long as I shall live."
Then he said farewell and let them go.
Edna said to Tobias,
"My child, may God bring you safely back,
and may I live long enough to see children
born of you and my daughter Sarah.
Before God I entrust my daughter to you.
Do nothing at all to grieve her
all the days of your life.
Go now in peace, my son.
From now on I am your mother,
and Sarah is your beloved wife.
May we all prosper together as family
all the days of our life."
Then she kissed them both and saw them off.
Tobias parted from Raguel with happiness and joy,
praising the God of heaven and earth
for making his journey successful.
Blessing Raguel and Edna, he said,
"God commands me to honor you
all the days of my life."

As they neared Nineveh, Raphael said,
"Let us hurry ahead of your wife
and prepare the house for her coming
while she is still on the way."
Anna embraced her son, saying,
"Now that I have seen you, my child,
I am prepared to die."
[Then Tobias applied the gall of a fish

to the blind eyes of his father,
and suddenly Tobit could see.]
Tobit rejoiced, praising God
for the safe return of his son and his sight.
Tobias told all about his journey,
that it had been successful —
he had the money,
he had gotten married —
and his bride was on her way,
was even now at Nineveh's gate.
Tobit went to the gate of Nineveh
to meet his daughter-in-law,
rejoicing and praising God.
The people of Nineveh
were amazed to see him,
full of vigor and energy,
with no one leading him.
Tobit acknowledged that God had been merciful.
God had restored his sight.
When Tobit met Sarah, his son's wife,
he blessed her with these words,
"Come, my daughter, and welcome.
Blessed be your God who has brought you to us.
Blessed be your father and mother.
Blessed be my son, Tobias.
And blessed be you, daughter Sarah.
Come now to your home, and welcome,
with blessing and with joy.
Come with me, my daughter."
There was rejoicing all that day
among all the Jews in Nineveh.

Then Raphael took Tobias and Tobit aside
and said to the two of them,
"Bless God in the presence of all the living
for the good things done for you.
Sing praise and bless God's name.
Tobit, when you and Sarah prayed,
it was I who read the record of your prayer
before the glory of God.
God knew whenever you buried the dead;
and I was sent to test you.
God also sent me to heal you and Sarah
who is now your daughter-in-law.
I am Raphael.
I am one of the seven angels

who are always standing ready
to enter the glory of God."
Then they blessed God, singing praises
for all God's marvelous deeds.

After Tobit and Anna had died,
Sarah and Tobias and their children
returned to Media,
to the home of her parents,
and settled there in Ecbatana.

◇ **Points for Shared Reflection**

- Discuss the plight of an unmarried woman in those days. What is the position of single women today? Is this true of other cultures?

- While demonic possession is a reality, do you think Sarah really had a demon? What other explanation is there for what happened to her before and with Tobias?

- Sarah came close to suicide. Suicide is a major cause of death among adolescents today. Why do our children commit suicide and how might we prevent it? What are the root causes of this social tragedy and in what ways must our systems change?

- Raphael was a healing angel, but he functioned also as a guardian angel. Belief in angels is very biblical. Do you believe in angels? Do you believe you have a guardian angel?

◇ **A Psalm for Casting Out Demons** (see page 226)

◇ **Prayer**

Almighty, All-Powerful Force for Good
Who overcomes all evil,
destroys demonic power
and casts out devils daily,
we beg You to take possession of us
so that we belong to You only,
and we ask You to protect us
against all that can do us harm.
We are afraid of demons,
but we have faith in You.
Amen.

## ◇ A PSALM FOR CASTING OUT DEMONS ◇

*Choir 1*   We are possessed by demons.
All of us.
No matter how many times we pray,
they won't go away completely.
Moods, habits, devilish desires
inhabit the regions of our subconscious
and break out suddenly, inexplicably,
taking us over,
making us someone we would rather not be,
someone we really are not.

*Choir 2*   We are obsessed with demons,
surrounded daily by demonic forces:
drink, drugs, illicit sex,
money, power, acquisition;
they are taking control of our neighborhoods,
trying to break down the doors of our homes
and too often breaking our hearts.

*Choir 1*   Beware of the guise of demons.
Seductive, sweet-talking,
pleasurable companions,
they are eager to befriend you,
but the demon who shares a meal with you
will never leave your home.

*Choir 2*   God can cast out demons.
Through a rock-solid faith,
the power of prayer,
and an unrelenting discipline,
God brings demons down.

*Choir 1*   Cast out the demons
treacherously lurking
within us
and around us.

*Choir 2*   Cast out the evil propensities
that threaten our very lives.

*Voice*   Drugs are demons.

*All*   Cast out the demons of drugs.
Prevent them from overpowering us.

*Voice*   Drink is a demon.

   By M. T. Winter, Crossroad Pub. Co., © 1991 Medical Mission Sisters

*All*    Cast out the demon of drink.
Let it not control our lives.

*Voice*   Rape and incest are demons.

*All*    Cast out the demons of rape and incest.
Prevent them from overpowering us.

*Voice*   Violence and abuse are demons.

*All*    Cast out the demons of violence and abuse.
Let them not control our lives.

*Voice*   Avariciousness and greed are demons.

*All*    Cast out the demons of avariciousness and greed.
Prevent them from overpowering us.

*Voice*   Uncontrollable anger is a demon.

*All*    Cast out the demon of uncontrollable anger.
Let it not control our lives.

*Voice*   Envy is a demon.

*All*    Cast out the demon of envy.
Prevent it from overpowering us.

*Voice*   Injustice is a demon.

*All*    Cast out the demon of injustice.
Let it not control our lives.

*Voice*   Oppression is a demon.

*All*    Cast out the demon of oppression.
Prevent it from overpowering us.

*Voice*   War is a demon.

*All*    Cast out the demon of war.
Let it not control our lives.

*Choir 1*   Let us put ourselves in the hands of God
Who has overcome the demons.

*Choir 2*   O God Who destroys demonic forces,
strengthen our determination
and please acknowledge our prayer.

*All*    We will not give in to demons.
They will not overpower us.
They will not control our lives.

By M. T. Winter, Crossroad Pub. Co., © 1991 Medical Mission Sisters      *WomanWisdom* /

# ANNA

◇ **Scripture Reference**    Tob 1:3, 9, 16–17, 19–21; 2:1, 9–14
Tob 4:1–4, 20; 5:3–6, 9, 17–22
Tob 6:1; 10:1–7; 11:5–6, 9–15; 14:2, 10, 12

◇ **Biography**

Anna was the wife of Tobit, a devout Jew whose grandmother's name
was Deborah and whose father's name was Tobiel. She was of the same
lineage as her husband and they had a son named Tobias. They lived in
exile in Nineveh where Anna did piecework to support her family after
her husband lost his sight.

◇ **Context**

Anna and her husband Tobit were observant Jews living in diaspora after
the fall of the Northern Kingdom in Israel. Tobit was pious, generous,
and charitable, but it was not easy being married to him. When it was
discovered that he was burying the dead who had been lying around

228

unattended, he left his wife and their young son Tobias and went into hiding until a new regime came to power. Shortly after they were reunited, he injured his eyes in a freak accident and before long, he was blind. Anna did piecework at home which she sold for money to maintain her family. When her employer gave her a bonus, a goat, her husband accused her of stealing. The man who had been so good to others took out his frustrations on his wife and was very hard on her. Finally he came up with a money-making scheme which entailed sending their son on a journey, and this nearly broke her heart. Her son delayed returning. When she was certain that he would never come back, she suddenly had a series of joyful experiences: Tobias came home, alive and well, accompanied by a wife; her husband's sight was restored; there was sufficient money to meet their needs — a happy ending to the story of Anna, a woman who was so often anxious because of what she had to endure and because of her inner fears. (For the historical and literary setting of Anna's story, turn to "Context" on page 216).

◇ **Lectionary Reading**

I, Tobit, walked in the ways of truth
and integrity,
all the days of my life.
When I was grown I married a woman,
a member of our own family,
and by her I became the father of a son
whom I named Tobias.
In the days of King Sennacherib,
I performed many acts of charity
to the members of my tribe.
I would give my food to the hungry
and my clothing to the naked;
and if I saw the dead body
of any of my people
behind the wall of Nineveh,
I would bury it.
Then one of the Ninevites told the king
that I was burying bodies,
so I had to go into hiding,
but they searched for me to put me to death,
and in fear, I ran away.
They confiscated my property
and added my assets to the royal treasury.
Nothing at all was left to me
but my wife Anna
and Tobias my son.
A short while later, Sennacherib died.

With the new regime, I returned home
and my wife Anna and my son Tobias and I
were reunited.
During the feast of Pentecost,
the festival of weeks,
I sat at table and ate my meal,
then later that night I washed myself
and went out into my courtyard,
sat down, and fell asleep.
My head was propped against the wall
uncovered, because of the heat.
I did not see the sparrows there,
lined up on the wall.
Their fresh droppings fell into my eyes,
causing white films to form.
Physicians could not heal me.
The more they treated me with ointments,
the more my vision blurred,
until I was totally blind.
For four years I was unable to see.
Everyone felt sorry for me.

At that time also my wife Anna
earned money doing women's work.
She would send what she made to her employers
and they would pay wages to her.
One day after sending a part of her weaving,
they paid her wages in full
and gave her a goat for a meal.
"Where did you get this goat?" I asked,
thinking it had been stolen.
"Return it to the owners.
We cannot eat stolen food."
She said, "It was given to me as a gift
in addition to my wages."
But I did not believe her.
I was flushed with anger against her.
Then Anna said to me,
"Where are all those acts of charity,
all your good deeds,
for which you are so well known?"

One day I remembered
I had left some money in trust
with a relative in Media.
So I called my son Tobias

and told him about the money.
"My son, when I die,"
I instructed him,
"give me a proper burial.
Honor your mother the whole of her life.
Do not abandon her.
Do whatever pleases her.
Do nothing to cause her grief.
Remember she faced many dangers for you
while you were in her womb.
And when she dies,
bury her beside me in my grave.
Now, my son, let me tell you about the silver
I left in trust with Gabael, our relative,
at Rages in Media."

Then I said to my son Tobias,
"Go find a trustworthy man
who can accompany you to Media,
and we will pay him wages
when you return again with the money.
So Tobias went out to look for a man
and he found the angel Raphael
standing in front of him.
He did not know he was an angel.
Tobias said, "Where do you come from?"
He answered, "From the Israelites.
I am here to look for work."
"Do you know the way to Media?"
"Yes, I do," he answered.
"I have been there many times.
I know all the roads.
I have often stayed with our kinsman Gabael
who lives in Rages of Media."
Before he began his journey
Tobias kissed me and his mother.
I said to him, "Have a safe journey,"
but his mother began to weep.
"Why have you sent my child away?
Is he not the staff of our hand
as he goes in and out before us?
Forget what is in Media.
Do not heap money upon money —
let it be a ransom for our child.
For surely the life that is given to us by God
is enough for us."

I said to her, "Do not worry.
He leaves in good health
and will return in good health.
Your eyes will see him on his return,
so I beg you, say no more.
An angel will accompany him,
his journey will be successful,
and he will return in good health."
So Anna wept no more.

From the time Tobias left I counted
how many days were needed for going
and how many to return.
When the days had passed and he had not come,
I said, "Could it be that he has been detained?
Or perhaps Gabael has died
and there is no one to give him the money."
And so I began to worry.
His mother said, "My child has perished.
He is no longer living."
She began to weep and mourn for her son.
"Woe to me, light of my eyes,
that I let you make this journey."
I tried to calm her by saying to her,
"Stop worrying, my dear; he is all right.
Something unexpected happened.
The man who went with him is trustworthy.
He is one of our kin.
Do not grieve for him, he will soon be here.
Be quiet now, don't worry."
She said to me, "Be quiet yourself!
Stop trying to deceive me!
My only child has perished."
She hurried out early every morning
and watched the road her son had taken,
ignoring everyone.
When the sun set, she went inside
and wept the whole night long,
getting no sleep at all.

Anna sat looking intently
down the road her son had taken
when she caught sight of him coming.
"Look, your son is coming," she said,
"and also the man who went with him."
Then Anna ran to meet her son.

She threw her arms around him and said,
"Now that I have seen you, my child,
I am prepared to die."
I stumbled out through the courtyard door
and my son caught hold of me firmly.
I felt him put medicine on my eyes —
he said it was the gall of a fish —
then he blew in my eyes
till they started to sting,
peeled the white films from them,
and suddenly, I could see.
"Tobias, my son, I see you," I said.
"Blessed be God," I shouted and wept.
"Blessed be God's great name.
Blessed be God's holy angels.
God has had mercy upon us.
I can see my son Tobias!
May God's holy name be blessed!"
Tobias told all about his journey,
that it had been successful —
he had the money,
he had gotten married —
and his bride was on her way,
was even now at Nineveh's gate.

Tobit died in peace when he was
one hundred twelve years old.
He was buried with honor in Nineveh;
and when Anna died,
Tobias buried his mother
beside her husband.

◇ **Points for Shared Reflection**

- Name some of the joys and some of the sorrows Anna experienced as wife of Tobit and mother of Tobias. In what ways was her marriage similar to a typical marriage today? Does her family life in any way resemble yours?

- To all outward appearances Tobit was the perfect husband — a good provider, dedicated, charitable, devout. Comment on the statement: spouses are not always what they appear.

- A change in Tobit's health changed his personality and changed a lot of things at home. What are the consequences of ill health on the physical and emotional resources of a family? Have you ever had to cope with an extended illness in your family or in yourself?

- Anna seemed overly protective of her son who was already an adult. In what ways do we smother our children? In what ways are we not protective enough?

◇ **A Psalm of Healing**  (see page 235)

◇ **Prayer**

Rise up
from the valley of suffering, O God,
with healing in Your wings.
Heal the hurt within us.
Heal the wounds inflicted upon us.
Heal the memories that haunt us.
Heal the feelings that drag us down.
Place within us the potential
to facilitate our own wellness.
Be wholly in us
who hunger for wholeness
every day of our lives.
Amen.

# ◊ A PSALM OF HEALING ◊

*Choir 1*    If we had faith
the size of a grain of sand,
we could move mountains of misery
by God's hand.

*Choir 2*    If we had love
the length of the universe,
no one would suffer
who lived with us
for better or for worse.

*Choir 1*    Sometimes
only time heals
the wounds inflicted
against our will:
we all know how that feels.

*Choir 2*    Scars have a way
of hanging on
long after love regenerates,
leave memories that fester
long, long after
the experience is gone.

*Choir 1*    Touch the source
of the illness in you
with the healing power
of prayer.

*Choir 2*    Call on Her healing Spirit
to restore in you
the fullness of life
that deep down
is already there.

*Choir 1*    Sit with the broken-hearted,
the broken in body,
the broken in spirit.
Reach out to them
tenderly,

*Choir 2*    and the God Who cares
about all such things
will hover over you,
a Brooding Bird
with healing in Her wings.

By M. T. Winter, Crossroad Pub. Co., © 1991 Medical Mission Sisters    *WomanWisdom* **/ 235**

# CLEOPATRA

◇ **Scripture Reference**    1 Macc 10:51–60; 11:1, 8–12

◇ **Biography**

Cleopatra III Thea was the daughter of Ptolemy VI Philometer who was married to his sister Cleopatra II. Her father gave her in marriage to Alexander Balas, ruler of Syria, then took her away from him and gave her to his rival Demetrius II. Her politically motivated marriages are the substance of her story.

◇ **Context**

After Alexander the Great conquered Palestine in 332 B.C.E., Israel became part of the Hellenistic world and suffered centuries of foreign occupation and war by Ptolemaic and Seleucid forces. When Alexander Balas came into power in Syria, he asked the Egyptian Ptolemy for the hand of his daughter Cleopatra. It was a mutually beneficial alliance and a large wedding took place in the summer of 150 B.C.E. When Alexander proved to be an incompetent king, Philometer took his daughter away from him and gave her to Demetrius II, the teenage son of the previous ruler who was determined to be king. There was a prophecy in the book of Daniel that said there would be a marriage between two dynasties of the divided Graeco-Macedonian empire, and that one would be strong as iron and the other weak as clay (Dan 2:43–44). Shortly after that happened, the pagan empires would collapse. This was the reason for including the mar-

236

riage of Cleopatra and Alexander in the Maccabean account. To the writer Alexander and his successor Demetrius II were both weak as clay, and Ptolemy VI seemed strong as iron. Jewish deliverance was near at hand. There had been two previous disappointments, but the marriage of Cleopatra Thea to the Seleucid Alexander seemed to suggest that the prophecy would soon be fulfilled. It was not long before Alexander Balas fell, Ptolemy VI was killed leaving the Ptolemaic kingdom weakened, and Demetrius II was judged unfit to rule.

Who and where was Cleopatra in all this political and prophetic intrigue? After a splendid wedding in the Seleucid city that bore the Egyptian dynastic name, she disappeared from the records and remains difficult to trace through the line of Cleopatras who share her name. She was wed successively to two unpopular men of enormous political ambitions and was queen in turn to two inept men who battled to be king. There is no easily accessible evidence that gives hint of her personal integrity, her personality, or her feelings. She was a pawn in the world of conquest, an object exchanged for political advantage in the game that conquerors play. She was even used by biblical authors as proof of prophecy.

◇ **Lectionary Reading**

Alexander crushed Demetrius and his army
to gain control of the country.
Then Alexander king of Syria sent word
to Ptolemy king of Egypt, saying,
"Since I have returned to my kingdom
and now sit on the throne of my ancestors,
let us be friends with one another.
Give me your daughter as my wife
and I will become your son-in-law
and will make gifts to you and to her
appropriate to your position."
Ptolemy the king replied to Alexander,
"Happy the day on which you returned
to rule the land of your ancestors
and to sit on the throne of their kingdom.
And now I will do for you as you wrote.
Meet me at Ptolemais
so that we might see one another,
and I will become your father-in law,
just as you have said."
So Ptolemy set out from Egypt
with his daughter Cleopatra
in the one hundred sixty-second year

and came to Ptolemais.
King Alexander met them there,
and Ptolemy gave his daughter Cleopatra
in marriage to Alexander
and celebrated her wedding
with pomp and splendor at Ptolemais,
as kings are prone to do.
Alexander wrote to Jonathan
to come and meet with him.
So Jonathan went to Ptolemais
and met the two kings there;
and he gave them silver and gold and gifts,
and he found favor with them.

◇

Then the king of Egypt assembled countless forces,
like the sand by the seashore,
and together with a fleet of ships,
he tried to gain possession of Alexander's kingdom by deceit.
King Ptolemy took the coastal cities
as far as Seleucia by the sea
and plotted against Alexander.
He sent envoys to Demetrius, saying,
"Come, let us make a covenant,
you and I together,
and I will give to you in marriage
my daughter who was Alexander's wife.
I now regret I gave him my daughter,
for he has tried to kill me.
You are the one who will reign
over the kingdom of your father."
Ptolemy accused Alexander
because he coveted his kingdom.
So he took his daughter away from him
and gave her to Demetrius.
He severed his ties with Alexander,
and their distrust and hatred for one another
was soon made manifest.

◇ **Points for Shared Reflection**

- Have you ever had a major life decision made for you by your father or your husband or someone else? How did you feel about
  that?

- Is it possible to maintain one's integrity in an environment of violence
  and intrigue? What would one have to do?

- Sensitive people often retreat into a private world within themselves where they can survive the pain and stress of difficult times. Do you have such an inner sanctuary? What is it like? When do you go there? What does it do for you?
- If all the rulers on earth were women, do you think we would have fewer wars and less tendency toward domination? Give reasons for your response.

◇ **A Psalm on Separation** (see page 240)

◇ **Prayer**

O One to Whom
we are connected
by unbreakable bonds of love,
You tell us
that nothing can separate us
from Your providential mercy
and Your covenant of care.
Our grateful beings praise You.
You are the substance of our hope
that life can and will go on.
Pour out on all our relationships
the possibility of forever,
and when we must sever
an inseparable bond,
strengthen us
and support us
so that life may continue
around us and in us,
forever and ever.
Amen.

*All*    Help us, Shaddai,
        to bear the pain

*Choir 1*    when someone we love
        stays away
        for no apparent reason,
        does not call,
        does not come,

*Choir 2*    and we are felled
        by the force of rejection,

*Choir 1*    feeling as You must feel, Shaddai,

*Choir 2*    when we do not call
        and we do not come.

*All*    Help us, Shaddai,
        to understand

*Choir 1*    when someone we love
        walks away
        from what we feel
        is important

*Choir 2*    and we are filled
        with confusion,

*Choir 1*    feeling as You must feel, Shaddai,

*Choir 2*    when we walk away from You.

*All*    Help us, Shaddai,
        to endure the wait

*Choir 1*    when someone we love
        runs away
        from home,
        from hope,
        from the help we offer,

*Choir 2*    leaving us
        feeling empty,

*Choir 1*    feeling as You must feel, Shaddai,

*Choir 2*    when we run away from You.

*All*    Help us, Shaddai,
        not to lose faith

    By M. T. Winter, Crossroad Pub. Co., © 1991 Medical Mission Sisters

| | |
|---|---|
| *Choir 1* | when someone we love<br>wanders away<br>from a covenant<br>or a commitment |
| *Choir 2* | and we must stand by helplessly, |
| *Choir 1* | feeling as You must feel, Shaddai, |
| *Choir 2* | when we wander away from You. |
| *All* | Help us, Shaddai,<br>to be open and fair |
| *Choir 1* | when someone we love<br>falls away<br>from the faith we shared together, |
| *Choir 2* | and we fear<br>the alienation<br>and are hurt<br>by the sense of loss, |
| *Choir 1* | feeling as You must feel, Shaddai, |
| *Choir 2* | when we fall away from You. |
| *All* | Help us, Shaddai,<br>to carry on |
| *Choir 1* | when someone we love<br>is taken away<br>suddenly,<br>by force,<br>without any warning,<br>without our permission, |
| *Choir 2* | and the heart of our being<br>is cut in two, |
| *Choir 1* | caught in the isolating grip<br>of unspeakable loneliness, |
| *Choir 2* | and a part of us dies<br>like a flower dies<br>when it is deprived of sun. |
| *All* | Help us at times like these, Shaddai,<br>to endure the separation,<br>to feel Your comforting Presence,<br>to know that nothing can separate us<br>from You<br>or the ones we love. |

# BRIDE OF JAMBRI

◇ **Scripture Text**   1 Macc 9:28–42

◇ **Biography**

The anonymous daughter of a wealthy family was about to marry a
man from the Jambri clan when her wedding party was ambushed by
the Maccabean hero Jonathan and his troops to avenge the murder of
his brother John. Many were killed or wounded, others escaped, and
the bride was never heard from again.

◇ **Context**

The Jews had undergone a period of intense persecution under Antiochus IV who sacked Jerusalem, plundered the temple, and prohibited
the Jews from following the prescriptions of the Torah. After his death
and a period of relative calm, his successor Demetrius waged battles
against the Jews. Judah the Maccabee was killed and leadership of the
Jewish resistance passed to his brother Jonathan. Bacchides the Seleucid general tried to destroy Jonathan, and renegades among the Jews
once again rose up in rebellion against him. Oppression from within
and without drove Jonathan and his troops into the Judean desert.
Jonathan sent his brother John, who was in charge of noncombatants,
to ask their friends the Nabateans to store excess baggage for them, but
the delegation was attacked by visiting Jambrites who confiscated the
baggage and murdered John. To avenge his death, Jonathan and his
brother Simeon and their men took advantage of a wedding celebra-

tion among the Jambrites, intending to take them by surprise. As the bridal party was met by the groom and members of the Jambri family, they were ambushed by Jonathan's army, who attacked and killed a number of them, leaving others wounded as survivors retreated to the hills.

That is the story of the bride's wedding day. Commentators speculate at length on just whose daughter she was — did she come from Canaan or was she an Arab? No one asks how she might have felt or why she should have been made to suffer such an injustice. She had nothing to do with the offense committed by her betrothed. Once again women are innocent victims of the wars between men and nations. It is probably safe to assume they left the bride physically unharmed although emotionally devastated. The final line of her story may well sum up the remainder of this woman's life. "So the wedding was turned into mourning and the voice of their musicians into a funeral dirge."

◇ **Lectionary Reading**

The friends of Judah said to Jonathan,
"Since the death of your brother Judah,
there has been no one comparable
to go against our enemies
and to deal with those who hate us
among the people of our own nation.
Therefore we have chosen you
to take his place as our ruler
and to be our leader in battle."
So Jonathan accepted the leadership
in place of his brother Judah.
When Bacchides [the Seleucid general] heard,
he tried to kill Jonathan,
but he and his brother Simeon
and all those who were with them
fled into the wilderness of Tekoa
and camped by the pool of Asphar.
Bacchides found him on the sabbath day
and crossed the Jordan with his army.
So Jonathan sent his brother John
who was leader of the multitude
to beg his friends the Nabateans
for permission to store with them
their large amount of baggage.
But the family of Jambri from Medeba came out
and seized John and all that he had
and carried it away.

Then Jonathan and Simeon heard this report.
"The family of Jambri
is celebrating a big wedding.
The bride is a daughter of a nobleman
and a large company is escorting her from Nadabath."
Remembering how their brother John had been killed,
they went up into the mountain and hid.
Looking down they saw a tumultuous procession
with a large amount of baggage,
saw the bridegroom come out
with his friends and his brothers
to meet them with tambourines
and musicians and many weapons.
Then they attacked the wedding party
and began killing the participants.
Many fell, many were wounded,
and the rest fled to the mountain,
and the Jews took all their goods.
So the wedding was turned into mourning
and the wedding music became a funeral dirge.
After they had fully avenged
the blood of their brother John,
they returned to the marshes of the Jordan.

◇ **Points for Shared Reflection**

- Wars leave millions of innocent victims, mostly women and children. Recall a recent war in which our nation was involved and try to see it from the other side, through the eyes and experiences of women. Share your insights with each other.

- Women are particularly vulnerable on their wedding day. How did you feel on your wedding day? Try to identify with the bride of this story and share how she might have felt and what she might have done. Let those who have been married respond to the questions and others listen and build on their comments.

- There is something completely incompatible about a wedding and a war. Compare these two realities from the perspective of values and systemic justice.

- Discuss the wedding traditions of our culture. What do you find especially meaningful? What would you like to add? What would you like to change, and why?

◇ **A Psalm about Interruptions** (see page 246)

◇ **Prayer**

The whirlwind
of unyielding grace
rips into my solitude
and cuts across
my rigid will
with unrelenting force.
All I really know
of Love
is what I have experienced,
whether organized
or by the way
or simply Her
interrupting me
with a wild, quick, warm embrace.
Let me welcome You
whenever You come,
however You come,
in whomever You come,
when You come to me.
Amen.

## ◇ A PSALM ABOUT INTERRUPTIONS ◇

*All*   Where are You, O Holy One?
Are You in the whirlwind?
Or are You in the still,
small voice
of existential calm?

*Choir 1*   The path
to eternal blessedness
is filled
with interruptions.

*Choir 2*   A whirlwind
unexpectedly
cuts into our precious time
and takes us
from our task.

*Choir 1*   The telephone rings, interrupting us.

*All*   Are You in the whirlwind?

*Choir 2*   The doorbell rings, interrupting us.

*All*   Are You in the whirlwind?

*Choir 1*   The churchbell sounds, interrupting us.

*All*   Are You in the whirlwind?

*Choir 2*   The shofar sounds, interrupting us.

*All*   Are You in the whirlwind
or in the voice of calm?

*Choir 1*   Human need interrupts us.

*All*   Are You in the whirlwind?

*Choir 2*   Human pain interrupts us.

*All*   Are You in the whirlwind?

*Choir 1*   A lonely person interrupts us.

*All*   Are You in the whirlwind?

*Choir 2*   Someone we love interrupts us.

*All*   Are You in the whirlwind
or in the voice of calm?

*Choir 1*   Life always interrupts us.
Wise ones understand.

   By M. T. Winter, Crossroad Pub. Co., © 1991 Medical Mission Sisters

| Choir 2 | One day death will interrupt the schedule we had planned. |

| Choir 1 | God always interrupts us, calling us to do something or go somewhere or be someone beyond our anticipation. |

| Choir 2 | Love always interrupts us, calling us out of self-pity or doubt or the residue of ancient guilt or present expectation. |

| Choir 1 | Where are You, O Holy One? Are You in the whirlwind? |

| Choir 2 | Or are You in the still, small voice of existential calm? |

| All | I will seek You in the whirlwind, and listen to Your still, small voice in the silence of this psalm. |

By M. T. Winter, Crossroad Pub. Co., © 1991 Medical Mission Sisters

# WIDOWS

⬥ **Scripture Reference**   See lectionary texts

⬥ **Biography**

Widows were women whose husbands were deceased and who had not yet remarried. The goal of a childless widow was to enter into a levirate marriage where possible and bear a child in her deceased husband's name. Widows were often without economic resource and had to depend on public charity for their survival.

⬥ **Context**

Widowhood was an extremely vulnerable state in ancient Israelite society. No provision was made for women whose husbands died before them. Considered inferior to other women, frequently poor, sometimes reduced to servitude, often harshly treated, they had no recourse under the law and were solely dependent on the providence of God and the charity of others. Women had no rights of inheritance, and hard as it is

248

to comprehend, their husbands rarely had a plan to provide for them after their death. Death before old age was a calamity and thought to be a punishment for sin, therefore it was a disgrace to be a widow. Isaiah spoke of the reproach of widowhood (54:4) and Naomi bewailed her misfortune (see the Book of Ruth). The narratives of the widow of Zarephath (page 313) and the prophet's widow (page 318) show how close these women came to lives of abject poverty, even to the point of being sold into slavery. The widow image was used symbolically by the prophets to describe the devastation that would befall Israel and Jerusalem.

The only consideration the law offered widows was the possibility of a levirate marriage whereby the brother of the deceased was obliged to take a childless widow and give her children in her husband's name. This was not a guarantee, and if the deceased had no brothers or his brothers were too poor to take another wife, or if the woman already had children, she was completely on her own. The law said the daughter of a priest could return to her father's house to await a levirate marriage. Ironically, the law gave widows a modicum of independence denied married women, for it said that if a widow made an oath, it stood, since she had no husband to revoke it (Num 30:9). Deuteronomy called for reapers to leave some sheaves in the field to be gleaned by widows and orphans and linked this to a blessing (24:19). The same source also stated that the tithe of the produce in the third year was to be given to the Levite, the sojourner, the fatherless, and the widow (26:12; 27:19). Widows with children were free to remarry. So were childless widows who had been released from the levirate bond. For the stories of widows who were exceptions to the norm, see Abigail (page 347), and Bathsheba, Ruth, and Judith in the companion volume *WomanWitness*.

◇ **Lectionary Reading**

A tenth of my grain, wine, olive oil,
pomegranates, figs, and fruits
I would give to the orphans, widows, and converts
who had attached themselves to Israel. (Tob 1:8)

◇

The high priest explained to Heliodorus,
the king's representative,
that there were some deposits
belonging to widows and orphans
in the temple treasury,
and some money belonging to a very prominent man,
and that it totaled four hundred talents of silver
and two hundred of gold. (2 Macc 3:10–11)

◇

After the sabbath they gave some of the spoils
to those who had been tortured
and to the widows and orphans
and distributed the rest among themselves
and their children. (2 Macc 8:28)

◇ **Points for Shared Reflection**

- Discuss the irony of the plight of widows in a deeply religious covenant community with strong familial bonds.

- Compare the situation of widows today with that of ancient Israel. How has their situation improved? What significant problems remain?

- Statistics say that women outlive men. In what ways might this be an advantage to women and in what ways a disadvantage?

- One of the injustices of the present — and the past — is the feminization of poverty. Why are women poor? What can be done to assist women in providing for themselves?

◇ **A Psalm about Grieving** (see page 251)

◇ **Prayer**

O Comforting One,
Compassionate One,
be with us all
when we suffer loss
and ache with the pain of grieving.
Give us a glimpse
of the way it will be
when love will never be taken away,
when life itself will not be diminished,
when all that we hold most precious
will live and remain with us forever.
Amen.

## ◇ A PSALM ABOUT GRIEVING ◇

*Choir 1*   I turned to the wind
who howled
and sighed
the whole time I was healing.

*Choir 2*   I turned to a tree
who had lost its leaves —
she knew how I was feeling.

*Choir 1*   I turned to the rain
who was in tears,
for I too felt like crying.

*Choir 2*   I turned to the earth
who understood
what it meant to live with dying.

*Choir 1*   I turned to a thistle
in a field,
I could see she too was lonely.

*Choir 2*   I turned to a rock
who knew how hard it was
to be one and only.

*Choir 1*   I turned to a blade of grass
because there were bonds
I had to sever.

*Choir 2*   I turned to the sea
who returned to me
and taught me about forever.

*Choir 1*   I turned to a mountain
who seemed secure
and I asked for strength
and endurance.

*Choir 2*   I turned to wildflowers
in a wood
and they gave me some assurance.

*Choir 1*   I turned to a friend
who sat with me
until she had to be leaving.

*Choir 2*   I turned to Shaddai
Who stayed with me
and helped me through my grieving.

# WIVES

◇ **Scripture Reference**  See lectionary texts

◇ **Biography**

From the beginning Canaanite, Hittite, Moabite, Midianite, Ammonite, Amorite, Philistine, Egyptian, and Cushite women, as well as Hebrew women, married Hebrew men. The women left their family home to marry into their husband's clan and they gave birth to the children who built the nation of Israel. Many of the women of other cultures continued to worship their own goddesses and gods.

◇ **Context**

In ancient Israel a man had power over his wife, who was subordinate to her husband in every way. She was classified as the property of her husband. Her patriarchal marriage was characterized by a desire for sons who were named by their father and who traced their descent through him. Genealogies rarely listed a mother or a daughter. However, there are hints of some possible matriarchal marriages early on. For instance both Jacob and Moses lived in the homes of their wives; Rebekah "ran and told her mother's household" (Gen 24:28) about her visitor; Naomi pleaded with her Moabite daughters-in-law to return "each of you to your mother's house" (Ruth 1:8). These may have been situations in which relationships were determined by the mother.

Polygyny was widespread in ancient Israel. A man married more than one woman primarily, but not exclusively, to have more sons. Levirate marriage promoted polygyny, for the marriage of a widow to her deceased husband's brother often meant she was a second wife. Marriage was strongly encouraged within a kinship circle, although marriage beyond the clan was allowed. From the very beginning the prohibition against marrying outside the Hebrew tradition was virtually ignored. Patriarchs, leaders, ordinary men all took non-Hebrew wives. Note Esau's Hittite wives, Judith and Basemath; Judah's Canaanite wife, Bathshua; Joseph's Egyptian wife, Asenath; Zipporah, the Midianite wife of Moses, and his second wife, the enigmatic Cushite; Samson's Philistine wife; Ruth the Moabite who married Boaz; and a legion of other women, including the hundreds of alien women in Solomon's royal harem. The paradox continued for centuries: foreign women who were continually disparaged continued to marry Hebrew men. Nevertheless women of foreign cultures were considered inferior to Hebrew women and often their children came second to those of pure Hebrew parentage. Abraham's firstborn son Ishmael was rejected in favor of Isaac; Jacob was sent to find a wife from among his own people; Jacob's sons slaughtered Shechem and his people supposedly to avenge their sister's rape but more likely to repulse the proposal to intermarry.

Women of other cultures were often identified with idolatry and that is really why they were despised and feared. It had been assumed that as wives they would adopt the religion of their husbands, but their own religious practices continued to flourish through the centuries and no doubt exercised some influence on their husbands and their children. For this reason the prophets and other writers spoke scathingly against them and strong indictments of intermarriage became prevalent. In order to preserve the cultural and religious identity of the community in post-Exilic Israel, Ezra and Nehemiah excommunicated those families who refused to dismiss their foreign wives. In one sense the severity of the threat posed by the wives is an indication of the influence these women had, particularly on their husbands. Women are usually the ones who worship and who transmit traditional values. Husbands may have owned their wives, but religion seems to have been one area that remained beyond their control. These women were blamed for all that was wrong in Israel and were constantly held up as the cause of the sin of Hebrew men and the apostasy of the nation. There is much to be learned from a closer study of the religious practices of Israel's foreign-born wives. It is especially revealing to note that after marrying into the culture, birthing its heroes, and being part of the tradition for generation upon generation, individual women continued to be remembered as "foreign" wives.

◇ **Lectionary Reading**

**Narrator:** We remember **wives whose names are known**
We remember **Adah and Zillah**

**Reader**
Lamech took two wives.
One's name was Adah,
and the name of the other was Zillah.
Adah gave birth to Jabal,
the ancestor of those who have livestock and live in tents.
His brother's name was Jubal,
and he was the ancestor of all those who play the lyre and pipe.
Zillah gave birth to Tubal-cain,
who made all kinds of bronze and iron tools.
The sister of Tubal-cain was Naamah.
Lamech said to his wives: "Adah and Zillah, hear my voice;
you wives of Lamech, listen to what I say.
I have killed a man for wounding me, a young man for striking me.
If Cain is avenged sevenfold, truly Lamech seventy-sevenfold."
(Gen 4:19-24)

◇ ◇ ◇

**Narrator:** We remember **Abihail**

**Reader**
The name of Abishur's wife was Abihail,
and she gave birth to Ahban and Molid. (1 Chr 2:29)

◇ ◇ ◇

**Narrator:** We remember **Abijah**

**Reader**
After the death of Hezron, in Caleb-ephrathah,
Abijah wife of Hezron gave birth to Ashhur, the father of Tekoa.
(1 Chr 2:24)

◇ ◇ ◇

**Narrator:** We remember **Ahinoam**

**Reader**
The name of Saul's wife was Ahinoam daughter of Ahimaaz.
(1 Sam 14:50)

◇

Saul was angry at Jonathan.
He said to him,
"You son of a perverse, rebellious woman!
Do I not know that you have chosen
the son of Jesse to your own shame
and to the shame of your mother's nakedness?" (1 Sam 20:30)

◇ ◇ ◇

**Narrator:** We remember **Atarah**

**Reader**
Jerahmeel also had another wife,
whose name was Atarah.
She was the mother of Onam. (1 Chr 2:26)

◇ ◇ ◇

**Narrator:** We remember **Azubah and Ephrath**

**Reader**
Caleb son of Hezron had children by his wife Azubah (Jerioth).
These were her sons: Jesher, Shobab, and Ardon.
When Azubah died, Caleb married Ephrath,
who gave birth to Hur. (1 Chr 2:18–19)

◇ ◇ ◇

**Narrator:** We remember **Baara, Hodesh, and Hushim**

**Reader**
Shaharaim had sons in the country of Moab
after he had sent away his wives Hushim and Baara.
He had sons by his wife Hodesh:
Jobab, Zibia, Mesha, Malcam, Jeuz, Sachia, and Mirmah.
These were his sons who were heads of ancestral houses.
He also had sons by Hushim: Abitub and Elpaal. (1 Chr 8:8–11)

◇ ◇ ◇

**Narrator:** We remember **Bathshua, the wife of Judah**

**Reader**
Judah settled near a certain Adullamite
whose name was Hirah.
There Judah saw the daughter of a certain Canaanite
whose name was Shua.
He married her and she conceived
and gave birth to a son,
and he named him Er.
Again she conceived and gave birth to a son
whom she named Onan.
Yet again she gave birth to a son,
and she named him Shelah.
She was in Chezib when he was born.
In the course of time
the wife of Judah, Shua's daughter, died. (Gen 38:1–5, 12)

◇

The sons of Judah were Er, Onan, and Shela.
These three the Canaanite woman Bathshua bore to him. (1 Chr 2:3)

◇ ◇ ◇

**Narrator:** We remember **Helah and Naarah**

**Reader**
Ashhur father of Tekoa had two wives, Helah and Naarah.
Naarah gave birth to Ahuzzam, Hepher, Temeni, and Haahashtari.
These were the sons of Naarah.
The sons of Helah were Zereth, Izhar, and Ethnan. (1 Chr 4:5–7)

◇ ◇ ◇

**Narrator:** We remember **Maacah, wife of Machir**

**Reader**
Maacah the wife of Machir son of Manasseh
gave birth to a son, and she named him Peresh;
and his brother's name was Sheresh. (1 Chr 7:16)

◇ ◇ ◇

**Narrator:** We remember **Maacah, wife of Jeiel**

**Reader**
Jeiel the father of Gibeon lived in Gibeon,
and the name of his wife was Maacah.
Her firstborn son was Abdon,
then came Zur, Kish, Baal, Nadab, Gedor,
Ahio, Zecher, and Mikloth,
who became the father of Shimeah. (1 Chr 8:29–32)

◇ ◇ ◇

**Narrator:** We remember **Mahalath**

**Reader**
Rehoboam took as his wife Mahalath
daughter of Jerimoth son of David
and of Abihail daughter of Eliab son of Jesse.
She gave birth to sons: Jeush, Shemaria, and Zaham. (2 Chr 11:18–19)

◇ ◇ ◇

**Narrator:** We remember **Peninnah**

**Reader**
Elkanah an Ephraimite had two wives.
One's name was Hannah.
The name of the other was Peninnah.
Peninnah had children, but Hannah did not.
On the day when Elkanah sacrificed,
he would give portions to his wife Peninnah
and to all her sons and daughters,
but to Hannah he gave a double portion
because he loved her,
though God had closed her womb.
Her rival used to provoke her severely
in order to irritate her,
because God had closed her womb. (1 Sam 1:1–2,4–6)

◇ ◇ ◇

**Narrator:** We remember **Zeresh**

**Reader**
Haman was happy that day,
but when he saw Mordecai at the king's gate,
saw that he did not bow to him
nor did he tremble before him,
he was infuriated, but he restrained himself.
At home he called his wife Zeresh
and a gathering of friends,
and he boasted of his riches and the number of his sons,
his promotions and his advancements,
and announced to everyone,
"Even Queen Esther invited me
to her banquet with the king.
Yet tell me, what good is all of this
when I see that Jew Mordecai sitting at the king's gate."
Then his wife Zeresh and his friends replied,
"Build a gallows and tell the king
to have Mordecai hung on it.

Then go to the banquet in good spirits
and make merry with the king."
This advice pleased Haman,
and he had the gallows made.

"What shall be done for the man the king would honor?"
the king asked Haman.
"He must be thinking of me," thought Haman,
so this was his reply.
"For the man whom the king would honor,
let royal robes be brought to him,
and a horse which the king has ridden,
and a royal crown for his head.
Let the one to be honored be robed
by the king's most notable official,
who will then lead the man on horseback
through the city's public square, proclaiming,
'Thus shall it be done for the man
whom the king wishes to honor.'"
Then the king said to Haman, "Quickly,
take the robes and the horse, just as you said,
and honor the Jew Mordecai who sits at the king's gate."
So Haman did as the king commanded,
parading Mordecai in public, proclaiming,
"Thus shall it be done for the man
whom the king wishes to honor."
Then Mordecai returned to the king's gate
while Haman went home humiliated and deeply distressed.
He reported to his wife and friends
who offered advice to him.
"If Mordecai is a Jew, then you will not prevail against him.
It is you who will surely fall."
While they were speaking, eunuchs arrived
and hurried Haman off to the banquet
that Esther had prepared. (Esth 5:9–14; 6:6–14)

◇ ◇ ◇

**Narrator:** We remember **wives whose names are unknown**
We remember the **wives of Noah's sons**

**Reader**
God said to Noah:
"I will establish my covenant with you;
and you shall come into the ark,
you, your sons, your wife, and your sons' wives with you.
And Noah with his sons and his wife and his sons' wives

went into the ark to escape the waters of the flood.
The rain fell on the earth forty days and forty nights.
On the very same day, Noah with his sons,
Shem and Ham and Japheth, and Noah's wife,
and the three wives of his sons entered the ark.
In the second month,
on the twenty-seventh day of the month,
the earth was dry.
Then God said to Noah,
"Go out of the ark, you and your wife,
and your sons and your sons' wives with you."
So Noah went out with his sons and his wife and his sons' wives.
These are the descendants of Noah's sons,
Shem, Ham, and Japheth and their wives;
for children were born to them after the flood.
The descendants of Japheth and his wife were Gomer,
Magog, Madai, Javan, Tubal, Meshech, and Tiras.
The descendants of Ham and his wife were
Cush, Egypt, Put, and Canaan.
To Shem also, the elder brother of Japheth,
and to his wife, children were born.
The descendants of Shem and his wife were Elam,
Asshur, Arpachshad, Lud, and Aram.
These are the families of Noah's sons and their wives,
and from these the nations
spread abroad on the earth after the flood.
(Gen 6:18; 7:7, 12–13; 8:14–16, 18; 10:1–2, 6, 21–22, 31–32)

◇ ◇ ◇

**Narrator:** We remember the **wife of Abimelech**

**Reader**
Abraham prayed to God;
and God healed Abimelech,
and also healed his wife and female slaves
so that they bore children.
For God had closed tight all the wombs
of the house of Abimelech
because of Sarah, Abraham's wife. (Gen 20:17–18)

◇ ◇ ◇

**Narrator:** We remember **the wife of Ishmael**

**Reader**
Ishmael lived in the wilderness of Paran;
and his mother got a wife for him from the land of Egypt. (Gen 21:21)

◇ ◇ ◇

**Narrator:** We remember **the wives of Jacob's sons**

**Reader**
Then Jacob set out from Beer-sheba;
and the sons of Israel carried their father Jacob,
their little ones, and their wives
in the wagons that Pharaoh had sent to carry him.
They also took their livestock
and the goods that they had acquired
in the land of Canaan, and they came into Egypt,
Jacob and all his offspring with him,
his sons and his sons' sons with him,
his daughters, and his sons' daughters,
all his offspring he brought with him into Egypt.
The children of Simeon were Jemuel, Jamin, Ohad,
Jachin, Zohar, and Shaul, the son of a Canaanite woman.
(Gen 46:5–7, 10)

◇ ◇ ◇

**Narrator:** We remember the **wives of Dathan and Abiram**

**Reader**
Now Korah son of Izhar,
along with Dathan and Abiram sons of Eliab,
and On son of Peleth — descendants of Reuben —
took two hundred fifty Israelite men,
leaders of the congregation
chosen from the assembly, well-known men,
and they confronted Moses.
They assembled against Moses and against Aaron
and said to them, "You have gone too far!
All the congregation are holy, everyone of them,
and God is among them.
Why then do you exalt yourselves
above the assembly of God?"
Moses sent for Dathan and Abiram,
but they said, "We will not come!
Is it too little that you have brought us
out of a land flowing with milk and honey
to kill us in the wilderness,
that you must also lord it over us?"
So Moses got up and went to Dathan and Abiram
and the elders of Israel followed him.
He said to the congregation,
"Turn away from the tents of these wicked men,
and do not touch anything of theirs,
or you will be swept away for all their sins."

So they moved away from the dwellings
of Korah, Dathan, and Abiram;
and Dathan and Abiram came
and stood at the entrance of their tents
with their wives, their children, and their little ones.
And Moses said, "This is how you shall know
that God has sent me to do all these works.
It has not been of my own accord.
If these people die a natural death
or if a natural fate comes upon them,
then God has not sent me.
But if God creates something new,
and the ground opens and swallows them up
and everything that belongs to them,
and they go down alive into Sheol,
then you shall know that these men have despised God."
As soon as he finished speaking,
the ground under them split apart.
The earth opened its mouth and swallowed them up,
along with their households —
everyone who belonged to Korah
and all their goods. (Num 16:1–3,12–13,25–32)

◇ ◇ ◇

**Narrator:** We remember the **wife of Ephraim**

**Reader**
The sons of Ephraim and his wife
were Shuthelah, Bered, Tahath, Eleadah,
Zabad, Ezer, and Elead.
Now the people of Gath who were born in the land
killed them because they came down to raid their cattle.
And their father Ephraim mourned many days,
and his brothers came to comfort him.
Ephraim again had intercourse with his wife
and she conceived and gave birth to a son;
and Ephraim named him Beriah,
because disaster had fallen on his house. (1 Chr 7:20–23)

◇ ◇ ◇

**Narrator:** We remember the **Judean wife of Mered**

**Reader**
Mered's Judean wife gave birth to Jered father of Gedor,
Heber father of Soco, and Jekuthiel father of Zanoah. (1 Chr 4:18)

◇ ◇ ◇

**Narrator:** We remember the **wife of Hodiah**

**Reader**
The sons of the wife of Hodiah,
the sister of Naham,
were the fathers of Keilah the Garmite
and Eshtemoa the Maacathite. (1 Chr 4:19)

◇ ◇ ◇

**Narrator:** We remember the **wives of Gideon**

**Reader**
Now Gideon had seventy sons, his own offspring,
for he had many wives.
His concubine who was in Shechem
also bore him a son,
and he named him Abimelech.
Abimelech went to his father's house at Ophrah
and killed his brothers, seventy men on one stone;
but Jotham the youngest survived,
because he had hidden himself. (Judg 8:30–31; 9:5)

◇ ◇ ◇

**Narrator:** We remember the **wife of Gilead**

**Reader**
Now Jephthah the son of a prostitute,
Gilead's son, was a mighty warrior.
The wife of Gilead also had sons
and when these sons were older,
they drove Jephthah away, saying,
"You shall not inherit in our father's house,
for you are the son of another woman."
So Jephthah fled from his brothers
to the land of Tob. (Judg 11:1–3)

◇ ◇ ◇

**Narrator:** We remember the **wife of Naaman**

**Reader**
Naaman, commander of the Syrian army,
was highly favored by the king
because through him God had given victory to Syria.
He was a great man and a valiant warrior,
but he had leprosy.
Now the Syrians on one of their many raids
had taken a young girl captive from the land of Israel,
and she served Naaman's wife.

She said to her mistress,
"If only my master were with the prophet who is in Samaria,
he would cure him of his leprosy." (2 Kings 5:1–3)

◇ ◇ ◇

**Narrator:** We remember the **eighteen wives of Rehoboam**

**Reader**
Rehoboam king of Judah loved Maacah daughter of Absalom
more than all his other wives and concubines.
He took eighteen wives and sixty concubines,
and became the father of twenty-eight sons
and sixty daughters. (2 Chr 11:21)

◇ ◇ ◇

**Narrator:** We remember the **fourteen wives of Abijah**

**Reader**
Abijah king of Judah grew strong.
He took fourteen wives and became the father
of twenty-two sons and sixteen daughters. (2 Chr 13:21)

◇ ◇ ◇

**Narrator:** We remember the **wives of Jehoram**

**Reader**
A letter from the prophet Elijah
came to Jehoram king of Judah saying,
"God will bring a great plague on your people,
your children, your wives, and all your possessions,
and you yourself will have a severe sickness. . . . "
God aroused against Jehoram the anger of the Philistines
and the Arabs who are near Ethiopia.
They invaded Judah, carried away all the possessions
found in the king's house,
along with his sons and his wives,
so that no son was left except Jehoahaz,
his youngest son. (2 Chr 21:12, 14–17)

◇ ◇ ◇

**Narrator:** We remember the **wives of Joash**

**Reader**
Joash reigned forty years in Jerusalem.
Jehoiada got two wives for him,
and he became the father of sons and daughters. (2 Chr 24:1, 3)

◇ ◇ ◇

**Narrator:** We remember the **wives of King Ahab**

**Reader**
King Ben-hadad of Aram marched against Samaria.
He sent messengers to King Ahab of Israel saying,
"Your silver and gold are mine,
your fairest wives and children also are mine."
The king of Israel answered,
"As you say, O king, I am yours with all that I have."
The messengers came again, saying,
"I sent to you saying, 'Deliver to me
your silver and gold, your wives and children.'
I will send my servants again tomorrow at this time,
and they will search your house
and the houses of your servants,
and take whatever pleases them."
Then the king of Israel called the elders of the land,
saying, "This man sent to me for my wives and my children,
my silver and my gold, and I did not refuse him."
Then all the elders and the people said to him,
"Do not listen or give consent."
Then the king of Israel went out and defeated the Arameans.
(1 Kings 20:1–8, 21)

◇ ◇ ◇

**Narrator:** We remember the **wives of the priests**

**Reader**
The priests were enrolled with all their little children,
their wives, their sons, and their daughters,
the whole multitude; for they were faithful
in keeping themselves holy. (2 Chr 31:18)

◇ ◇ ◇

**Narrator:** We remember the **wife of Job**

**Reader**
Job's wife said to him,
"Do you still persist in your integrity?
Curse God and die." But he said to her,
"You speak as any foolish woman would speak.
Shall we receive the good at the hand of God
and not receive the bad?" (Job 2:9–10)

"My breath is repulsive to my wife;
I am loathsome to my own family." (Job 19:17)

◇ ◇ ◇

**Narrator:** We remember the **wife of Ezekiel**

**Reader**
The word of God came to me:
"Mortal, with one blow
I am about to take away the delight of your eyes;
yet you shall not mourn or weep,
nor shall your tears run down.
Sigh, but not aloud;
make no mourning for the dead.
Bind on your turban,
and put your sandals on your feet;
do not cover your upper lip
or eat the bread of mourners."
So I spoke to the people in the morning,
and at evening my wife died.
And on the next morning
I did as I was commanded. (Ezek 24:15–18)

◇ ◇ ◇

**Narrator:** We remember the **wife of King Artaxerxes**

**Reader**
King Artaxerxes said to me —
the queen was sitting beside him —
"How long will you be gone,
and when will you return?" (Neh 2:6)

◇ ◇ ◇

**Narrator:** We remember the **queen**
  **and other wives of King Belshazzar**

**Reader**
King Belshazzar made a great festival
for a thousand of his nobles,
and he was drinking wine in their presence.
Under the influence of the wine,
Belshazzar commanded that they bring in
the vessels of gold and silver
that his father Nebuchadnezzar had taken
out of the temple in Jerusalem, so that the king and his nobles,
his wives and his concubines might drink from them.
So they brought in the vessels of gold and silver
that had been taken out of the temple,
the house of God in Jerusalem,
and the king and his nobles,
his wives and his concubines drank from them.

They drank the wine and praised the gods of gold
and silver, bronze, iron, wood, and stone.
Immediately the fingers of a human hand appeared
and began writing on the plaster of the wall
of the royal palace, next to the lampstand.
Not one of the king's wise men
was able to read or interpret the writing.
The queen heard the discussion of the king and his nobles
and came into the banqueting hall.
She said, "O king, live forever!
Do not let your thoughts terrify you or your face grow pale.
There is a man in your kingdom
who is endowed with a spirit of the holy gods.
In the days of your father King Nebuchadnezzar
he was found to have enlightenment, understanding,
and wisdom like the wisdom of the gods.
Your father made him chief of the magicians,
enchanters, Chaldeans, and diviners,
because an excellent spirit, knowledge, and understanding
to interpret dreams, explain riddles, and solve problems
were found in this Daniel,
whom the king named Belteshazzar.
Now let Daniel be called, and he will give the interpretation."
Daniel said in the presence of the king,
"You have exalted yourself against the God of heaven!
The temple vessels have been brought in before you,
and you and your nobles, your wives and your concubines
have been drinking wine from them.
You have praised the gods of silver and gold,
of bronze, iron, wood, and stone,
which do not see or hear or know;
but the God in whose power is your very breath,
and to whom belong all your ways,
you have not honored.
So the hand was sent to you from God's presence . . .
God has numbered the days of your kingdom
and brought it to an end." (Dan 5:1–26, excerpts)

◇ ◇ ◇

**Narrator:** We remember the **wives of Daniel's accusers**

**Reader**
King Belshazzar gave a command,
and those who had accused Daniel were brought
and thrown into the den of the lions —
they, their children, and their wives.

Before they reached the bottom of the den
the lions overpowered them
and broke all their bones in pieces. (Dan 6:24)

◇ ◇ ◇

**Narrator:** We remember the **wives of the priests of Bel**

**Reader**
King Cyrus said to Daniel,
"Do you not think that Bel is a living god?
Do you now see how much he eats and drinks each day?"
And Daniel laughed and said,
"Do not be deceived, O King,
for this thing is only clay inside and bronze outside,
and it never ate or drank anything."
Now there were seventy priests of Bel,
besides their wives and children.
The priests of Bel said,
"Set out the food and prepare the wine yourself, O King,
and shut the door and seal it with your signet.
When you return in the morning,
if you do not find that Bel has eaten it all,
we will die; otherwise Daniel will die,
who has been telling lies about us."
They were unconcerned,
for beneath the table they had made a hidden entrance,
through which they would enter regularly
and consume all the provisions.
During the night the priests came as usual,
with their wives and children,
and they ate and drank everything.
Early in the morning the king came with Daniel.
The king said, "Are the seals unbroken?"
"They are unbroken, O king," answered Daniel.
As soon as the doors were opened,
the king looked at the table and shouted,
"You are great, O Bel, and in you there is no deceit!"
But Daniel laughed and said,
"Look at the floor and notice whose footprints these are."
The king said, "I see the footprints
of men and women and children."
The king was enraged and arrested the priests
and their wives and children;
and he put them to death. (Bel 6–22, condensed)

◇ ◇ ◇

**Narrator:** We remember the **wives of the Exodus**

**Reader**
Aaron said to the people in the wilderness,
"Take the gold rings from the ears of your wives,
your sons, and your daughters,
and bring them to me."
So all the people took the gold rings from their ears,
and brought them to Aaron.
He took the gold, molded it, and made an image of a calf.
And they said, "These are your gods, O Israel,
who brought you up out of the land of Egypt." (Ex 32:2–4)

◇

"Although God has given you this land to occupy,
all your troops shall cross over armed
as the vanguard of your Israelite kin.
Only your wives, your children, and your livestock
shall stay behind in the towns which I have given you."
                              (Deut 3:18–19)

◇ ◇ ◇

**Narrator:** We remember the **wives who suffered**
              **and the wives who died**

**Reader**
Now there was a great outcry of the men
and their wives against their Jewish kin.
For there were those who said,
"With our sons and our daughters, we are many;
we must get grain, so that we may eat and stay alive."
There were also those who said,
"We are having to borrow money
on our fields, our vineyards, and our houses
in order to get grain during the famine."
And there were those who said,
"We are having to borrow money
on our fields and vineyards
to pay the king's tax.
Now our flesh is the same as that of our kindred;
our children are the same as their children;
and yet we are forcing our sons and daughters to be slaves,
and some of our daughters have been ravished.
We are powerless, and our fields and vineyards
now belong to others." (Neh 5:1–5)

◇

All the men of Bethulia,
their wives, their children,

every resident alien, hired laborer, and purchased slave,
all put sackcloth around their waists.
They cried out in unison praying to God
not to allow their infants to be carried off
and their wives to be taken as booty.
When the whole Assyrian army
had surrounded them for thirty-four days
and their water containers were empty,
they cried out with a loud voice,
"It would be better for us to be captured by them.
We shall indeed become slaves, but our lives would be spared,
and we would not see our children and our wives
die before our eyes." (Jdt 4:10, 12; 7:20, 23 27)

◊

Many who sought justice went into the wilderness
with their sons and wives and livestock
because troubles pressed heavily upon them.
The enemy pursued them and attacked them on the sabbath,
and they died with their wives and their children
and their livestock, about a thousand persons. (1 Macc 2:29, 30, 38)

◊

Judah said to the people,
"They come arrogantly and lawlessly against us
to destroy us and our wives and our children,
but we fight for our lives and our laws." (1 Macc 3:20–21)

◊

The Jews in Gilead wrote to Judah,
"The Gentiles around us have gathered to destroy us.
Come and rescue us from their hands,
for many of us have fallen.
All our relatives in the land of Tob have been killed.
They have captured their wives and children and goods,
and have destroyed about a thousand persons." (1 Macc 5:9–13)

◊

The Romans attacked the Greeks.
Many of them were wounded or killed,
and the Romans captured their wives and children. (1 Macc 8:10)

◊

Simon said to the people of Jerusalem,
"I will avenge my nation and the sanctuary
and your wives and children,
for all the nations have gathered together
out of hatred to destroy us." (1 Macc 13:1, 6)

◊

Some of the governors in various places
would not let the Jews live quietly and in peace.

The people of Joppa did an ungodly deed.
They invited the Jews who lived among them,
together with their wives and children,
to embark on boats which they had provided,
as though there were no ill will toward them.
This was done by public vote of the city.
The Jews accepted because they suspected nothing,
and the people of Joppa took them out to sea
and drowned at least two hundred of them. (2 Macc 12:2–4)

◇

Their concern for their wives and their children,
and for their brothers and sisters and relatives,
lay upon them less heavily than their concern
for the consecrated sanctuary,
which was their first and greatest fear. (2 Macc 15:18)

◇ ◇ ◇

**Narrator:** We remember the **foreign wives**

**Reader**
So the Israelites lived among the Canaanites, the Hittites,
the Amorites, the Perizzites, the Hivites, and the Jebusites;
and they took their daughters as wives for themselves,
and their own daughters they gave to their sons;
and they worshiped their gods. (Jdg 3:5–6)

◇

The word of God came to Jeremiah
for all Judeans living in the land of Egypt.
Then a very large assembly answered Jeremiah.
It consisted of all the men who were aware
that their wives were making offerings to other gods
and of all the women who stood by. They said,
"As for this word you have spoken in the name of God,
we are not going to listen to you.
Instead we will do what we have vowed,
make offerings to the queen of heaven
and pour out libations to her,
just as we and our ancestors,
our kings and our officials used to do
in the towns of Judah and in the streets of Jerusalem.
We used to have plenty of food.
We prospered and experienced no misfortune.
But ever since we stopped making offerings
and pouring our libations to the queen of heaven,
we have lacked everything,
and we have perished by the sword and by famine."

The women said, "Indeed we will go on
making offerings to the queen of heaven
and pouring out libations to her.
Do you think that we made cakes for her
marked with her image
and poured out libations to her
without our husbands' being involved?"
Then Jeremiah said to the men and women,
"As for the offerings you made in the towns of Judah
and in the streets of Jerusalem, you and your ancestors,
your kings and your officials, and the people of the land,
God could not bear the sight of your evil doings
and the abominations that you committed,
so your land became a wasteland and a curse,
uninhabited to this day.
It is because you burned offerings,
it is because you sinned against God,
because you did not obey the voice of God
nor walk in God's ways and decrees and statutes
that this disaster has befallen you
as is still evident today."
Then Jeremiah said to the men and women,
"Hear God's word all you Judeans who live in the land of Egypt.
Thus says the God of Israel:
You and your wives have accomplished in deeds
what you declared in words, saying,
'We are determined to perform the vows we have made,
to make offerings to the queen of heaven
and to pour out libations to her.'
By all means, keep your vows and make your libations!
All the people of Judah who are living in Egypt
shall perish by the sword and by famine,
until not one person is left.
Only a few will escape the sword
to return to the land of Judah.
The remnant of Judah that has settled in Egypt
shall know whose words will stand,
mine or theirs!" (Jer 44:1, 15–28)

◇

Ezra prayed and wept before the house of God,
and a very large assembly of men, women, and children
wept bitterly with him.
"We have broken faith with our God
and have married foreign women from the peoples of the land,
but still there is hope for Israel," said Shecaniah son of Jehiel.
"So now let us make a covenant with God

to send away all these wives and their children,
and let it be done according to the law.
Take action, for it is your duty; be strong and do it."
Then Ezra stood up and made the chief priests,
the Levites and all Israel swear
that they would do as had been said.
Ezra fasted and mourned
over the faithlessness of the exiles
as a proclamation sent throughout Judah
ordered all returned exiles
to assemble in Jerusalem within three days
or be banned from the congregation.
The people came and sat in the open square
before the house of God,
trembling because of this concern
and because of the heavy rain.
Then Ezra the priest stood up and said,
"You have sinned by marrying foreign women
and thereby increased the guilt of Israel.
Now confess to the God of your ancestors
and separate yourselves from the peoples of the land
and from your foreign wives."
The assembly replied with a loud voice,
"It is so. We must do as you have said.
But the people are many, the rains are heavy,
and we cannot remain out here in the open.
This is not a task for a day or two,
for many of us have sinned.
Let our officials represent the assembly,
and let all in our towns who have taken foreign wives
come at appointed times,
with the elders and judges of their respective towns,
until the matter is settled
and God's fierce wrath is averted from us."
So this is what they did.
Ezra the priest selected men who were heads of families
and they sat down to examine the matter
until they came to the end of all the men
who had married foreign women.
And all who had married foreign women
sent them away with their children.

(Ezra 10:1–17, 44; 1 Esd 8:91–96; 9:1–17, 36)

◇

The rest of the people, the priests, the Levites,
the gatekeepers, the singers, the temple servants,
and all who have separated themselves

from the peoples of the land
to adhere to the law of God,
their wives, their sons, their daughters,
all who have knowledge and understanding,
join with their kin, their nobles,
and enter into a curse and an oath to walk in God's law,
which was given by Moses the servant of God,
and to observe and do all the commandments
and the ordinances and the statutes of God.
We will not give our daughters to the peoples of the land
or take their daughters for our sons. (Neh 10:28–30)

◇

In those days also I saw Jews
who had married women of Ashdod, Ammon, and Moab;
half of their children spoke the language of Ashdod
and could not speak the language of Judah,
but spoke the language of various peoples.
I contended with them and cursed them
and beat some of them and pulled out their hair,
and I made them take an oath in the name of God, saying,
"You shall not give your daughters to their sons,
or take their daughters for your sons or yourselves.
Did not King Solomon sin on account of such women?
There was no king like him among the nations.
He was king over Israel, beloved by God,
yet foreign women caused even Solomon to sin.
Shall we then act treacherously against our God
by marrying foreign women?" (Neh 13:23–27)

◇ ◇ ◇

**Narrator:** We remember **all the faithful wives
whose stories are lost to us**

**Reader**
All Judah stood before God with the little ones,
their wives, and their children. (2 Chr 20:13)

◇

The heads of ancestral houses were chosen to go up to Jerusalem,
according to their tribes,
with their wives and sons and daughters,
and male and female servants, and their livestock.
And Darius sent with them a thousand cavalry
to take them back to Jerusalem in safety,
with the music of drums and flutes;
all their relatives were making merry.
And he made them go up with them. (1 Esd 5:1–2)

**Narrator:** We remember **all the wives not mentioned in scripture who are implicitly present in the stories of their husbands and their children**

[*Pause for silent reflection.*]

◇ **Points for Shared Reflection**

• List all the different ways a husband had power over his wife in the patriarchal marriage of ancient Israel and evaluate these from a woman's perspective.

• Comment on the practice of polygyny in which the husband had more than one wife. How would you fare in such a setting? How could such a practice be condoned by biblical religion?

• Was the continual castigation of women of other cultures and other religions really the word of God or the prejudicial opinion of biblical writers, prophets, and other religious leaders? Elaborate on your response.

• As an American, comment on the phrase "foreign wife" as it has been applied to biblical women throughout the centuries. Who would qualify as a "foreign wife" in America?

◇ **A Psalm on Love**  (see page 275)

◇ **Prayer**

I love You, O God,
my Love,
my Warmth,
my Solace,
my Fulfillment.
All that I am,
all that I do
finds meaning and purpose in You.
Fill me with the full force
of Your Love
and its passionate splendor,
so that I might hold
and heal all those
who are crying out for love.
Love through me
all the unreconciled
whose homes and hearts
are broken,
and let them know
I am able to love
because You have first loved me. Amen.

*All*  There are three things the heart must know.
The first is: what is love?

*Choir 1*  Love is
the whole of us handed over
wholeheartedly to another.

*Choir 2*  Love is
the inside out of us
in harmony with another.

*Choir 1*  Love is
being there
day after day
for one
for many
for any who need to know
what it means
to be loved.

*Choir 2*  Love is
simply knowing
Love is,
and growing to know
the Love that is
and will be for us forever.

*All*  There are three things the heart must know.
The second is: how do we love?

*Choir 1*  We love
when we simply sit and wait
and never lose faith in another.

*Choir 2*  We love
when we listen to another life
and affirm that life into being.

*Choir 1*  We love
when we take initiative
to forgive and forget,
to be and become,
to shoulder the burden
and share the pain,
to try to see things through another's eyes
and feel with another's passion.

*Choir 2*   We love
in all those little ways
we fill our lives
and crowd our days
with genuine gestures of loving.

*All*   There are three things the heart must know.
The third is: are we loved?

*Choir 1*   We are loved
when we are called into life
and invited into meaning.

*Choir 2*   We are loved
when we are healed inside
deep down
in the empty hole of our being,
where shame and shadows
seek to define us,
struggle to own us
and occupy so much sacred time.

*Choir 1*   We are loved
when we feel we are whole
and at ease
with what is
and was
and may be,
and at ease
with who we have become
and who we are becoming.

*Choir 2*   We are loved,
yes we are loved and embraced
by the Love that lasts forever,
unquestioningly,
unconditionally,
empowering us
to love another,
to love all others
in the way that we are loved.

*All*   She is Love.
We are loved,
and we learn to love
when we imitate Her loving.
Hers is an everlasting love.
I love You with all my heart, Shaddai.
May my own love live forever.

   By M. T. Winter, Crossroad Pub. Co., © 1991 Medical Mission Sisters

# CONCUBINES

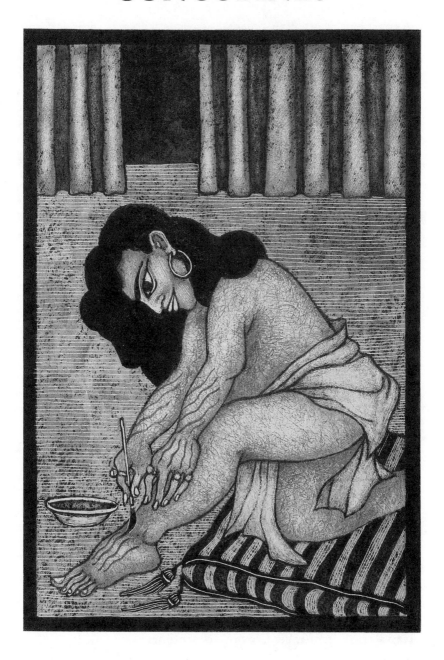

◇ **Biography**

A concubine was a man's marital associate who was secondary to his wife. In many ways she functioned as a wife but had the status of a slave. She was either the man's personal property or she was given to him temporarily by his wife to achieve surrogate motherhood for her, for the child of a concubine on behalf of a wife was the wife's adoptive child. Concubines were morally acceptable in Israel. Many men had concubines, including Abraham, Jacob, David, and Solomon. The rights of a Hebrew girl sold into concubinage were guaranteed by biblical law.

◇ **Context**

One of the primary purposes of concubines was to give birth to children, especially sons. When a man's wife was barren, it was her prerogative to give him her slave that she might have children through her. Four of the twelve tribes of Israel were descendants of concubines. Ishmael, Abraham's firstborn son, was born of a concubine. A concubine gained status if she gave birth to sons because she would be remembered. Hagar, Zilpah, Bilhah, Rizpah are remembered because they had sons. The kings of Judah had many concubines, according to the Bible. David had ten or more, Solomon supposedly had three hundred. A man challenged another man's authority by having sex with his concubine. When Absalom assaulted ten of his father's concubines publicly on the palace roof, it was a declaration of war. Undoubtedly there were some warm and loving relationships between individual women and the men to whom they were concubines. Nevertheless, the double enslavement of concubinage and of gender was a systemic violation to women who lived during biblical times.

◇ **Lectionary Reading**

**Narrator:** We remember **Ephah and Maacah, Caleb's concubines**

**Reader**
Ephah, Caleb's concubine, bore Haran, Moza, and Gazez.
Maacah, Caleb's concubine, bore Sheber and Tirhanah.
She also bore Shaaph father of Madmannah,
Sheva father of Machbenah and father of Gibea;
and the daughter of Caleb was Achsah. (1 Chr 2:46, 48, 49)

◇ ◇ ◇

**Narrator:** We remember **Gideon's concubine**

**Reader**
Jerubbaal son of Joash
[who was also called Gideon]
went to live in his own house.

Now Gideon had seventy sons,
his own offspring,
for he had many wives.
His concubine who was in Shechem
also bore him a son,
and he named him Abimelech.
Now Abimelech son of Jerubbaal
went to Shechem to his mother's family
and said to them and to the whole clan of his mother's family,
"Say in the hearing of all the nobles of Shechem,
'Which is better for you,
that all seventy of the sons of Jerubbaal rule over you,
or that one rule over you?'
Remember also that I am your bone and your flesh."
So his mother's relatives
spoke all these words on his behalf
in the hearing of all the nobles of Shechem;
and their hearts were inclined to follow Abimelech,
for they said, "He is our brother."
Abimelech went to his father's house at Ophrah,
and killed his brothers,
the sons of Jerubbaal,
seventy men on one stone;
but Jotham the youngest survived,
for he had hidden himself.
Then all the nobles of Shechem and Beth-millo
made Abimelech king
by the oak of the pillar at Shechem.
When Jotham was told of it,
he went and stood on the top of Mount Gerizim
and cried aloud to the people of Shechem,
"You have risen up against my father's house,
killing this day seventy men on one stone,
and have made Abimelech,
the son of his slave woman,
king over all the nobles of Shechem,
because he is your kinsman.
If you have acted with good faith and honor
with Jerubbaal and his house this day,
then rejoice in Abimelech,
and let him also rejoice in you;
but if not, let fire come out from Abimelech,
and devour the lords of Shechem and Beth-millo,
and devour Abimelech." (Judg 8:29–31; 9:1–3, 5–7, 18–20)

◇ ◇ ◇

**Narrator:** We remember **Manasseh's Aramean concubine**

**Reader**
Manasseh's Aramean concubine
gave birth to a son Asriel,
and then gave birth to a second son Machir,
who was the father of Gilead. (1 Chr 7:14)

◊ ◊ ◊

**Narrator:** We remember **Reumah, Nabor's concubine**

**Reader**
Milcah bore eight children to Nabor, Abraham's brother.
Nabor's concubine, whose name was Reumah,
gave birth to Tebah, Gaham, Tahash, and Maacah. (Gen 22:23–24)

◊ ◊ ◊

**Narrator:** We remember **Timna, the concubine of Eliphaz, Esau's son**

**Reader**
Timna was a concubine of Eliphaz, Esau's son,
and she gave birth to Amalek.
The sons of Lotan were Hori and Herman;
and Lotan's sister was Timna. (Gen 36:12, 22; 1 Chr 1:39)

◊ ◊ ◊

**Narrator:** We remember the **concubines in the royal harem**
**of Ahasuerus**

**Reader**
After twelve months under custody
for cosmetic preparation,
each girl in turn went in to the king
and returned the following morning,
but to a different harem,
the one for concubines
under custody of Shaashgaz, the king's eunuch.
She did not return to the king again
unless she was summoned by name. (Esth 2:12, 14)

◊ ◊ ◊

**Narrator:** We remember the **concubines in the royal harem**
**of Belshazzar**

**Reader**
King Belshazzar made a great festival
for a thousand of his nobles,
and he was drinking wine in their presence.

Under the influence of the wine,
Belshazzar commanded that they bring in
the vessels of gold and silver
that his father Nebuchadnezzar had taken
out of the temple in Jerusalem,
so that the king and his nobles,
his wives and his concubines might drink from them.
So they brought in the vessels of gold and silver
that had been taken out of the temple,
the house of God in Jerusalem,
and the king and his nobles,
his wives and his concubines drank from them.
They drank the wine
and praised the gods of gold and silver,
bronze, iron, wood, and stone.
Immediately the fingers of a human hand appeared
and began writing on the plaster of the wall
of the royal palace, next to the lampstand.
Daniel said in the presence of the king,
"You have exalted yourself against the God of heaven!
The temple vessels have been brought in before you,
and you and your nobles,
your wives and your concubines
have been drinking wine from them.
You have praised the gods of silver and gold,
of bronze, iron, wood, and stone,
which do not see or hear or know;
but the God in whose power is your very breath,
and to whom belong all your ways,
you have not honored.
So the hand was sent to you from God's presence. . . .
God has numbered the days of your kingdom
and brought it to an end." (Dan 5:1–5, 17, 23, 24, 26)

◇ ◇ ◇

**Narrator:** We remember **Antiochis, concubine of Antiochus**

**Reader**
The people of Tarsus and of Mallus revolted
because their cities had been given as a present
to Antiochis, the king's concubine. (2 Macc 4:30)

◇ **Points for Shared Reflection**

- How did you feel when you learned that so many male heroes of the Bible had female concubines? When did you first learn of this?

- Why were we not taught about all the women in the lives of the men whom the Bible says were chosen by God? Would that have made a difference in how they were perceived? Does it make a difference now with you?

- Compare the biblical concubine with the contemporary mistress. What are the similarities? What are the differences? What are the justice issues for women involved in both these styles of relationship?

- Concubinage is a form of sexual slavery. What forms of sexual slavery exist in our own society today? What can we do to liberate women from bondage to these forms?

◇ **A Psalm on Being There** (see page 283)

◇ **Prayer**

We look for You,
Shekinah-Shaddai,
for this is what You promised:
I will be with you forever
as an everlasting Presence
in the wisdom of Sophia,
in the shadow of Shekinah,
in the breath of abiding Spirit,
in a covenant of Shalom.
Be there for us
when we need You most
and remain with us forever,
for we are lost without You
and we live on the strength
of Your love,
now and forever.
Amen.

## ◇ A PSALM ON BEING THERE ◇

*Choir 1*   I will be there
for you
to try to do
what you are asking.
I only ask this in return,
that you be there for me.

*Choir 2*   I will be there
for you, my friend,
to be what you are asking:
that I be there for you.

*All*   Will You be there for me, Shaddai,
whenever I call on You?

*Choir 1*   I will be there
for you
through all the sharp edge
of your grieving,
when pain sometimes
becomes so great
you fear your world will end.

*Choir 2*   I will be there
for you, my friend,
whenever a need arises
and you have nowhere else to turn
for comfort and for love.

*All*   Will You be there for me, Shaddai,
whenever I turn to You?

*Choir 1*   I will be there
for you
when all the world
has turned against you,
and will never question
your faithfulness
or your integrity.

*Choir 2*   I will be there
for you, my friend,
when you have turned
against yourself,
helping you gain perspective,
helping you see
the one I see.

By M. T. Winter, Crossroad Pub. Co., © 1991 Medical Mission Sisters      *WomanWisdom* / **283**

*All*    Will You be there for me, Shaddai,
whenever I run to You?

*Choir 1*    Being there
brings stability
to a life that is always
in motion.

*Choir 2*    Being there
brings continuity;
that is the meaning
of love,
the essence
of devotion.

*All*    Where will You be
when I need You, Shaddai?
Will You be there for me?
What will You say?
What will You do?

*Voice*    I will be there
as a loving Presence
in those who are there
for you.

    By M. T. Winter, Crossroad Pub. Co., © 1991 Medical Mission Sisters

## ◇ III ◇
# Memorable Women

# ORPAH

◇ **Scripture Reference**   Ruth 1:1–15

◇ **Biography**

Orpah, a Moabite, married Chilion, the son of Naomi and Elimelech from Bethlehem in Judah. They had emigrated to Moab because of the famine in Judah during the time of the judges. Elimelech died, then Chilion died, leaving his widow childless. Naomi decided to return to Judah. She encouraged Orpah and Ruth, widow of her other son, to stay among their own people. Ruth chose to accompany Naomi. Orpah decided to remain in Moab and returned to her family home.

◇ **Context**

Orpah was the other woman in the well-known story of Ruth and Naomi. She too was a Moabite, a widow, and childless, and quite at home with her mother-in-law and sister-in-law. At first she was determined to go with Naomi and Ruth to live in Judah. She accompanied them part of the way, but at Naomi's insistence, she finally turned back. It may have been the bleak prospects for marriage that finally convinced her, for Naomi was quite clear that she knew of no husband that she might provide. Certainly the thought of a life without children was enough incentive to return to familiar surroundings and try to begin again. Orpah emerges from the narrative as an ordinary woman, a good, solid, sensible woman, the kind that families and cultures depend on from one generation to the next.

In the days when the judges ruled,
there was a famine in the land.
A certain man of Bethlehem in Judah
went to live in the land of Moab
with his wife and his two sons.
The man's name was Elimelech
and his wife's name was Naomi.
The names of his sons were Mahlon and Chilion.
Elimelech died in Moab,
and his sons took Moabite wives.
One of the wives was named Orpah;
the name of the other was Ruth.
They had lived there together about ten years
when Mahlon and Chilion died,
leaving Naomi without a husband and sons.
She prepared to return with her daughters-in-law
to the country from which she had come,
for word was about in Moab
that the famine had come to an end.
They began the journey together,
and on the way to the land of Judah,
Naomi said to her daughters-in-law:
"Go back now to your mother's house,
and may God deal kindly with you,
as you have dealt with my sons and me.
May God grant you security with a husband of your own."
Then she kissed them and they wept,
and the women then said to her,
"We will go with you to your people."
But Naomi said, "Turn back, my daughters.
Why will you go with me?
Do you think I still have sons in my womb
that might become your husbands?
Turn back, my daughters, and go your way.
I am too old to marry again.
Even if I thought there was such a hope,
would you wait until my sons were grown?
Would you then refrain from marrying?
No, my daughters, life has been bitter,
for me more than for you,
because God's hand has turned against me."
The three women wept again.
Then Orpah kissed her mother-in-law
and returned to her own people.

◇ **Points for Shared Reflection**

- Do you think Orpah made the right choice? Why?
- If the choice were yours, would you have gone with Naomi or returned home to your family?
- In the preceding narrative, with which woman do you most identify — Naomi, Ruth, or Orpah — and why?
- Naomi, Ruth, and Orpah, three women from three separate traditions, became a close-knit and loving community. How might these women serve as role models for women-church or another type of female support group to which you or your friends belong?

◇ **A Psalm for Ordinary People**  (see page 289)

◇ **Prayer**

O One Who is in Relationship,
blessed are the bonds
of solidarity and love
that make the community of believers
into a family of friends.
May we be there for each other
in the high times and the low times,
courageously accompanying one another
on our journey into Life.
Be there for us
and with us
at the crossroads of decision,
and make our choices fruitful
and our opportunities clear.
Extraordinary God of ordinary people,
we thank You for Your gentle way
with those who trust in You.
Amen.

# ◇ A PSALM FOR ORDINARY PEOPLE ◇

*All*    What about us? We are ordinary people.
Have You a blessing for us?

*Choir 1*    We are not risk takers,
we who make up the majority
of the community of believers.
We are simply ourselves,
ordinary people,
living ordinary lives.

*Choir 2*    We are not in the headlines
or the deadlines
or the front lines
of the big parade,
but rather prefer
the more mundane conviviality
of the crowd.

*All*    What about us? We are ordinary people.
Have You a blessing for us?

*Choir 1*    You will not find us there
in the glare
of demand and expectation,
although some worlds depend on us,
knowing we will come through.

*Choir 2*    You will not see us
seeking applause,
except from those who love us,
for we are content
with doing our bit
and our best
in our own milieu.

*All*    What about us? We are ordinary people.
Have You a blessing for us?

*Choir 1*    We in the background
nuance and highlight
the Spirit of God among us.

*Choir 2*    We are the backbone,
we are the structure
supporting the goodness around us.

*All*    Remember us, Shaddai. We are ordinary people.
Bless our ordinary lives.

By M. T. Winter, Crossroad Pub. Co., © 1991 Medical Mission Sisters     *WomanWisdom* / **289**

# HEROINE OF THEBEZ

◇ **Scripture Reference**   Judg 9:50–56

◇ **Biography**

Nothing is known of the anonymous woman who killed the tyrant Abimelech by crushing his skull with a millstone, thereby liberating Thebez.

◇ **Context**

Abimelech was the son of Gideon by his Canaanite concubine who lived in Shechem. Gideon, one of the major judges of Israel, had seventy other sons by his many wives. In his bid for power, Abimelech killed all of his brothers but the youngest, Jotham, and in violation of the tribal confederacy, he prevailed upon his Canaanite relatives to make him king. Abimelech's kingship was only local. He ruled over Shechem and several of the surrounding towns, including Thebez, until they revolted. He retaliated by razing Shechem and setting siege to Thebez.

The people of Thebez barricaded themselves in the *migdal*, usually translated "strong tower" but perhaps more accurately called "fortress-temple of the Strong One," that is, of the deity El. Abimelech had destroyed Shechem's stronghold by fire and was preparing to do the same in Thebez when he was stopped by a woman. To avoid the shame of dying by the hand of a woman, he had his armor-bearer kill him. Nothing is known of this anonymous heroine of Thebez. Was she Jewish or was she Canaanite? Was she a believer in Elohim, the God of Israel, or El, the Canaanite deity, or an integration of both? She accomplished what warriors had failed to do, yet she is known to us simply as one of the countless courageous women who wove their experience into the strong fabric of life during the time of the judges in Israel.

◇ **Lectionary Reading**

Abimelech marched to Thebez,
then besieged and stormed the city.
All the men and women, all the local leaders
fled to the fortified tower
standing within the city walls,
barricaded themselves inside it,
and climbed up to the roof.
When Abimelech came to set fire to the tower,
a woman threw a millstone on his head,
crushing Abimelech's skull.
Calling his armor-bearer to him, he said,
"Draw your sword and kill me,
so it will not be said about me,
'He was killed by a woman.'"
The young man stabbed him, and he died.
When the Israelites saw that Abimelech was dead,
they went safely to their homes.
So God repaid Abimelech
for murdering his seventy brothers.

◇ **Points for Shared Reflection**

- In your personal or professional life, have you ever been resented because you were a woman? Share your experience.

- Has anything you have done ever been resented, or disparaged, or made light of, or ridiculed, or rejected, because you were a woman? Share your experience.

- Have you ever been deprived of opportunity or advancement in your religious or professional life because you were a woman? Share your experience.

- Are there Abimelechs in your life who have forced you to wall off a piece of yourself and who are keeping you under siege? Share only what you feel comfortable sharing and feel free to ask for prayers for your liberation.

◇ **Because-I-Am-a-Woman Psalm** (see page 293)

◇ **Prayer**

Can we share a moment, please,
woman to Woman, friend to Friend?
There are things I need to ask for:
strength to make it through tomorrow,
time to make it through today,
healing of memories from the past,
courage to deal with life's frustrations,
patience in times of discrimination,
forgiveness for those who patronize me,
gentleness, just because I need it,
compassion because so many others need it.
Be with me now and when I need You most.
And thank You for listening.
Amen.

## ◇ BECAUSE-I-AM-A-WOMAN PSALM ◇

*Voice* I couldn't go to certain schools,
*All* because I am a woman.

*Voice* I had to follow different rules,
*All* because I am a woman.

*Voice* I had to act a certain way,
*All* because I am a woman.

*Voice* They never gave me equal pay,
*All* because I am a woman.

*Voice* I was the one they would harass,
*All* because I am a woman.

*Voice* I was the one who was second class,
*All* because I am a woman.

*Voice* Religion was especially rough,
*All* because I am a woman.

*Voice* I've never felt quite good enough,
*All* because I am a woman.

*Voice* Then God, Shaddai, reached out to me,
*All* because I am a woman.

*Voice* And there were things I learned to see,
*All* because I am a woman.

*Voice* Things I am committed to,
*All* because I am a woman.

*Voice* Things that I intend to do,
*All* because I am a woman.

*Voice* God made me and I am good,
*All* because I am a woman.

*Voice* I share in God's own Motherhood,
*All* because I am a woman.

*Voice* The image of God is image of me,
*All* because I am a woman.

*Voice* God will give the victory,
*All* because I am a woman.

*Voice* God said, Daughter, don't be sad
because you are a woman.

*All* And I said, I am very glad,
because I am a woman!

# WITCH OF ENDOR

◇ **Scripture Reference**    1 Sam 28:3–25

◇ **Biography**

The woman at Endor was a sorcerer who could conjure up the dead. She risked her life to call up Samuel at Saul's request, for Saul himself had banished such practices from Israel. No biographical information has been found to identify her.

◇ **Context**

Saul was desperate. He had lost religious power and he felt forsaken by God. About to face the Philistines in armed combat, he consulted God concerning his chances of success, but God did not answer. In his earlier religious fervor, Saul had outlawed all forms of sorcery and divination, but now he turned to what he had previously denounced. The word he received took all the spirit out of him, for it confirmed his own condemnation. It is difficult to put a label on the woman he consulted. Designations such as witch, sorcerer, shaman, diviner, wizard, necromancer, clairvoyant, medium, magician had shades of meaning lost to us now. The sweeping biblical denunciation of all that fell beyond the scope of its own definition makes it impossible for us to separate authentic experience and its expression from the truly idolatrous and demonic.

This story confirms the presence and the importance of sorcery and similar practices in the lives of the Israelite people, particularly at times of personal and national crisis. When Saul requested a medium, his servants knew exactly where to find one. It also suggests a confidence in women at such times. Saul specifically requested a woman, even though other texts clearly indicate that such practitioners were also male. In Hebrew the woman of Endor is called *ba'alat 'ob*, which means "mistress of the spirits," whereas elsewhere such professionals are called *'obot*, "raisers of spirits."

The woman of Endor was experienced and skilled in her craft. Her reputation enabled Saul's people to find her, and the word used to describe her to others confirms what they found. The woman herself conveys a rich tapestry of character and feeling in the narrative concerning her. To the stranger she was a law-abiding citizen. To the sincere seeker she was a professional who was both competent and honest. When she saw more clearly, she was terrified, and yet she spoke her truth. Careful to protect herself from self-incrimination, she did not name the shade she conjured up but left that to the one who sought him. Suddenly she shifted roles, moving adroitly from conjurer to caregiver. Concerned for Saul's well-being, she sympathetically offered him something to eat. Concerned for her own personal safety, she killed her fatted calf and prepared a special meal. Saul kept his word not to harm her. It is not unreasonable to suspect that after her experience with Saul, word would have spread and she would have been particularly distinguished among her peers.

Now Samuel was dead
and was buried in Ramah.
All Israel mourned for him.
Early on, Saul had expelled from the land
all mediums and sorcerers.
Now the Philistine forces were assembled at Shunem.
Saul and his troops were encamped at Gilboa.
When Saul saw the Philistine army,
terror filled his heart,
and he turned to God for counsel,
but God did not answer him,
either through oracle or prophet or dream.
So Saul said to his servants,
"Find me a woman who conjures up spirits
that I might consult with her."
His servants confided to him,
"There is a medium at Endor."
Saul disguised himself with a change of clothes
and went to see the woman,
accompanied by two of his men.
He came to her under cover of night, saying,
"Conjure up a spirit for me,
the one I will name for you."
The woman said to him,
"Surely you know what Saul has done.
He has banished all sorcerers from the land.
Are you setting a trap for me?
Do you want to have me killed?"
But Saul swore to her this oath,
"As God lives, no punishment will come to you
for what you are about to do."
Then the woman said,
"Whom shall I call up for you?"
And he replied, "Samuel."
Then the woman recognized Saul.
She let out a cry
and turned and said,
"Why have you deceived me?
I know that you are Saul!"
The king said, "Have no fear,
just tell me what you see."
"I see a ghost rising out of the ground,"
the woman said to Saul.

"What does he look like?" he asked her.
"I see an old man wrapped in a robe."
Then Saul knew it was Samuel,
and he bowed to the ground and did homage.
Samuel said to Saul,
"Why have you disturbed me by bringing me back?"
Saul answered, "I am greatly distressed,
for the Philistines are warring against me
and God has turned away from me
and answers me no more,
neither by prophets nor by dreams.
So I have summoned you to advise me."
Samuel said, "Why do you come to me
if God has turned against you?
God is doing what God foretold to me
and is tearing your sovereignty out of your hand
to give it to your neighbor, David.
Because you did not obey God's voice
when you failed to inflict the wrath of God
on Amalek, you will pay for it now.
God will deliver you and Israel
into the hands of the Philistines.
And I say to you, tomorrow
you and your sons will die."
Saul fell to the ground,
overcome with fear
and faint from lack of food,
for he had not eaten all day and all night.
Seeing his terror, the woman said,
"Because I have obeyed your command to me,
I have taken my life in my hands.
Listen now to your servant.
Let me set before you a morsel of bread,
that you may eat
and gain strength for your journey."
But Saul refused.
"I will not eat," he said to her,
but the woman and his servants insisted
until he gave in to them.
The woman slaughtered a fatted calf,
baked some unleavened loaves of bread
and set these before Saul and his servants,
and they ate,
and then rose
and went into the night.

⬦ **Points for Shared Reflection**

- What do you know about witches? Do you think they are good or bad? Would you be willing to get to know one?

- Saul privately embraced something he had publicly condemned. Discuss the ethical and moral obligations of those who write the laws. Discuss also the importance of practicing what we preach.

- Why would Saul specifically have requested a woman? Are there times when women, or men, prefer to relate to a woman? When? Are there times when you specifically request a woman? What are those times?

- We often condemn what we do not understand, particularly in the religious arena. What are some religious practices you condemn but do not fully understand?

⬦ **A Psalm in Search of the Goddess** (see page 299)

⬦ **Prayer**

Goddess of Wisdom
and Earth
and Sky
Who lives in the songs
and memories
of countless generations,
how manifold are Your ways.
How dare we say we know You
when we do not even know the names
our sisters know You by.
Instill in us a deep desire
to open ourselves to Your wisdom
and to entrust ourselves to Your grace,
that we may follow wherever You lead
in the name of Love.
Amen.

# ◇ A PSALM IN SEARCH OF THE GODDESS ◇

*Chorus*  Who are You, O Holy One?
How have Your daughters named You?

*Voice*  I Am Shekinah,
your Dwelling Place,
your All-Embracing Presence.

*All*  Draw us to You, Shekinah,
that we may live and move and be
within Your blessedness.

*Chorus*  Who are You, O Holy One?
How have Your daughters named You?

*Voice*  I Am the Prehistoric Goddess.
I have many names
and myriad manifestations.

*All*  O Prehistoric Goddess,
reveal to us Your names
so we can call You when we need You.

*Chorus*  Who are You, O Holy One?
How have Your daughters named You?

*Voice*  I Am Ishtar and Inanna.
The ancient Near East praised Me
from generation to generation.

*All*  O Ishtar and Inanna,
image of the Holy One,
we praise Her when we praise You.

*Chorus*  Who are You, O Holy One?
How have Your daughters named You?

*Voice*  I Am Sophia,
Wisdom, Discernment.
Who loves Me knows My ways.

*All*  Inhabit our hearts, Sophia.
Teach us to know Your ways.

*Chorus*  Who are You, O Holy One?
How have Your daughters named You?

*Voice*  I Am Isis of Egypt,
manifest Wisdom,
eye of Re the sun god,
Universal Goddess.

By M. T. Winter, Crossroad Pub. Co., © 1991 Medical Mission Sisters         *WomanWisdom* / **299**

*All*    Isis, show us Wisdom
in everything and in everyone.

*Chorus*    Who are You, O Holy One?
How have Your daughters named You?

*Voice*    I Am Hathor, Egypt's Golden One.
Look for Me in the sycamore.
Look for Me in the sky.

*All*    Hathor, help us to cherish the trees
of the forest
and reach for the sky.

*Chorus*    Who are You, O Holy One?
How have Your daughters named You?

*Voice*    I Am Shaddai.
I Am Nurturing Mother.
You know Me by My name.

*All*    You are a Mother to us, Shaddai.
We know You and we love You.

*Chorus*    Who are You, O Holy One?
How have Your daughters named You?

*Voice*    I Am Cybele,
the Great Mother Goddess
of ancient Anatolia.

*All*    Fill us, Cybele, Great Mother Goddess,
with Your long-lived nurturing Spirit.

*Chorus*    Who are You, O Holy One?
How have Your daughters named You?

*Voice*    I Am Nut
of the sky, of Egypt,
Goddess of Affection.

*All*    Nut, we call upon Your name
and long for Your affection.

*Chorus*    Who are You, O Holy One?
How have Your daughters named You?

*Voice*    I Am Shalom,
River of Peace.
I Am Wholeness and Well-Being.

*All*    We pray to You, for You are Shalom,
the Fullness of our being.

**300** / *WomanWisdom*    By M. T. Winter, Crossroad Pub. Co., © 1991 Medical Mission Sisters

| Chorus | Who are You, O Holy One? |
| | How have Your daughters named You? |

| Voice | I Am Hera and Athene, |
| | Aphrodite and Artemis, |
| | Demeter and Persephone — |
| | the Goddesses of Greece. |

| All | The more we call You by these names, |
| | the more we will come to know You. |

| Chorus | Who are You, O Holy One? |
| | How have Your daughters named You? |

| Voice | I Am Anath-Astarte, |
| | and Lady Asherah of the Sea |
| | from the biblical land of Canaan. |

| All | Anath and Asherah, forgive us, |
| | for all we have done to You. |

| Chorus | Who are You, O Holy One? |
| | How have Your daughters named You? |

| Voice | I Am Gaia, |
| | Earth Mother, |
| | Who was and is the earth. |

| All | We love You, Gaia, Goddess of Earth, |
| | and we make our home within You. |

| Voice | I Am Gods and Goddesses. |
| | My stories and images differ. |
| | I Am many manifestations, |
| | but I Am One and the Same. |
| | I, Shaddai, created a world |
| | where nobody knows My Name. |

| All | We praise You, God of Heaven and Earth, |
| | and call You Goddess of Heaven and Earth |
| | as we come to know Your name. |

# WOMAN OF TEKOA

◇ **Scripture Reference**   2 Sam 14:1–24

◇ **Biography**

We know that this unnamed woman from Tekoa lived during David's reign, and we can conclude from her narrative that she was courageous, convincing, articulate, and honest. More specific biographical data is unknown.

◇ **Context**

Absalom, David's son, had been in exile in Geshur for three years because he had killed his brother Amnon for raping their sister Tamar. David had finally become reconciled to Amnon's death and was secretly longing for Absalom's return. Joab, commander of David's army, sensed what the king was feeling but did not dare to address the matter directly, so he arranged a morality play of sorts and engaged a woman from Tekoa, a village just south of Bethlehem, to play the leading role. The remainder of the narrative unfolds on two levels. The woman pretends to be a widow whose story about her son who murdered his brother differs from David's story in detail but is parallel to it in meaning. In getting the king to solve her problem concerning the surviving son, she also gets him to solve his own problem concerning Absalom. David finally saw through the subterfuge and insisted on knowing who was behind it. The woman told him it was Joab, and that she had agreed under coercion to go along with the ruse. Instead of being angry with Joab, David gave him permission to bring Absalom home. The woman must have been an able performer, because even in the narrative she deftly switched roles, slipping between fiction and reality with the skill of a survivor.

If her story had been true, she had every right as a widow to bring her case before the king, but because it was not, she risked the king's wrath by her impertinence, and the penalty could have been death. The woman from Tekoa had been asked to play a role that had been devised for her, but she skillfully rewrote the script to include the more critical roles of mediator and facilitator of reconciliation. The phrase describing her, *'issa hakama*, has been variously translated as "wise woman," "quick-witted," or by implication from the narrative, "one who can act." She was more than a skilled performer, however, as the analysis above indicates. Her qualities included an ability to sense a situation, seize it, and turn it to her advantage; ability to adapt to a changing situation; and ability to get people to work with her, not against her. She must have been fairly intuitive and discerning, truly a woman of wisdom.

◇ **Lectionary Reading**

Joab, son of David's sister Zeruiah
and commander of David's army,
knew that David was preoccupied
with Absalom his son
[who had been hiding out for three years
since killing his brother Amnon].
Joab sent to Tekoa for a woman of wisdom.
"Pretend to be a mourner," he told her,
"and put on your mourning garments.
Do not anoint yourself with oil
but behave like a woman who has been grieving
for many days for the dead.
Go to the king and say this to him,"
and he told her what to say.
When the woman of Tekoa came to the king,
she fell to the ground and did homage.
"Help me, my lord!" she pleaded.
"What troubles you?" asked David.
And the woman told this story.

"Alas, I am a widow, my husband is dead.
Two sons had I, your servant;
they fought with each other out in the field
and one struck the other and killed him.
My clan has risen up against me, demanding,
'Surrender your son that we may avenge
his murdered brother's blood,
even if we destroy the heir.'
They would quench my one remaining ember,
leaving me and my husband
with neither remnant nor name
to light the face of the earth."
Then David said to the woman,
"Go home, I will deal with this myself
and speak on your behalf."
The woman of Tekoa said to the king,
"The guilt be on me and my ancestors' house;
let the king and his throne be guiltless."
"If anyone should threaten you," David replied,
"bring him here to me
and he will never hurt you again."
"Remember, my lord, to call on your God
to stay the hand of the avenger of blood
so that my son may live," she said.
"As God lives,
not a single hair of your surviving son
shall fall to the ground," said David.
"Please, let your servant speak yet another word
to my lord the king," she persisted.
"Speak," said David, and she did.
"Why has the king,
who in deciding for me convicts himself,
not brought his banished son home again
for the benefit of all the people?
We must all die;
we are all like water
poured out upon the ground
which can never be gathered up again.
Neither does God bring back the dead,
but God will bring back an exile.
Make plans then to bring the exile home.
I have come to say this to my lord the king
because people have made me afraid.
I said, I will speak to the king.
Perhaps the king will fulfill my request.
Perhaps the king will hear my words

and save me and my son from being cut off
from the heritage of God,
and in speaking the word that sets me at rest,
the king will discern between good and evil,
for the king is like the angel of God.
Now may your God be with you!"
Then the king said this to the woman.
"Reveal to me whatever I ask you."
"Let my lord the king speak," she replied.
"Is the hand of Joab behind all of this?"
he asked, and the woman responded,
"Yes, it was Joab who sent me here
and who put these words in my mouth.
He disguised his intent,
but my lord has wisdom
like the wisdom of the angel of God
to discern all things on earth."
The king then turned to Joab and said,
"Very well, your request is granted.
Go and bring Absalom home."
Joab prostrated himself on the ground
and did homage and blessed the king and said,
"Today your servant has found favor before you,
for the king has granted my request."
So Joab set out for Geshur
and returned to Jerusalem with Absalom.
"Let him stay in his own house," David said,
"he is not to come into my presence."
So Absalom retired to his own house
and was not received by his father.

◇ **Points for Shared Reflection**

- Men have often tried to put words in women's mouths or write their scripts for them. Has this ever happened to you? Share the circumstances, if it has.

- Joab did not want to confront the king himself, so he approached him indirectly, through a woman. Tell about a time when you were placed in the position of mediator or go-between by a man.

- Many women have the gift of discernment or a strong sense of intuition that enables them to see beneath the surface to the heart of things. Are you strongly intuitive? Have you the gift of discernment?

- Women are skilled at effecting reconciliation. Is this a particular skill you can claim? Name some areas involving women in religion that are in need of reconciliation.

◇ **A Psalm Celebrating Wisdom**  (see page 307)

◇ **Prayer**

O Wise One
Who waits for those
who come in search of Sophia
in order to bestow the gift of wisdom
and a truly discerning heart.
You come to us
when we come to You
and together we strive
to become one heart,
one mind,
one will,
one spirit.
Truly, the gift of wisdom
is the gift to be one with God,
now and forever.
Amen.

# ◇ A PSALM CELEBRATING WISDOM ◇

*Choir 1*  They are wise
who can get to the heart
of an issue or a person.

*All*  Make us women* of wisdom, Sophia,
women who see to the heart.

*Choir 2*  They are wise
who are not afraid
to trust their intuition.

*All*  Make us women of wisdom, Sophia,
women of intuition.

*Choir 1*  They are wise
who know what is real
and know when one is only pretending.

*All*  Make us women of wisdom, Sophia,
who are real and not pretending.

*Choir 2*  They are wise
who can empathize
with another's situation.

*All*  Make us women of wisdom, Sophia,
women who can empathize.

*Choir 1*  They are wise
who can clearly discern
the path they ought to follow.

*All*  Make us women of wisdom, Sophia,
women who are clearly discerning.

*Choir 2*  They are wise
who use their heads
when others around them panic.

*All*  Make us women of wisdom, Sophia,
women who seldom panic.

*Choir 1*  They are wise
who listen well
and are not afraid to be honest.

*All*  Make us women of wisdom, Sophia,
women unafraid to be honest.

---

*Inclusive groups may substitute "people" for "women" in the response marked for *All*.

By M. T. Winter, Crossroad Pub. Co., © 1991 Medical Mission Sisters     *WomanWisdom* **/ 307**

*Choir 2*   They are wise
who are vulnerable
and can open their heart to another.

*All*   Make us women of wisdom, Sophia,
women open to others.

*Choir 1*   They are wise
who are warm and loving,
who truly care about people.

*All*   Make us women of wisdom, Sophia,
women who care about people.

*Choir 2*   They are wise
who dwell in God
and are filled with God's own Spirit.

*All*   Make us women of wisdom, Sophia,
women filled with Your Spirit.

   By M. T. Winter, Crossroad Pub. Co., © 1991 Medical Mission Sisters

# WISE WOMAN OF ABEL-BETH-MAACAH

⬦ **Scripture Reference**   2 Sam 20:14–22

⬦ **Biography**

A wise and courageous woman in Abel-beth-maacah, a fortified city in northern Israel, was instrumental in lifting the city's siege during the reign of David. Scripture does not record her name.

⬦ **Context**

Abel-beth-maacah was a center of conservatism where the best of Israel's traditions were preserved. It was called "a mother in Israel" because surrounding villages depended on it. When Joab laid siege to the city, he did so in order to contain and defeat a minor insurrection before it could spread to the rest of the Northern Kingdom and pose a major threat to David's reign. Conventional wisdom said that the elimination of an enemy of the nation, in this case Sheba and his troops, justified the destruction of an innocent city and its inhabitants, including women and children. However, a woman of Abel-beth-maacah, where so much historic wisdom was preserved, challenged that view with some intuitive wisdom of her own. Why waste your heritage? she asked. She meant, why destroy a center of so much tradition, of so much value to the nation? Why shed innocent blood? Why kill us? It would only escalate the problem. Many more people would be incensed and would join the counterforce against him. Exactly what was he trying to accomplish? There was more than one way to achieve a goal. Her womanwisdom found the appropriate strategy to satisfy both Joab's agenda and her own. She had to confront and convince her own people, but before long, Sheba's head was thrown over the wall and Abel-beth-maacah was saved. Ironically, the city's name means "mourning the house of Maacah." Maacah was the name of Absalom's mother, David's wife.

◊ **Lectionary Reading**

David said to Abishai,
"Sheba son of Bichri will do us more harm than Absalom.
Take forces and pursue him
or he will find fortified cities for himself
and manage to escape from us."
So Joab and his brother Abishai pursued Sheba son of Bichri.
(2 Sam 20:6, 10)

Sheba passed through Israel to the city of Abel-beth-maacah,
and all of his forces assembled around him
and followed him inside.
Joab's army put the city under siege,
set a ramp against its rampart
and began battering the wall to break it down.
A woman of wisdom called out from the city.
"Listen! Come here. Tell Joab I said, 'I want to speak to you.'"
Joab approached and the woman asked,
"Are you Joab?" He answered, "I am."
"Listen to the words of your servant," she said.
"I am listening," he replied.
"They used to say in the old days,
'Let them ask in Abel and in Dan
whether anything has been discontinued
which the faithful in Israel ordained.'
I am a peaceable and faithful Israelite.
Why do you destroy a mother-city of Israel
and devour God's heritage?"
Joab defended himself. "Far be it from me to devour or destroy.
That is not the issue here.

Sheba son of Bichri of the hills of Ephraim has turned against King David.
Surrender him and I will withdraw."
The woman said to Joab,
"His head shall be thrown over the wall to you."
Then the woman explained to her people the wisdom of her plan,
and they beheaded Sheba and threw his head over the wall to Joab.
So the Israelites blew the trumpet and the troops
dispersed from the city and everyone went home.
Joab returned to Jerusalem and reported to the king.

◇ **Points for Shared Reflection**

• Women usually seek a solution where everybody wins. Is this your style when groups are divided or opinions differ? Can you recall a situation where such an approach was particularly effective?

• Why was the heroine of this story a woman of wisdom? Analyze her approach to conflict resolution and her personal style. What have you learned from her?

• Women are often accused of not using their heads. Men are often accused of being too much into their heads. Would you care to comment? In this narrative, a woman uses her head and a man loses his. What is the message here?

• A woman accomplished what a besieging army and a besieged male leadership could not do. Can you think of a similar instance in modern times? In your own life?

◇ **A Psalm for Women under Siege** (see page 312)

◇ **Prayer**

When our back is up against the wall,
we seek You, Shalom,
to empower us,
to encourage us,
to enlighten us
with a vision of hope,
a pledge of support,
a promise of peace
in the midst of all the power
amassed to besiege us.
Then peace will descend
like a singing bird,
like a lilting word,
and our moment of liberation
will come in the name of Shalom.
Amen.

*Choir 1*  When we get the job we have always wanted
and think we cannot do it:

*All*  Empower us, Shalom.

*Choir 2*  When we get the job we have never wanted
and know we cannot do it:

*All*  Strengthen us, Shalom.

*Choir 1*  When so much more is demanded of us
because of our female gender:

*All*  Energize us, Shalom.

*Choir 2*  When no opportunity is given to us
because of our female gender:

*All*  Open a path, Shalom.

*Choir 1*  When we have no resources and cannot manage
to support ourselves and our children:

*All*  Provide for us, Shalom.

*Choir 2*  When there is no recourse and no one
to hear our case or plead our cause:

*All*  Intercede for us, Shalom.

*Choir 1*  When we have a prophetic message
but are terrified of speaking:

*All*  Give us a word of Shalom.

*Choir 2*  When we have a prophetic task
but no support or affirmation:

*All*  Encourage an act of Shalom.

*Choir 1*  When our back is up against the wall
and patriarchy surrounds us:

*All*  Lead us forth in Shalom.

*Choir 2*  When our insecurities rise up
and threaten to defeat us:

*All*  Reach out to us in Shalom.

*Choir 1*  It is You, Shalom, Who liberate
those under siege, Who end a war.

*Choir 2*  Peace frees those held hostage.
That's what Shalom is for.

*All*  To You be glory and praise, Shalom,
now and forevermore.

  By M. T. Winter, Crossroad Pub. Co., © 1991 Medical Mission Sisters

# WIDOW OF ZAREPHATH

◇ **Scripture Reference**    1 Kings 17:8–24

◇ **Biography**

An impoverished widow who lived in Zarephath, a port city on the Phoenician coast between the cities of Tyre and Sidon, gave hospitality to the prophet Elijah at the height of a devastating famine. She shared what little she had with him and in return he performed two miracles. Her meager supply of grain was continually replenished and her son was restored to life.

◇ **Context**

There was a famine in the land of Israel, but God provided for the prophet Elijah. Ravens brought him bread and meat in the morning and in the evening, and he drank from a stream east of the Jordan until its waters dried up. Then God sent Elijah to the Phoenician widow in Zarephath (or Sarepta), saying she would provide for him. In a series of life-giving exchanges, he gave her the means whereby she was able to prepare food to keep them going, and he restored to life the child who was her life, just as she sustained life in him. It is true that the widow needed Elijah, but the prophet first needed her. Desperately thirsty, he asked her for water. Hungry, he asked her for bread. Her generous response was rewarded with an undiminished supply. Both miracles have parallels in the Elisha cycle in Second Kings, where the widow's jar of oil keeps flowing and a dead son is restored to life. These are common folkloric themes and

**313**

may represent some legendary embellishment of the facts. Some commentators suggest that the boy did not die but was unconscious or in a coma. Whatever the specifics, the widow and the prophet were mutually dependent on each other to the point of maintaining life. That a widow was chosen to provide for the prophet is a particularly poignant point, for she herself had no provisions and no one to provide for her. A childless widow was a family responsibility in terms of securing an heir, but a widowed mother was on her own and had to struggle to survive. Nevertheless God sent the prophet to the woman so that he might be nourished by her. This relationship between the religious figure and the woman should not be overlooked.

◇ **Lectionary Reading**

The word of God came to Elijah,
the Tishbite of Tishbe in Gilead, and said,
"Go to Zarephath and stay there.
It is in the region of Sidon.
A widow will give you food to eat,
according to my instruction."
So Elijah set out for Zarephath,
and when he reached the city gate,
he saw a widow gathering sticks.
Elijah called to her,
"Please give me a sip of water,
I am desperate for a drink."
As she was about to do it,
he called to her again.
"Please give me a scrap of bread to eat."
"As God lives," the woman said,
"I have nothing baked
and only a handful of meal in a jar
and a little oil in a jug.
Here I am, gathering sticks
so that I might prepare one final meal
to eat with my son before we die."
Elijah said, "Do not be afraid.
Go do as you have said.
Only first make me a tiny cake
and bring it here to me,
before you make something for you and your son.
For thus says the God of Israel:
The jar of meal will not be emptied
and the jug of oil will not run dry
until God sends rain to wash the earth."
The woman did as Elijah had said,

and she and he and her whole household
ate for many days.
While Elijah was still in the widow's house,
her son became critically ill
and was on the verge of dying.
The widow cried out to Elijah,
"What have I done,
O prophet of God?
Have you come to bring my sin to remembrance
and to cause the death of my son?"
"Give me your son," he said to her,
and he took the boy from his mother's arms
and carried him into the upper room
where he himself had been lodging
and laid him on his own bed.
Then Elijah cried out,
"O God my God,
why have you brought this calamity
on the widow with whom I am staying?
Will you take away her son?"
Then he stretched himself upon the child
three times, and cried aloud to God:
"Let life return to this child again!"
God listened to Elijah
and the child was fully alive again.
Then Elijah took him and brought him down
and gave him to his mother.
"Your son will live," Elijah said.
"Now I know," the woman replied,
"that you are a prophet of God
and that God's word in your mouth is truth."

◇ **Points for Shared Reflection**

- The elements of bread and water and oil are sacramental symbols. Here in the hands of a woman, they give life to God's anointed. What parallels can you draw with the present? Has something similar happened within your own experience?

- We are reminded of the widow's mite in the Gospel of Luke. This widow too gave generously of the little she had. In what ways might you incorporate this biblical principle into your own life? Do you believe that God will give back to you whatever you need to survive?

- In times of extreme deprivation, people need each other. When was the last time you turned to another for something essential to your physical or spiritual or emotional life?

- The widow's story is all about the basic necessities of life. Have you thought about getting back to basics? What would that entail? What would you have to do differently? In what ways would you have to change, both inside and out?

◇ **A Psalm about Getting Back to Basics** (see page 317)

◇ **Prayer**

Help us get back to basics,
O Heart and Soul of Our Existence,
the necessities of life,
the necessities of love,
the realities of joy and sorrow.
Assuage our hunger and thirst for You
and our craving for justice and peace.
Be staff for the journey
inward and outward
and rest when our spirits falter,
for You are our Hope,
You are our Strength,
You are our Ongoing Life,
today and forever.
Amen.

# ◇ A PSALM ABOUT GETTING BACK TO BASICS ◇

*Choir 1* It is time to get back to basics.
    We seem to have lost our touch.

*Choir 2* We are satiated with superfluity:
    too often, too many, too much.

*Choir 1* Give us some bread for the journey,
    dry, with a bit of crust,

*Choir 2* a map for the pilgrimage inward,
    and a guru we can trust.

*Choir 1* Give us some life-giving water
    from a clear, existential spring.

*Choir 2* See that we have a vision,
    and a song that we can sing.

*Choir 1* Give us strength for the struggle,
    and hope, to move us along,

*Choir 2* the capacity to forgive ourselves
    and those who do us wrong.

*Choir 1* Empower us to empower others,
    for that's what it's all about,

*Choir 2* and may our resources never diminish,
    our energy never give out.

*Choir 1* Inspire us so that we might know
    the penetrating power of prayer.

*Choir 2* Touch us in ways that help us feel
    Your providential care.

*Choir 1* Let us live life with a passion
    for justice and integrity.

*Choir 2* Bless us with compassion
    and the wisdom to let life be.

*Choir 1* May the love we feel find all the right words
    forever, in a poem,

*Choir 2* and may we find the perfect friend
    with whom we are at home.

*All* To get back to basics, the rules are few.
    It means basically, God, getting back to You.

By M. T. Winter, Crossroad Pub. Co., © 1991 Medical Mission Sisters     *WomanWisdom* / 317

# PROPHET'S WIDOW

◇ **Scripture Reference**   2 Kings 4:1–7

◇ **Biography**

The prophet's widow was an ordinary woman who had fallen on hard times. With the death of her husband she was deep in debt and had no way to pay her bills or to support herself and her two children. She pleaded with Elisha to prevent her creditor from confiscating her children as slaves and he gave her a bottomless jar with just enough oil to meet all her needs.

◇ **Context**

This narrative is the first of a series of miracle stories with independent traditions involving the prophet Elisha recorded in the Second Book of Kings. The stories focus on Elisha's legendary involvement with ordinary people and suggest a continuity with Elijah's concern for the destitute and the dead. In this pericope, the widow, whose late husband had been a member of a prophetic guild, was on the verge of losing everything when Elisha intervened. He had known her husband, although he was not associated with the man's prophetic community. Elisha came up with a strategic plan for helping the woman help herself and a miracle was performed, not by Elisha, but by the widow. Through God's power, she was able to take charge of her situation and do what was necessary to provide for herself and for her children.

◇ **Lectionary Reading**

The wife of a member of the company of prophets
cried out one day to Elisha,
"Your servant my husband is dead.
You know that he was a God-fearing man,
but now a creditor is about to take my two children
and make them his slaves."
Elisha said to her,
"What shall I do for you?
What do you have in the house?"
She answered, "Only a jar of oil."
Then Elisha said to the widow,
"Go, borrow from your neighbors
all the empty jars they can find.
Then go in the house
and shut the door behind you and your children.
Pour oil into those empty jars.
When each jar is full, set it aside."
So she left Elisha and shut the door
and began filling the jars.
Her children kept bringing jars to her
and she kept right on pouring.
When the jars were full, she said to her son,
"Bring me another jar."
"There are no more," he said to her,
and then the oil stopped flowing.
She went to tell the prophet of God
and Elisha said to her,
"Go sell the oil and pay your debts,
and you and your children live on the rest."

◇ **Points for Shared Reflection**

- The widow was so economically dependent upon her husband that she was left destitute when he died. Reflect on this in light of women's experience in general. Has this been true of anyone in your family?

- Elisha helped a woman in need by helping her help herself. How might you help someone in need in your community in this way?

- A completely helpless widow was suddenly able to take charge of her situation when given the means to do so. Has this ever happened to you? Have you ever wished it had?

- Do you sometimes feel so poured out that there is nothing left of you to spare? How can the widow's experience be of help to you at such times?

◇ **A Psalm for Helping Us Help Ourselves** (see page 321)

◇ **Prayer**

Helper of All Who Are Helpless,
we call on You
in times of stress
and in times of devastation.
Pick up the broken pieces
of our hearts, our homes, our history
and restore them to the way they were,
or give us the means of starting over
when everything seems lost.
O God, Our Help in Ages Past,
we place all our hope in You.
Amen.

## ◇ A PSALM FOR HELPING US HELP OURSELVES ◇

*Choir 1*   Help me, O God, to help myself
when I feel so utterly helpless,
when I am deprived of human help
and human consolation.

*Choir 2*   Help me help others help themselves
in whatever ways are helpful,
wherever Your grace is present
and the occasion justifies.

*Choir 1*   If You intervene with miracles,
I will wait until they happen.
Inspire me and miracles
may start to come from me.

*Choir 2*   If I give the hungry bread,
they will be hungry again tomorrow,
but if I give them a field and seed,
they will grow their own supplies.

*Choir 1*   Exercise power over me
and I will passively follow.
Empower me and I will lead others
to come with me to You.

*Choir 2*   A bunk bed in a shelter
is a one night stand for someone,
but a marketable skill and a living wage
takes a household off the streets.

*Choir 1*   Replace a tree with another tree
and the forest lives forever.
Replace a smile with another smile
and the joy goes on and on.

*Choir 2*   Give love and you will have love
around and within you forever.
We truly love others only when
we have learned to love ourselves.

*All*   Help us, O God, to help ourselves,
and help us help others help themselves.
Praise to You, God our Helper.

# SHUNAMMITE WOMAN

◇ **Scripture Reference**    2 Kings 4:8–37; 8:1–6

◇ **Biography**

The Shunammite woman was wealthy, childless, and married to an elderly man. Because of her admiration for Elisha, she became his benefactor and provided the prophet with room and board whenever he was in the area. In return, Elisha performed a miracle. She gave birth to a son and when the child died, Elisha restored him to life. At the prophet's urging, she relocated to Philistine territory during the seven years of famine. Because of her past association with Elisha, her house, land, and lost income from the land were restored to her on her return.

◇ **Context**

The Shunammite woman's story is the focal point of the anthology of miracle stories featuring the prophet Elisha in chapter 4 of the Second Book of Kings. For a time their lives were interwoven with reciprocal significance. The well-to-do Shunammite made a home in her house for the itinerant prophet, and in return, Elisha made a home of her house for her by promising her a child. The boy died and was brought back to life by Elisha, restoring her inner world. Later on in the book and in her life, her confiscated property and possessions were returned because of her association with the prophet, restoring her outer world. The Shunammite's story is a story of loss and restoration. It is also a story of her coming into her own. She offered the prophet hospitality, not only because she admired him, but primarily because she wanted to be included in his sphere of blessing, and the blessing she received was the unfolding of a dimension of herself. She stood in the background, bound by formality, when the prophet promised her a child, but she pushed forward, forcefully, past every obstacle to confront the prophet directly when the child he had promised her died. She called him to account for his miracle and forced him to an action he had not intended by insisting he return with her. She challenged the prophet and won. For a moment she was his equal, for she knew something that he did not know, the condition of her child, but his privileged status of beloved miracle worker was restored to him when the child was restored to life.

◇ **Lectionary Reading**

One day when Elisha was passing through Shunem,
a wealthy woman urged him to stop
and have a meal with her.
Whenever he came that way again
he would always eat with her.
The woman said to her husband,
"This man who regularly passes our way
is surely a holy person.
Let us make a room for him on the roof
with a bed, a table, a chair, and a lamp
so he will have a place to stay
whenever he comes again."
One day when Elisha was in the area,
he went up to his room to rest.
Suddenly he said to his servant Gehazi,
"Call the Shunammite woman."
She came and stood before him
and Elisha said to Gehazi,
"Say to her, you have taken such trouble
and have done so much for us,
what then can we do for you?
Should we speak a word on your behalf
to the king or the chief of the army?"
She answered, "I live among my people."

Elisha said, "What then may we do for her?"
Gehazi answered, "She has no son
and her husband is getting old."
"Come here," said Elisha, for she stood at the door.
Then he told the Shunammite woman,
"This time next year, this very season,
you will hold a son in your arms."
She replied, "My lord, holy one of God,
do not deceive your servant."
Well, the woman conceived
and gave birth to a son
at that time the following year,
just as Elisha had said.
One day when the child was older,
he went out among the reapers.
He complained to his father,
"My head is hurting,"
and his father said to his servant,
"Carry him to his mother."
She cradled her child on her lap until noon,
and then the little boy died.
She went up to the room on the roof,
laid her son on Elisha's bed,
closed the door, and left.
Then she called to her husband and said to him,
"Send me one of the servants with a donkey,
so that I may hurry to the prophet of God
and return again today."
"Why go today?" he said to her.
"It is neither new moon nor sabbath."
"It will be all right," she said to him,
then she saddled her donkey
and said to her servant,
"Urge the animal on.
Do not hold back unless I tell you."
And so she came to Elisha
who was residing at Mount Carmel.
When Elisha saw her coming,
he said to his servant Gehazi,
"Look, the Shunammite woman!
Hurry to her and say to her,
Are you all right?
Is your husband all right?
Is your little boy all right?"
She answered, "It is all right."
When she came to Elisha,

she threw herself down before him
and stayed there, clinging to his feet.
Gehazi tried to push her away,
but Elisha said, "Let her alone,
for she is in bitter distress
and God has hidden it from me."
Then she said, "Did I ask you for a son?
Did I not say, Do not mislead me?"
Then Elisha said to Gehazi,
"Take my staff in your hand and go.
If you meet anyone, do not greet them,
and if anyone greets you, do not respond.
Lay my staff on the face of her child."
The mother of the boy responded,
"As God lives and as you live,
I will not leave here without you."
So Elisha got up and followed her home.
Gehazi went on ahead of them
and he laid the staff on the face of the child
but there was no sign of life.
He went back to meet Elisha and said,
"The child has not awakened."
When Elisha entered the Shunammite's house,
he saw her son lying dead on his bed.
He closed the door on the two of them
and he prayed aloud to God.
He got up on the bed
and lay on the child,
his mouth on his mouth,
his eyes on his eyes,
his hands on his hands;
and as he lay upon the child,
the flesh of the boy grew warm.
He got up and walked around the room,
then covered him again.
The boy sneezed seven times,
and then he opened his eyes.
Elisha summoned Gehazi and said,
"Call the Shunammite woman."
When she came, Elisha said,
"Take your son."
She fell at the feet of Elisha,
then took her son and left.

◇

Now Elisha had said to the woman
whose son he restored to life,

"Take your family and leave this place
and settle wherever you can,
for God has called for a famine
that will last for seven years."
The woman heeded the prophet's words
and left for the land of the Philistines
where she settled for seven years.
When seven years had passed,
she returned and set out to see the king.
Now the king was conversing with Gehazi, saying,
"Tell me about all that Elisha has done."
While he was telling the king how Elisha
had raised a dead child to life,
the child's mother arrived to appeal to the king
for the return of her house and her land.
"My lord," said Gehazi,
"here is the woman
and here is the woman's son
whom the prophet Elisha restored to life."
The king questioned the woman
and she confirmed what Gehazi had said.
So the king appointed an official, saying,
"Restore to her all that was hers,
together with all the revenue
that the fields have earned
from the day she left
until the moment of her return."

◇ **Points for Shared Reflection**

- The Shunammite woman wanted to be closer to holiness so she invited holiness into her home. Have you made room for the Holy One in your home? In your heart?

- The woman's faith was tenacious. She believed her son would live. How do you handle death? How strong is your faith when a person you love dies? When a dream dies? When hope dies?

- As a woman, have you ever had to challenge religious authority and insist on getting your way? Or have you ever wanted to and refrained? Share the circumstances with the group.

- The Shunammite woman who was reticent and submissive grew to be confident, determined, and forceful. What is the story of your own growth as a woman? Is your unfolding similar to hers?

◇ **A Psalm of Confidence** (see page 328)

⬦ **Prayer**

O One Who Is All-Confident,
reach out to us
who are so unsure,
so insecure,
so hesitant,
and fill us with Your confidence
in all we say and do.
Give us the strength
to hold our own,
be firm in us
and steadfast,
so that we may grow,
in our own way,
as confident as You.
For this we pray.
Amen.

*Choir 1*   Be confident, you who are tentative.
Her Spirit-Force is with you.

*Choir 2*   Throw off the inner and outer ways
of submission and subservience.

*Choir 1*   Look up and look life straight in the eye
and do not cringe before it.

*Choir 2*   Take charge of who and what you are
and what you intend to be.

*Choir 1*   When they put you down or take you on,
stand up for what you stand for,

*Choir 2*   and let nothing diminish the woman-spirit
sustaining and strengthening you.

*Choir 1*   You are largely what you think you are,
so set your mind in order.

*Choir 2*   Know that God knows who you are
and one day, so may you.

*Choir 1*   We can go forth and conquer worlds
if we trust the Force within us.

*Choir 2*   We can transform our hesitant ways
if we entrust ourselves to Her.

*Choir 1*   Praise to Shaddai the Summit and Source
of the confidence we engender.

*Choir 2*   Praise to the One Who intimately understands
our female gender.

   By M. T. Winter, Crossroad Pub. Co., © 1991 Medical Mission Sisters

# SLAVE TO NAAMAN'S WIFE

◇ **Scripture Reference**   2 Kings 5:1–15

◇ **Biography**
The young Israelite girl who served Naaman's wife had been captured by Naaman who was commander of the Syrian army in the days of the prophet Elisha. She told her mistress that a prophet in Israel could cure her husband of his leprosy, and he did. Nothing more is known of her.

◇ **Context**
In biblical times the term "leprosy" was the general designation for any disease of the skin. Naaman did not have what we today consider leprosy (it is now known as Hanson's disease) or he would have been socially ostracized. Whatever the diagnosis, the condition was probably very visible and very embarrassing so that when his wife informed him that her

Israelite slave girl knew of a cure, he pursued the possibility immediately and without question.

This narrative holds some important hermeneutical insights regarding the status and role of women. There are stark contrasts between the army commander and the young girl who is the catalyst for his physical cure and his religious conversion. There is the contrast between age, gender, culture, and religion. The slave is young, female, Jewish, and a believer in the God of Israel. There is a contrast between position and status, between have's and have-not's, and between other less tangible characteristics. The girl is a slave and powerless. She has nothing. The man is the enslaver who has power. He has everything. The girl hovers in the background, barely visible. The man is out front with a flourish, visible to the point of spectacle with his ostentatious display. She is inexperienced. He has years of experience. But she has something he does not have. She has wisdom and she has faith; and she knows of a cure for his debilitating condition. He is a foreigner and a non-believer, but her faith is enough for him, and it is enough for God. Naaman is willing to transcend cultural and religious barriers simply on the strength of her word. And God comes through for her.

◇ **Lectionary Reading**

Naaman, commander of the Syrian army,
was highly favored by the king
because through him
God had given victory to Syria.
He was a great man
and a valiant warrior,
but he had leprosy.
Now the Syrians on one of their many raids
had taken a young girl captive
from the land of Israel,
and she served Naaman's wife.
She said to her mistress,
"If only my master were with the prophet
who is in Samaria,
he would cure him of his leprosy."
So Naaman went and told the king
what the girl from Israel had said
and the king replied to Naaman,
"Go then to Israel,
and I will send along with you
a letter to the king."
So Naaman went to Israel.
He took with him ten talents of silver,
six thousand shekels of gold,

and ten sets of garments.
He went to the king of Israel
and gave him the letter, which read,
"When this letter reaches you,
you will know that I have sent to you
Naaman who is my servant,
that you may cure his leprosy."
When the king of Israel read the letter,
he tore his clothes and said,
"Am I God, giver of life and death,
that this man sends word to me
to cure a man of his leprosy?
Is he trying to pick a quarrel with me?"
When Elisha the prophet heard
that the king of Israel had torn his clothes,
he sent a message to the king,
"Send him to me so that he may learn
there is a prophet in Israel."
So Naaman came with his horses and chariots
and halted at the entrance to Elisha's house.
Elisha sent him a message, saying,
"Go, wash in the Jordan seven times
and your flesh shall be restored
and you shall be clean."
But Naaman was angry and left, saying,
"I thought he would surely come out for me
and stand and call on the name of his God
and wave his hand over the spot
and cure the leprosy!
Are not the rivers of Damascus,
the Abana and the Pharpar,
better than all the waters of Israel?
Could I not wash in them and be clean?"
He turned and went away in a rage.
But his servants approached him and said to him,
"Master, if the prophet had commanded you
to do something that was difficult,
would you not have done it?
So why not do this simple thing
that the prophet has said to do,
'Wash, and be clean'?"
So Naaman went down to the river Jordan
and immersed himself seven times,
according to the word of the prophet of God,
and his flesh was restored
like that of a boy

and he was cured of his leprosy.
Then Naaman returned to the prophet of God
with all of his retinue,
and he stood before the prophet and said,
"Now I know that there is no God
anywhere else on earth
except in Israel."

◇ **Points for Shared Reflection**

- The young girl who had been abducted from her family and enslaved in a foreign land came to the aid of her captor. Do you think he returned the favor? Have you ever been in a similar situation where you had the chance to do good to an adversary? Did you?

- The Bible ordinarily stresses a close connection between faith and healing. Naaman did not have faith, either in the God of Israel or in the healing process. Why did God heal Naaman?

- The Bible cites many instances when the God of Israel healed, welcomed, supported persons of other cultures and other religions. What might this be saying to us and to the world in which we live?

- We are growing more and more conscious of the issues surrounding the so-called have's and have-not's in our global society. What new perspective have you gained from the story of the slave to Naaman's wife?

◇ **A Psalm for the Have's and Have-not's** (see page 333)

◇ **Prayer**

O God You have us firmly
in the palm of Your loving hand
and You have not forsaken any of us
in our time of trial or need.
Help us to see that what we have
has to be for the good of others,
and what we have not
ought not to be our ultimate concern.
Bless us with enough for us to be
forever faithful to You,
and thank You for Your generous love.
Amen.

## ◊ A PSALM FOR THE HAVE'S AND HAVE-NOT'S ◊

*Choir 1*    Some people seem to have it all,
more than they need,
all they desire
all the while
they are alive.

*Choir 2*    Some seem to have so little,
much less than they want,
sometimes even less
than they really need to survive.

*Choir 1*    Some have a house high on a hill
with every material convenience,
but have never had a home.

*Choir 2*    Others in ghettos or shanty-towns
know each day
as the sun goes down
the meaning of shalom.

*Choir 1*    Some can travel the world at will,
moving here or there,
but cannot say
just where their roots are planted.

*Choir 2*    Others occupy limited space
but are open to hear about anyplace
and take none of their world for granted.

*Choir 1*    Some accumulate to have enough
so as not to worry
about having enough
but then they worry
about what they have;
there is always anxiety.

*Choir 2*    Others with less
to worry about
have
in the midst of poverty
sometimes
an inner security.

*Choir 1*    The rich can be rich
in material things
and in other ways, impoverished,
so that life as a whole
lacks meaning.

| Choir 2 | The poor can be rich |
| | in friendship and faith |
| | and other such things of value, |
| | though their context is demeaning. |

| Choir 1 | Whoever has love |
| | has everything |
| | and is rich beyond all measure. |

| Choir 2 | Whoever lacks love |
| | has nothing of value |
| | no matter what else they treasure. |

| Choir 1 | O God of all of us, |
| | help us to have what we need |
| | for the fullness of living, |

| Choir 2 | and help us to share |
| | from the wealth that is there |
| | in Your goodness |
| | and Your giving. |

By M. T. Winter, Crossroad Pub. Co., © 1991 Medical Mission Sisters

# HULDAH

◇ **Scripture Reference**   2 Kings 22:11–20; 2 Chr 34:22–28

◇ **Biography**

Huldah was a prophet who lived in Jerusalem during the reign of King Josiah and during the time of the prophet Jeremiah. The king sent a delegation to Huldah for her interpretation of the "book of the law" which the high priest had found in the temple. She foretold God's wrath upon the nation and God's mercy toward Josiah. Huldah was the wife of Shallum and the daughter-in-law of Tikvah son of Harhas.

◇ **Context**

The Hebrew scriptures recognize only four female prophets as actually possessing legitimate prophetic powers: Miriam and Deborah of the pre-monarchical period; Huldah during the reign of Josiah in the latter part of the seventh century B.C.E.; and Noadiah during the time of Nehemiah in the fifth century B.C.E. Two separate biblical texts record Huldah's contribution. It is generally accepted that the scroll found by Hilkiah in the temple contained the core chapters of Deuteronomy, probably chapters 12–26. Why was Huldah consulted for an interpretation of the scroll and not the more prominent Jeremiah or Zephaniah? It may be that her opinions were more respected, or she, as wife of a minor temple official, may have been the cult prophet there. Huldah prophesied the destruction of Jerusalem and Josiah's death which would precede it, and Josiah took her predictions seriously, initiating widespread religious reform beyond Jerusalem to the local cult-centers throughout Judah. Huldah's prophetic response has been so redacted that it is impossible to recover the original oracle in her own words. Although her teachings have not survived, she may have been more prominent than history has allowed. The Mishnah states that the two southern gates to the Temple Mount were called the Huldah Gates (Middoth 1.3)

◇ **Lectionary Reading**

In the eighteenth year of King Josiah,
the high priest Hilkiah
said to Shaphan the secretary,
"I have found the book of the law
here in the house of God."
He gave the book to Shaphan to read,
and then Shaphan read it aloud to the king.
                                 (2 Kings 22:3, 8, 10)

When the king heard the words
of the book of the law,
he tore his garments and called together
Hilkiah the high priest,
Shaphan the secretary,
and his servant Asaiah and commanded,
"Go and inquire of God for me,
for the people, and for all of Judah
concerning this book that was found in the temple,
for the wrath of God is kindled against us
because our ancestors disobeyed the words
that are written here."
So Hilkiah, Asaiah, and Shaphan
joined Achbor and Ahikam,
deputies to the king,
to form a delegation
to visit the prophet Huldah
who lived there in Jerusalem
in the newer section of the city.
She was the wife of Shallum,
keeper of the wardrobe,

and they went to consult her at home.
"Thus says God, the God of Israel,"
the prophet declared to them.
"Tell the man who sent you to me,
Thus says God:
I will indeed bring disaster
upon this place and upon its inhabitants —
I will fulfill what is written
in the words of the book
that the king of Judah has read.
Because my people have abandoned me
and made offerings to other gods,
they have provoked me to anger
with the work of their hands
and my wrath will not be abated.
As for the king of Judah who sent you to inquire of me,
this is the message to him.
Thus says God, the God of Israel,
regarding the words you have heard:
because your heart has been penitent
and you humbled yourself before God
when you heard how I spoke against this place
and of the curse on its inhabitants,
foretelling their desolation,
because you have torn your garments
and wept before me, I have heard you.
Thus says God:
I will gather you to your ancestors
and you will go to your grave in peace,
for your eyes shall not behold the disaster
I will visit upon this place."
Then the delegation left the house of Huldah
and took her words to the king.

◇ **Points for Shared Reflection**

- Of the three Jerusalem prophets of this period, one is virtually
  unknown, and that one is a woman. Why is this?

- Huldah's original words were re-edited by men. Has this ever happened to you? How did you feel about it? Was your message more
  accurate before or after the editing? Why?

- When you are of a minority opinion or have an unpopular message
  to deliver, do you sometimes hesitate to speak? Why?

- Are there any female prophets today? What is their prophetic message? Is anybody listening?

◇ **A Psalm Proclaiming a Vision**  (see page 339)

◇ **Prayer**

O Dawn of the New Creation,
spill a ray of hope
to lift the hearts
of Your sons and daughters,
for we are bound by a vision
that is not always clear to see.
As we live into Your promises,
help us to help each other,
for we truly need each other,
as You need us
and we need You
every day of our lives.
Amen.

### ◇ A PSALM PROCLAIMING A VISION ◇

*Voice*   Prophet, tell me, what do you see?
        Will there be a New Creation?

*All*   I see a New Day dawning,
      with clean water,
      virgin forests,
      and fields and fields of grain;
      trees are doing a ring dance
      in praise of God, in praise of Gaia;
      we are like children
      and all of us
      are walking in the rain.

*Voice*   Prophet, tell me, what do you see?
        Describe the New Creation.

*All*   I see a New Age dawning,
      when no one will be hungry,
      when all will be sheltered
      and safe
      and secure
      and all of our work will be done,
      and all who praise Sophia
      will be sitting in the sun.

*Voice*   Prophet, tell me, what do you see?
        Are we the New Creation?

*All*   I see a New Beginning
      in all who overcome addiction,
      in all who will not go to war,
      in all those good and generous ones
      who witness to compassion,
      who struggle to bring about a time
      when no one is below another
      and no one is above,
      when we are all within Shalom,
      bonded together in love.

# MICHAL

◇ **Scripture Reference**   1 Sam 14:49; 18:17–29; 19:11–17
1 Sam 25:43–44
2 Sam 3:12–16; 6:12–23; 1 Chr 15:29

◇ **Biography**

Michal was Saul's younger daughter and David's first wife. Saul arranged the marriage primarily as a prelude to David's demise. One night Michal helped her husband escape a death squad sent by Saul, and a short while later, her father took her away from David and gave her in marriage to Paltiel the son of Laish. In the beginning Michal loved David but eventually she came to despise him. He reclaimed Michal after her father's death, taking her by force from her grief-stricken husband. While scripture states that Michal remained childless until her death, the masoretic text of 2 Sam 21:8 mentions five children.

◇ **Context**

Michal married David on the rebound after her father Saul had said he could have her older sister Merab and then changed his mind. Michal was in love with David. She saved him from certain death at the hands of her father's soldiers. Saul punished her by taking her from David and giving her to another man. Her new husband, Paltiel, truly loved her. Michal's life was traumatically changed again when David insisted on retrieving her and made his treaty with Abner after the death of Saul conditional on her return. Why did David want her back? Perhaps he sensed such a political alliance between the two alienated houses would unite warring factions under his reign. Or it may have been in retaliation for a bruised ego or because of a false sense of justice — he had paid a high price for her, a bounty of one hundred Philistines (according to the Septuagint) — but hardly out of love, for the change again in Michal's life must have cost the woman dearly. Michal, now one of a royal harem of wives and concubines, could barely stand the sight of David and castigated him for his behavior in accompanying the ark to Jerusalem. Scripture concludes this incident with the comment that Michal remained childless until her death. It may have been the writer's way of saying that David no longer slept with her because of her impertinence. One cannot conclude from this verse that Michal had no children, only that she had no children by David. It is hard to determine whether David ever loved Michal, the daughter of the man who so often tried to kill him, who had kept him for years in exile, who had deprived him of his women, whom David had fought long and bloody battles to overthrow.

◇ **Lectionary Reading**

Now the names of Saul's two daughters were:
Merab, the name of the firstborn,
and Michal, the name of the younger.

◇

Then Saul said to David,
"Here is my elder daughter Merab.
I will give her to you as a wife,
only be valiant for me
and fight God's battles."
For Saul thought,
"I will not raise a hand against him.
Let the Philistines deal with him."
David said to Saul,
"Who am I and who are my family
that I should be son-in-law to a king?"
But just at the time that Merab
should have been given by Saul to David,
he gave her instead to Adriel the Meholathite
as a wife.
Now Saul's daughter Michal loved David,
and Saul was told,
and it pleased him.
Saul speculated to himself,
"Let me give her to him.
Let Michal be a snare for him,
that the Philistines might overcome him."

So Saul said to David a second time,
"You shall now be my son-in-law."
Then Saul commanded his servants,
"Speak to David in private.
Say to him,
'See, the king is delighted with you
and all his servants love you.
Now then, become the king's son-in-law.'"
So Saul's servants spoke to David
and David said to them,
"Does it seem such a simple thing to you
for a man who is poor and insignificant
to become the king's son-in-law?"
The servants told Saul what David had said.
"Say this to David," he told them,
"The king desires no marriage gift,
just bring him a hundred foreskins
of his enemies, the Philistines,
that he may be avenged."
Now Saul planned that David would fall
by the hand of the Philistines.
When David was told the words of Saul,
he was pleased to be the king's son-in-law.
He got up, went out, assembled his men,
and killed one hundred Philistines
and brought one hundred foreskins to Saul
that he might become the king's son-in-law.
Saul gave him his daughter Michal as a wife.
But when Saul realized that God was with David
and that his own daughter Michal loved him,
he was even more afraid of David.
So Saul was David's enemy from that moment on.

&#9671;

Now Saul sent messengers to David's house
to keep him under guard that night,
for he planned to kill him in the morning.
David's wife Michal said to him,
"If you do not save your life tonight,
tomorrow you will be killed."
So Michal let David down through a window
and he escaped into the night.
Michal took an idol, covered it with clothes,
put a net of goat's hair on its head,
and laid it on David's bed.
When Saul sent messengers to take David,
Michal said, "He is sick."

Then Saul sent the messengers to see for themselves.
He said, "Bring him here to me in his bed,
so that I might see him and kill him."
When they saw the idol in David's bed,
they brought word back to Saul
and Saul sent for Michal.
"Why have you deceived me like this?
Why have you let my enemy go?
Why has he escaped?"
Michal said to her father,
"He said to me, 'Michal, let me go,
otherwise I will kill you.' "

◇

David also married Ahinoam of Jezreel;
both she and Abigail became his wives.
Saul had given Michal, David's wife,
to Paltiel son of Laish, who was from Gallim.

◇

Abner sent messengers to David at Hebron, saying,
"To whom does the land belong?
Make your covenant with me
and I will support you
and give all of Israel over to you."
David said, "Good, I will covenant with you,
but one thing first I require:
bring Saul's daughter Michal with you
when you come to see me again."
Then David sent word to Saul's son Ishbaal.
"Give me my wife Michal
for whom I paid one hundred Philistine foreskins
for having her."
Ishbaal took her away from her husband Paltiel
the son of Laish,
but her husband went with her,
weeping, and walking behind her
all the way to Bahurim.
Then Abner said to him, "Go back home!"
so he went back home without her.

◇

David went and brought up the ark of God
to Jerusalem with rejoicing.
When those who were bearing the ark of God
had gone six paces,
he sacrificed an ox and a fattened sheep.
David danced with all his might
before the ark of God.

He was clad with a linen vestment.
So David and all the house of Israel
brought up the ark to Jerusalem
with shouting and with trumpets.
As the ark came into the city of David,
Michal looked out of the window
and she saw King David
leaping and dancing with joy
before his God,
and she hated him in her heart.
They set the ark inside the tent
that David had prepared for it,
and David offered burnt offerings
and offerings of well-being
and blessed the people in the name of God.
He distributed food among all the people,
a cake of bread, a portion of meat,
and a cake of raisins
to all assembled,
both women and men of Israel.
Then the people returned to their homes.
David went to bless his household,
but Michal the daughter of Saul,
David's wife,
came to meet David and said,
"What a spectacle you made of yourself today,
you the king of Israel,
exposing yourself to the eyes of young maids,
as vulgar men might shamelessly do!"
David said to Michal,
"I danced before God who chose me
in place of your father and his household,
who appointed me prince over Israel,
to rule the people of God.
I will make myself yet more contemptible than this
and abase myself in my own eyes,
but as for the maids of whom you have spoken,
these hold me in high esteem."
And Michal the daughter of Saul
was childless to the day of her death.

## ◇ Points for Shared Reflection

- Michal lied to her father in order to save her husband's life,
  joining a tradition of biblical women who lied for the faith. When, if
  ever, is it permissible not to tell the truth?

- Why did Michal despise David during the latter years of their relationship? What do men today do to the women who love them that turns that love for them into revulsion?

- Was Michal's castigation of David's public behavior before the ark really an issue of propriety or one of hypocrisy? Give examples of current leaders whose religious fervor coincides with a reputation for violence and injustice.

- What is the connection between your own behavior and your attendance at religious services? What does ethics have to do with the rites and rituals of worship?

◇ **A Psalm to Guard against Hypocrisy** (see page 346)

◇ **Prayer**
O God of Grace and Glory,
You see us and You know us
in the integrity of our being;
lead us not into the temptation
to be what we are not.
Help us to more fully integrate
our rituals of meaning
with our services of life,
so that one informs the other
to the glory of Your name
and the good of all Your people
everywhere on earth,
now and forever.
Amen.

*Choir 1*   How easy it is to dance and sing
at our shrines and sacred places,
then deftly slay the tens of thousands
who seek our solicitude.

*Choir 2*   How glibly we go through the motions
of the rites of our tradition
and fail to connect such services
to an indigent's right to life.

*Choir 1*   We throw our handful of coins
into the coffers of congregations
and never tithe our conscience
to a global economy.

*Choir 2*   How can we shout a word of praise,
then raise our voice in anger?
What will a firm "so be it" mean
from lives that live a lie?

*Choir 1*   Give me a heart that lives its faith
by expressing it in practice.

*Choir 2*   Give me a faith that molds the heart
to walk in integrity.

*Choir 1*   Shield me, Shaddai, from shibboleths
meant to expose my flaws unjustly.

*Choir 2*   Guard me, O God, from giving in
to pressure to conform.

*Choir 1*   Blessed is she whose honesty
will dare to call the question.

*Choir 2*   Venerable is the vulnerable one
who sees things as they are.

*Choir 1*   Let our prayer like incense
dare to rise uninterrupted,
making of coal and ashes
fire and flame to light our way.

*Choir 2*   Let our lives be uncompromised by
temptations to pretension.
Let what we do and what we are
be true to what we say.

    By M. T. Winter, Crossroad Pub. Co., © 1991 Medical Mission Sisters

# ABIGAIL

⬧ **Scripture Reference**   1 Sam 25:1–42; 27:1–4; 30:1–18
2 Sam 2:1–4; 3:2–3; 1 Chr 3:1

⬧ **Biography**

Abigail of Carmel married David after the death of her husband, Nabal, a mean but wealthy man. She was a wise and beautiful woman who impressed David when she came to him to intercede for those of her household who were about to experience David's wrath. Abigail was the mother of Daniel (also called Chileab), David's second son.

⬧ **Context**

Saul, condemned by Samuel and rejected by God, sensed in David a threat to his monarchy that had to be destroyed. He pursued him in a jealous rage, but David managed to elude him, sparing Saul's life in the episode that preceded his encounter with Nabal. In this narrative we meet a different David, one who has decided to be less forgiving. Samuel is dead and he was the one who had championed David's kingship. Now David would have to cut his own path, and that would mean eliminating all who happened to get in his way. Nabal was nothing more than a nuisance, but he evoked David's wrath. David was about to kill him and all who were part of his household when Abigail stopped him in his tracks. Intelligent, sensitive, beautiful, she knew when to step forward and when to pull back, how to appeal to his rational side and how to appeal to his senses. Prophetically, she spoke of his kingship, then

347

cautioned him against an act of vengeance unbecoming to his rank. She deflected his anger, deterred him from senselessly shedding blood, and he blessed her for her insight. Her speech is a classic example of a capable, self-assured woman who uses all of her wit and wisdom to achieve a noble end. Abigail met and married David just as his star was rising. As widow of a Calebite chieftain, her allegiance could only benefit him in his effort to secure the throne.

◊ **Lectionary Reading**

Samuel died and all Israel
assembled and mourned for him,
and they buried him in Ramah
which was Samuel's hometown.
Then David arose and went down
into the wilderness of Paran.
Now there was a man in Maon
who had property in Carmel.
The man was very rich —
three thousand sheep, a thousand goats —
and he was shearing his sheep in Carmel.
The man's name was Nabal
and his wife's name was Abigail.
Abigail was beautiful and clever,
but her husband was surly and mean.
He was a Calebite.
When David heard in the wilderness
that Nabal was shearing sheep,
he sent ten men to Carmel,
instructing them with these words,
"Go to Nabal and greet him for me, saying,
'Peace be to you and to your house,
and peace to all that is yours.
Your shepherds will tell you we have done you no harm
all the time we have been in Carmel.
Please share some provisions with us and David,
for we come to you on a feast;
may we find favor with you.' "
When the men had said all this to Nabal,
he answered, "Who is David?
Who is the son of Jesse?
Today many servants escape from their masters.
Shall I take my bread and my water
and the meat I have butchered for my shearers
and give it to men who come here to me
from God alone knows where?"

So David's men returned to him
and told what had transpired.
"Every man strap on his sword!" he shouted,
and four hundred men strapped on their swords
and followed after David,
while two hundred stayed with the baggage.
One of Nabal's men told Abigail,
"David sent messengers out of the wilderness
who came and saluted our master,
and he shouted insults at them.
Yet the men were very good to us.
We suffered no harm
and we never lost anything
when we were in the fields;
as long as we stayed beside them,
they were a wall by day and by night,
all the while we were tending the sheep.
Consider now what you ought to do,
for revenge has been planned against our master
and against all of his household.
He is so ill-natured, no one can speak to him."
Then Abigail hurried,
took two hundred loaves,
two skins of wine,
five slaughtered sheep already prepared,
five measures of grain,
one hundred clusters of raisins
and two hundred cakes of figs,
and loaded it all on donkeys,
instructing her young men,
"Go on ahead. I am coming after you."
But she did not tell her husband.
As she rode her donkey she approached David
under cover of the mountain,
as David had finished saying,
"In vain I protected this man's goods
out here in the wilderness.
He has returned me evil for good.
May God so do to David and more
if a single male survives among all who belong to him."
When Abigail saw David,
she bowed to the ground before him and said,
"Upon me alone, my lord, be the guilt.
Please let your servant speak.
Do not take seriously this ill-natured man;
as his name is, so is he,

for Nabal means a fool.
I did not see the young men you sent.
Since God has restrained you from taking vengeance,
may your enemies be like Nabal.
Please accept this gift on behalf of your men,
and forgive our trespasses.
God will make a sure house of my lord.
No evil will dwell within you
for as long as you shall live.
If any pursue you to seek your life,
your life shall be bound in the bundle of life
that is under the care of God,
but the lives of your enemies God shall fling
like a stone from the hollow of a sling.
When God has done all the good
that God has spoken concerning you
and appointed you prince over Israel,
my lord shall have no cause for grief
or pangs of a guilty conscience
for having shed innocent blood without cause
or for having saved himself.
And when God has dealt well with you, my lord,
then remember me, your servant."
David said to Abigail,
"Blessed be the God of Israel,
who sent you to me today.
Blessed be your good sense,
and blessed be you
who have kept me clear
from bloodguilt and from avenging myself
by the force of my own hand!
For as surely as the God of Israel lives,
who has kept me from hurting you,
if you had not hurried to meet me today,
truly by morning not one single male
would have lived in the house of Nabal."
Then David received her gifts from her hand
and said to her, "Go to your house in peace.
I have granted your petition.
I have heard what you had to say."
When Abigail returned to her home and Nabal,
he was holding a lavish feast,
a feast fit for a king.
His heart was merry within him,
for he was very drunk,
so she spoke not a word to him until morning.

In the morning when Abigail had told him all,
his heart sank like a stone.
About ten days later,
God struck Nabal down, and he died.
When David heard that Nabal was dead,
he said, "Blessed be God
who has judged the case of Nabal's insult
and restrained me from doing evil."
Then David proposed to Abigail.
A delegation came to Carmel and said,
"David wants you as his wife."
Abigail rose and bowed to the ground, saying,
"Your servant is a slave
prepared to wash the feet of his servants."
Abigail got up quickly
and rode away on her donkey,
her five maids accompanying her.
She rode behind David's messengers,
and she became David's wife.

◇

One day David said to himself,
"I shall surely perish by the hand of Saul.
Let me leave for the land of the Philistines
and I will escape his wrath."
So David set out and crossed over,
he and six hundred men and their households,
to Achish king of Gath.
David and his two wives,
Ahinoam of Jezreel and Abigail of Carmel,
his troops and all their households,
settled there at Gath.
When Saul was told that David had fled,
he no longer searched for him.

◇

The Amalekites raided Ziklag;
they sacked it and burned it down,
capturing all who were in it,
women and children, young and old,
and carried them all away.
When David and his men returned to the city,
they found the city destroyed
and their families taken captive.
They wept until they could weep no more.
David was in danger of being stoned,
for people were very bitter
at the loss of their wives and children.

David's two wives had also been taken,
Ahinoam of Jezreel and Abigail of Carmel.
David prayed for strength,
asked the priest Abiathar for the vestment,
and then inquired of God,
"Shall I pursue the raiders?
Is there hope of overtaking them?"
God answered him, "Pursue them.
You will definitely overtake them
and rescue all the captives."
So David set out with six hundred men,
but two hundred dropped out at Wadi Besor,
too exhausted to go on.
They found an Egyptian out in the open
and brought the man to David.
He had been wandering three days and three nights,
deprived of food and water.
They fed him bread and water,
raisins and cakes of figs,
and when he had sufficiently revived,
David said to him,
"Where are you from? Who are you with?"
He said, "I am from Egypt,
a servant to an Amalekite.
I was part of the raid on the Negeb
when we burned Ziklag down,
but I fell ill so they left me behind."
"Will you lead me to the raiding party?" asked David.
"If you swear you will not kill me," he said,
"or return me to my master,
I will lead you down to them."
When they saw the raiders sprawled on the ground,
eating and drinking and dancing
because they had captured so many spoils
from the Philistines and from Judah,
David and his troops attacked and fought
from twilight to the following evening.
Only four hundred young men mounted on camels
managed to escape.
David recovered everything
and rescued all the captives,
including his two wives.

◇

Sometime later, David asked God,
"Shall I settle in the cities of Judah?"
God said to him, "Yes, go."

"To which shall I go?" asked David.
And God replied, "To Hebron."
So David went up to Hebron
with his wives Ahinoam and Abigail,
and brought all the men who were with him,
and everyone in his house.
They settled in the towns of Hebron.
The people of Judah came to him,
and there they anointed David as king
over the house of Judah.

◇

Sons were born to David at Hebron.
His firstborn was Amnon, son of Ahinoam.
His second was Daniel (or Chileab),
and this was Abigail's child.

◇ **Points for Shared Reflection**

- Can you recall a time when your intervention at home or at work had a calming effect and turned an explosive situation around?

- What special strengths do you bring to a crisis situation?

- Do you think a meal or some kind of gift helps the process of negotiation or the resolution of a crisis? When has this worked for you?

- Do you sometimes speak wise words? Does anybody listen?

◇ **A Psalm of Wise Words**  (see page 354)

◇ **Prayer**

O Wise One
Who speaks wise words
to all who stop to listen,
speak to us now
in ways that will bring
some sense to our confusion
and an end to our foolishness.
Call us to speech
in that power-filled mode
of the prophet and disciple,
so that all who hear our own
wise words
will turn from their ways
to You.
Amen.

## ◇ A PSALM OF WISE WORDS ◇

*Choir 1*  Help us to speak
wise words
when our world erupts
with a stinging blast
and no one on earth is listening.

*Choir 2*  Help us to speak
wise words
when our lives explode
with a vengeance
and we know we are out of line.

*Choir 1*  Help us to speak
wise words
when a best friend seeks our counsel.

*Choir 2*  Help us to speak
wise words
when a family member leans on us
for comfort or advice.

*Choir 1*  Help us to speak
wise words
when we face a hard decision
for ourselves
or someone we love.

*Choir 2*  Help us to speak
wise words
in response to troubling questions
about life
or love
or God.

*Choir 1*  Help us to speak
wise words
when we challenge
our traditions
and seek to offer alternatives
to the platitudes
and the rules.

*Choir 2*  Help us to speak
wise words
to ourselves
in our silent moments
as we shout Sophia's wisdom
from the top of our trusting hearts.

 By M. T. Winter, Crossroad Pub. Co., © 1991 Medical Mission Sisters

# WOMAN OF BAHURIM

◇ **Scripture Text**   2 Sam 17:15–21

◇ **Biography**

This unidentified wife of an anonymous man who lived in the village of Bahurim just outside Jerusalem saved the lives of David's messengers and thereby saved the king.

◇ **Context**

On hearing that Absalom was on his way from Hebron to kill his father and proclaim himself king of Judah, David took his family and fled from Jerusalem. Absalom met with his two counselors, Ahithophel, who had defected from David, and Hushai, who had remained loyal to the king, and asked their advice on how to gain victory over his father. Ahithophel's advice was swift and lethal — go immediately and slaughter the king and all his forces. Hushai, hoping to buy time so that he might warn David in advance of an attack, argued convincingly against a quick offensive, pointing out that night was fast approaching and that David was too good a warrior to be taken by surprise. He sent two messengers to warn David, but they were spotted leaving Jerusalem and followed to Bahurim. The messengers came to the house of a supporter whose wife hid them inside a well and lied to their pursuers. The episode is reminiscent of Rahab and the spies in Jericho in the book of Joshua. A number of women in biblical tradition lied on behalf of the covenant community or one of its representatives, among them Rebekah, Tamar, Rahab, Jael, and Judith. The action of the woman of Bahurim was truly courageous and historically significant, for David went on to defeat Absalom's forces and returned to Jerusalem.

◇ **Lectionary Reading**

Then Hushai said to the priests
Zadok and Abiathar,
"Thus and so did Ahithophel counsel Absalom
and the elders of Israel;
and thus and so have I counseled.
Therefore, go quickly to David and say,
'Do not lodge tonight at the fords
to the wilderness,
but make sure that you cross over;
otherwise the king
and all who are with him
will be destroyed.'"
Abiathar's son Jonathan
and Zadok's son Ahimaaz
were waiting at En-rogel.
A servant girl was their go-between.
She would come and deliver the message
and they would go and tell King David,
for they could not risk being seen
going in and out of the city.
But a boy saw them and told Absalom,
so both of them quickly disappeared
and went to the house of a man at Bahurim
who had a well in his courtyard,
and they lowered themselves into it.
The man's wife stretched a cover
over the mouth of the well
and spread out grain upon it.
Absalom's servants approached her and asked,
"Where are Ahimaaz and Jonathan?"
The woman said to them,
"They have crossed over the brook of water."

And when they had searched
and could not find them,
they returned to Jerusalem.

◇ **Points for Shared Reflection**

- A different kind of behavior is acceptable in life-and-death situations.
  What kinds of rules can be broken in order to save a life?

- Was the woman justified in lying? What would you have done if you
  were her?

- For a fleeting moment the life of a king is in the hands of a village
  woman. What does the biblical tradition have to say about that?

- In what ways do women who seem powerless today have power
  over the structures that oppress them?

◇ **A Psalm about Giving Thanks**  (see page 358)

◇ **Prayer**

We thank You
for the gift of life
and the gift of love,
O Holy One,
as we call upon You
confidently
with the names
we know You by.
Be here with us,
be here for us
whenever our need
spills over
in petition and in praise.
Amen.

### ◇ A PSALM ABOUT GIVING THANKS ◇

*All*   Give thanks to Shaddai,
for She is good;
Her love endures forever.

*Chorus*   She tends Her children tenderly;

*All*   Her love endures forever.

*Chorus*   She listens to us attentively;

*All*   Her love endures forever.

*Chorus*   She cares about us passionately;

*All*   Her love endures forever.

*Chorus*   She comforts us compassionately;

*All*   Her love endures forever.

*Chorus*   Give thanks to Shaddai,
for She is good;

*All*   Her love endures forever.
Give thanks to Sophia,
for She is wise;
Her wisdom endures forever.

*Chorus*   She teaches us discernment;

*All*   Her wisdom endures forever.

*Chorus*   She gifts us with intuition;

*All*   Her wisdom endures forever.

*Chorus*   She is the Source of our knowledge;

*All*   Her wisdom endures forever.

*Chorus*   She is our Inspiration;

*All*   Her wisdom endures forever.

*Chorus*   Give thanks to Sophia,
for She is wise;

*All*   Her wisdom endures forever.
Give thanks to Shekinah,
for She is here;
Her presence endures forever.

*Chorus*   She is present in all of creation;

*All*   Her presence endures forever.

*Chorus*   She is present in all our experience;

*All*   Her presence endures forever.

 By M. T. Winter, Crossroad Pub. Co., © 1991 Medical Mission Sisters

| Chorus | She is present in people around us; |
|---|---|
| All | Her presence endures forever. |
| Chorus | She is present here within us; |
| All | Her presence endures forever. |
| Chorus | Give thanks to Shekihah,<br>for She is here; |
| All | Her presence endures forever.<br>Give thanks to Shalom,<br>for She is at peace;<br>Her peace endures forever. |
| Chorus | She is peace in the midst of conflict; |
| All | Her peace endures forever. |
| Chorus | She is peace in the pain of upheaval; |
| All | Her peace endures forever. |
| Chorus | She is peace at the heart of our striving; |
| All | Her peace endures forever. |
| Chorus | She is peace surpassing all understanding; |
| All | Her peace endures forever. |
| Chorus | Give thanks to Shalom,<br>for She is at peace; |
| All | Her peace endures forever.<br>Give thanks to Shaddai,<br>for She is good;<br>Her love endures forever.<br><br>Give thanks to Sophia,<br>for She is wise;<br>Her wisdom endures forever.<br><br>Give thanks to Shekinah,<br>for She is here;<br>Her presence endures forever.<br><br>Give thanks to Shalom,<br>for She is at peace;<br>Her peace endures forever.<br><br>Give thanks to Shaddai,<br>for She is good;<br>Her love endures forever. |

By M. T. Winter, Crossroad Pub. Co., © 1991 Medical Mission Sisters

# ABISHAG

◇ **Scripture Reference**    1 Kings 1:1–4, 15; 2:13–25

◇ **Biography**

Abishag the Shunammite was a beautiful young virgin who was brought in to attend to David the king when he was very old. They brought her to him to keep him warm. Theirs was not a sexual relationship. Nobody knows what became of Abishag after David died.

◇ **Context**

David had an eye for beauty — his wives Bathsheba and Abigail were exceptionally beautiful women — so his attendants brought him a beautiful young girl to ease the hours of his final days. Abishag, a Shunammite virgin, was brought in to David not as a sexual partner but in order to minister to him, to attend to his needs, to brighten his days, to lay in his arms and warm him at night. She presents a striking contrast, her youth over against David's debilitating age, her innocence alongside of his lifetime

360

of experience and the political intrigue that encircled him concerning accession to his throne. Adonijah, Haggith's son and David's firstborn, expected to succeed his father by right of primogeniture, but David had long ago promised Bathsheba that Solomon would be his heir, and she made him keep his promise. After Solomon's coronation and David's death Adonijah, seemingly accepting defeat, asked one thing only of his brother Solomon and he made his request through Bathsheba. He asked for Abishag as his wife. When Bathsheba presented this request to her son, Solomon interpreted it as a challenge to his right to rule, for Abishag belonged to David who had bestowed the kingship on Solomon, and the claim to David's woman would surely be followed by a claim to David's throne. So Solomon had his brother executed because he had asked for Abishag. The young Shunammite never speaks and her story ends with David's. Even though she was not David's wife or concubine, she was still considered his woman, more accurately, his property. She apparently was not released after David's death, at least not immediately. Following the incident with Adonijah, there is no further word about her.

◇ **Lectionary Reading**

King David was old and advanced in years,
and although he was covered with layers of clothes,
he simply could not get warm.
One day his servants said to him,
"Let a young virgin be brought to the king
to serve as the king's attendant,
and let her lie in your arms at night
in order to keep you warm."
So they went and searched for a beautiful girl
throughout all of Israel,
and they found Abishag the Shunammite,
and they brought her to the king.
The girl was very beautiful.
She became the king's attendant
and she served him faithfully,
but he never had sex with her.
When Bathsheba went in to see the king,
Abishag was attending him.
The king was very old.

◇

Adonijah, son of Haggith,
came to Bathsheba, Solomon's mother.
She asked, "Do you come peaceably?"
He said, "I come in peace.
May I have a word with you?"
She said to him, "You may."

He said, "You know that the kingdom was mine.
All Israel thought I would reign.
The kingdom has now been turned around.
It has become my brother's,
because it was his from God.
I have one request to make of you.
Please do not refuse it."
"What is it?" Bathsheba asked him.
He said, "Please ask King Solomon —
he will not refuse you —
to give me Abishag as my wife."
"Very well," said Bathsheba,
"I will speak on your behalf."
So Bathsheba went to Solomon.
The king stood up to meet her,
bowed down to her, then sat on his throne
and had a throne brought for his mother,
who sat at his right hand.
She said, "I have one small request to make.
Please do not refuse me."
Her son, the king, responded,
"Make your request, my mother,
for I will not refuse you."
She said, "Give Abishag the Shunammite
to Adonijah as his wife."
King Solomon answered his mother,
"Why ask for Abishag the Shunammite?
Why not ask for the kingdom as well!
Adonijah is my elder brother;
Abiathar the priest and Joab
are completely committed to him."
Then Solomon swore an oath, saying,
"May God do to me and more besides,
for Adonijah has devised this scheme
at the risk of his own life!
By the God who placed me on this throne
and made me a house as promised,
today Adonijah dies!"
So Solomon dispatched Benaiah
who struck Adonijah dead.

◇ **Points for Shared Reflection**

- In what ways is Abishag an ideal role model for young girls today?
- In what ways does Abishag reflect the negative stereotypes patriarchy bestows on women?

- How important is physical beauty to you in establishing a relationship? What characteristics are beautiful to you?

- What are the potential strengths of a platonic male/female relationship? Have you ever experienced such a friendship? Has it been good for you?

◇ **A Psalm for Girls** (see page 364)

◇ **Prayer**

On the sixth day of creation,
You looked upon Your little girls
and saw that we were good.
Creator God,
good Mother God,
give us genuine delight
in all the mystery of being female.
Help us cherish our link to life
and our role in the new creation,
and help our virgin daughters
bear the burden of maturing
with humor and grace,
courage and delight,
every day of their lives.
Amen.

*Choir 1*   Remember the time,
the first time
you helped your mother
bake some bread
and marveled
at the way it rose
unassisted,
although you had tried
with all your might
to squeeze it into submission?

*All*   That was a blessing time,
little girl,
with your female awareness rising.

*Choir 2*   Remember the time,
the first time
you felt your breasts
begin to swell
and wondered if the milk had come
and if anyone around
could tell,
certain you heard God
wish you well?

*All*   That was a blessing time,
little girl,
for your female power was rising.

*Choir 1*   Remember the time,
the first time
you felt the blood
begin to flow,
and all the things you longed to know
about love and life
trickled forth
in a silent stream
from a wellspring deep within you?

*All*   That was a blessing time,
little girl,
in your own female transforming.

*Choir 2*   Remember the time,
the first time
you were there in the midst
of woman's world,

   By M. T. Winter, Crossroad Pub. Co., © 1991 Medical Mission Sisters

weaving a web of relationship,
testing the strength of gendering,
spinning a circle of solid support
for a future as yet unknown?

*All*  That was a blessing time,
little girl,
when your female bonds were forming.

*Choir 1*  Remember the time,
the first time
your mother gave the go-ahead
for you to try some grown-up things
like going out
on your first date
and coming home
a little late?

*All*  That was a blessing time,
little girl,
with your female gifts maturing.

*Choir 2*  Remember the time,
the first time
you heard a female name for God
and prayed to Her
with such delight
you knew She was delighted too?

*All*  That was a blessing time,
little girl,
for you knew Your God as female.
How beautiful are the little girls
who stand on the threshold of womanhood
and look at themselves
and know it is good.
Praise to You, Shekinah-Shaddai.
All Your daughters praise You.

By M. T. Winter, Crossroad Pub. Co., © 1991 Medical Mission Sisters    *WomanWisdom* /

# Psalm Title/Theme Index

# Index of Women

# WomanWitness
## Women of the Hebrew Scriptures
## Part Two

## CONTENTS